Managing Clergy
Lives

Managing Clergy Lives

Obedience, Sacrifice, Intimacy

by

Nigel Peyton

and

Caroline Gatrell

B L O O M S B U R Y

LONDON • NEW DELHI • NEW YORK • SYDNEY

Bloomsbury T&T Clark
An imprint of Bloomsbury Publishing Plc

50 Bedford Square
London
WC1B 3DP
UK

1385 Broadway
New York
NY 10018
USA

www.bloomsbury.com

Bloomsbury is a registered trade mark of Bloomsbury Publishing Plc

First published 2013
Reprinted 2013

British Library Cataloguing-in-Publication Data
A catalogue record for this book is available from the British Library.

ISBN: HB: 978-1-441-13792-0
PB: 978-1-441-12125-7

Library of Congress Cataloging-in-Publication Data
A catalogue record for this book is available from the Library of Congress.

Typeset by Newgen Imaging Systems Pvt Ltd, Chennai, India
Printed and bound in Great Britain

For priests everywhere in the Church of God, in admiration:
'Esteem them very highly in love because of their work'
1 Thessalonians 4.13

For Anne, Emily, Jennifer and Mark
Nigel Peyton

For Tony, Anna and Emma
Caroline Gatrell

CONTENTS

FOREWORD AND ACKNOWLEDGEMENTS

Joint authorship has been mutually challenging and great fun. There are a number of friends and colleagues who have helped shape this book. Thanks are due to Nick Abercrombie, Christopher Bates, Valerie Bevan, David Brown, Simon Burnett, George Cassidy, Elaine Dunn, Lorna Finley, Graham James, Hayley Matthews, Sarah-Jane Page, Anne Peyton, John Rodwell and Tony Watson who in varied ways encouraged the research and have critically reviewed our work. Our families, Anne Peyton, Emily and Mark, Tony Gatrell and Anna, Emma, Max, Pam and Mike have supported us through the hours of rewriting. Our editors Caroline Chartres and Anna Turton at T & T Clark Continuum have been patient and discerning. The authors are grateful for the following copyright permissions: For poems by R S Thomas, copyright Kunjana Thomas 2001: 'The Priest' *Not That He Brought Flowers* 1968; 'The Minister' *An Acre of Land* 1952; 'The Word' *Laboratories of the Spirit* 1975. Material from *Ordination Services* published by Church House Publishing, copyright Archbishops' Council 2007. Material from *Guidelines for the Professional Conduct of the Clergy,* published by Church House Publishing, copyright the Convocations of Canterbury and York 2003. Scripture quotations are from The New Revised Standard Version of the Bible, Anglicised Edition, copyright 1989, 1995 by the Division of Christian Education of the National Council of the Churches of Christ in the United States of America. Finally we must thank those without whom there would be no book: the clergy who took part in the 'Managing Clergy Lives' research project and who generously gave their time in conversation.

Nigel Peyton and Caroline Gatrell

THE PRIEST

The priest picks his way
Through the parish. Eyes watch him
From windows, from farms;
Hearts wanting him to come near,
The flesh rejects him.

Women, pouring from the black kettle,
Stir up the whirling tea-grounds
Of their thoughts; offer him a dark
Filling in their smiling sandwich.

Priests have a long way to go.
The people wait for them to come
To them over the broken glass
Of their vows, making them pay
With their sweat's coinage for their correction.

He goes up a green lane
Through growing birches; lambs cushion
His vision. He comes slowly down
In the dark, feeling the cross warp
In his hands; hanging on it his thoughts icicles.

'Crippled soul', do you say? Looking at him
From the mind's height; 'limping through life
On his prayers. There are other people
In the world, sitting at table
Contented, though the broken body
And the shed blood are not on the menu.'

'Let it be so,' I say. 'Amen and amen.'

R S Thomas Not That He Brought Flowers (1968)

1

In Search of Priesthood

*My ordination was just incredible . . . I felt that something had
happened and that I would never be the same again*

CAROLE

Researching clergy lives

Managing Clergy Lives explores the commitment of Church of England
parish clergy to their ordination vows, and affirms their positive staying
power. Priests who participated in *Managing Clergy Lives*, far from being
the Welsh clergyman R S Thomas's 'crippled souls, limping through life on
their prayers' press ahead faithfully, continuing to honour their ordination
promises across the years. Striving to be obedient in body and soul, they pay
the price of lost intimacies and sacrifice their own needs and desires. The
suggestion that 'priests have a long way to go' resonated with us and we
became curious to discover more about how contemporary clergy experience
and explain their priestly vocation in an often unreceptive world. In short,
why do they remain in the priesthood?

The *Managing Clergy Lives* research was undertaken by interviewing,
in depth, 46 parish clergy (14 women and 32 men) across 42 English
dioceses (Peyton 2009). R S Thomas wrote his poem 'The Priest' in 1968
from the perspective of the all-male priesthood when women remained far
from being ordained in the Church of England, so our research enables
some reflection on a gender-mixed priesthood a generation further on. The
clergy interviewed were all stipendiary (i.e. paid) and occupied in parish
ministry. The research participants were recruited entirely from those
clergy who additionally were appointed as Rural Deans (increasingly
called Area Deans), a voluntary 'middle management' role, comprising the
supervision of a local area of Anglican churches and their clergy. The data
set included a rich variety of personal and professional variables which

further enhanced a coherent sample of mature, 'key informants' (Collinson 1992: 235), clergy who could provide evidence of 'staying power'. We are aware that Area/Rural Deans might be seen to have a particular perspective of priestly ministry. However they often talk about 'having influence without authority' and as such Area/Rural Deans are able not only to reflect on their own lives in isolation but understand only too well the differing circumstances of many clergy colleagues. Lee and Horsman (2002) and Barley (2009) recognize that Area/Rural Deans provide frontline and safe relational space where the clergy can be themselves. As our interviewee Penny put it, 'I think we often do help other people in a way that we have been helped. I think that is kind of partly the wounded healer stuff'. The Area/Rural Deans perceive themselves as carrying a certain amount of accessible wisdom.

We believe therefore that our participants tell the story of contemporary clergy life in the Church of England with a refreshing openness. In the chapters which follow they frequently offer insights that are critical of themselves and the Church as well as describing their enduring efforts in mission and ministry in parishes. Our research examines the personal experiences and meanings of clergy lives in the Church of England in the 21st century: we are keen to describe the complex character of vocational work. What interests us is why clergy are who they are and what they believe and do – how they embody priesthood in an enduring vocational commitment. How do clergy keep 'body and soul together'?

We pursued these questions by means of the qualitative approach favoured by Silverman (1993, 2005), bringing to life the silent witness of clergy lives through semi-structured interviews with a particular sample of experienced clergy. Our qualitative approach looked at the everyday lives of clergy: what motivates clergy to press ahead despite difficulties and what strengthens their identity in the embodiment of priesthood? Warren (2002), reporting in largely psychotherapeutic terms, judged that more research was needed into the meaning of priesthood for the clergy and about clergy relationships. Here, and from a more sociological perspective, we provide fresh evidence about Church of England clergy, developing a new critique of Church literatures about the clergy, engaging creatively with the fields of theology, the social sciences and management studies, suggesting new connections and explanations.

Our research strategy – the 'search for priesthood' – reflects the approach towards organizational structures, practices and cultures characterized by Watson in his text *In Search of Management* (2001). This approach looks beyond the abstract and focuses on the everyday narratives of living a priestly life, listening to clergy talking about their lives in their own words. We are not arguing here that clergy are alone in experiencing the issues of discipline, self-sacrifice and the loss of intimacy which our research highlights. We believe however that our clergy participants have an interesting and particular vocational story to tell which is compelling.

Crippled souls?

Interest has focused a great deal on judging 'when things go wrong' with clergy, possibly over-much. Empirical research about clergy has tended to concentrate on the downside of being a priest. In *The Cracked Pot* Warren (2002) interviewed 60 Anglican parish clergy about the realities and meanings of their ordained ministries and family lives using a psychodynamic analytical approach. Her conclusion was that many clergy are struggling in the positions in which they find themselves, and that their internal emotional, or ego-identity, is poor. Burgess (1998, 2005) drew attention to the problems of assistant curates and the clergy 'drop-out' rate. Nash (1990) and Meyrick (1998) wrote about the experiences of clergy spouses and family life in the vicarage with some earthy and poignant insights while Burton and Burton (2009) explored clergy family stress. In their influential report Lee and Horsman (2002) proposed practical suggestions from a large scale consultation exercise on preventing clergy stress, sickness and ill-health retirement. This was followed by the publication of *Bruised Reeds?* a clergy wellbeing survey in two dioceses (Thomas 2006). InterHealth, an occupational health provider for Christians in ministry highlights the danger of clergy stress and offers 'a holistic approach to health, caring for body mind and spirit' (InterHealth 2008: 16) while the Victorian Anglican foundation which has become St Luke's Healthcare (2011) continues to care for clergy as they care for others.

Lee and Horsman refer medically to 'the identified patient' (2002: 3) arising from their work with burned-out clergy. It is important that we acknowledge the significance for the Church and for clergy of existing research on clergy ill-health. Some clergy do suffer anxiety and illness, some become depressed, others engage in financial or substance abuse or extra-marital relationships, some are in trouble with the Church authorities and a few with the criminal justice system. Our research, however, suggests a broader perspective. Early and ill-health retirements are monitored closely by the Church of England because of the pension costs and prevention lessons to be learned – sick clergy can damage themselves and their parishes. Yet, clergy record few sickness absence days each year compared with other occupational groups (Church of England 2005a), amounting to just 3.4 days in 2007, equivalent to 1.4 per cent of working days. Annual clergy turnover measured simply in terms of priests leaving the Church of England payroll is just 3 per cent compared with 11 per cent for nurses and 13 per cent for school teachers (Smithers and Robinson 2004, Church of England 2008a). The number of clergy early ill-health retirements, 13 per cent of all clergy retirements in 2008, is slowly reducing. However the component of mental health, stress and anxiety as the principle cause of many sickness days and early retirements remains a concern (Church of England 2010a). These factors notwithstanding clergy tend to record high job satisfaction in occupational surveys (Ashworth 1999, Rose, M 1999, Church of England 2001a) and are enjoying longer lives (Church of England 2006a). For a number of years the Anglican Diocese of Liverpool has surveyed its clergy and in 2011 found that 95 per cent of its clergy enjoyed their ministry and 92 per cent supported the aspirations of the diocesan strategy; during the previous year 65 per cent took no time off through sickness/ill health and a further 25 per cent fewer than 6 days off (Liverpool 2011). Although at best it seems that the clergy lifestyle is healthy and happy a *Church Times* article on clergy wellbeing highlighted the caution expressed by Webster (2002): 'clergy do not tend to be at war with themselves, as people are in some jobs, and obviously that has a positive effect on their health. By contrast however when there are things in the job that aren't congruent with them – as when there is a crisis of faith, which happens a lot more than people say, or there are issues which put them at odds with the institution – it can be personally devastating' (Paveley 2008). Nevertheless, as the poetry of R S Thomas sharply illustrates, it is not unusual for Christians in general, and priests in particular, to question their faith periodically. Bishop Richard Holloway's recent autobiographical *Memoir of Faith and Doubt* (Holloway 2012) focuses a great deal upon the dilemmas of personal and public uncertainty. The 'Patterns of Service' research pioneered by Barley (2009) indicates that although mid-career Church of England clergy are largely fulfilled, their vocation and role may be pulling in different directions – there is no evidence of a loss of vocation but some could be happier. Turton (2010) found in a socio-psychological study of clergy burnout an inherent paradox whereby clergy job satisfaction is accompanied by clergy stress. His respondents were glad to be ordained but experienced some suffering for the sake of a meaningful ministry.

Leaving ministry?

Recent Anglican literature about clergy follows a long tradition of spiritual and practical theological reflection on the life and work of a priest in contemporary society (Guiver 2001, Christou 2003, Cocksworth and Brown 2006, Pritchard 2007, Lewis-Anthony 2009, Ward 2011). Other, therapeutic (Warren 2002, Lee and Horsman 2002, Thomas 2006) and managerial-practitioner approaches (Church of England 2003a, 2003b, 2004a, 2005a, 2005b, 2006b, Rooms and Steen 2008) address the presence, performance and professional ministerial accountability of the clergy in the 21st century. The literature has frequently depicted the clergy as failing or dysfunctional, at odds with authority and parishioners. The titles of reports and articles in the church press, for example, 'Cracked Pots,' 'Bruised Reeds' and 'When It Gets Too Much' have tended to reinforce this impression. The Church of England has been described as a bad employer by Burgess (2002) and encouraged to take better care of its clergy (Lee and Horsman 2002, Warren 2002, Webster 2002, Jones et al. 2004, Savage 2006, Thomas 2006, Paveley 2008) and clergy families (Burton and Burton 2009). This emphasis is possibly partly explained by the essentially pastoral paradigm of ministry in the Church of England in which a dedicated priest cares for those suffering in the parish community, embodied as a Christ-like 'wounded healer' (Campbell 1981: 43) or 'wounded companion' (Pritchard 2007: 67).

Conversely, it has also been argued that relatively few clergy end up permanently 'on the analyst's couch' (Savage 2006) or leave ministry for good. Research by Towler and Coxon (1979) charted the career paths of Anglican clergy and suggested a broadly defined drop-out rate of 6 per cent. Research studies in the United States (Jud 1970, Smith 1974, Sandford 1984) explored the reasons for parochial clergy burn-out and departure. They concluded that while the reasons were complex, there was a convergence of clergy anxieties concerning role conflicts, relationship difficulties and a sense of personal and professional inadequacy. Because clergy experience and rationalize their occupation as not merely a job but as a life, there is a tendency to internalize problems in a magnified and unhealthy way. Interestingly Jud and his colleagues recognized a limitation in their analysis which was an added incentive for our research. They conceded that researchers need to interview just as intensively those clergy who stay as they do those who leave ministry and they noted the importance of understanding the different career outcomes among clergy who struggle with the same problems:

> if we were to go back and redo this whole study, it would almost certainly involve intense interviews with pastors as well as ex-pastors, and a more systematic attempt to focus upon the multiple sources of career pressures and the wider variety of clergy responses to them, rather than narrowing down to one type of response – that of leaving the field. (Jud 1970: 51)

A generation on from these early enquiries the world and the Christian churches and the social context of ministry in the Church of England have changed. Clergy do sometimes leave full time, stipendiary ministry and discovering the reasons why has attracted research and employer interest (Burgess 2005, Church of England 2005a). Percy explored contemporary cultural factors that may contribute to a loss of clergy morale and departure and alleges that the drop-out rate has risen to 10 per cent (Percy 2006: 163–4). From an autobiographical standpoint Lamont explored the reasons why clergy leave parish ministry for other ministries and concluded that, 'none of us have lost our faith: we still have our vocations, but they have moved out from the constraints of the Church . . . to leap the vicarage wall requires nerve' (Lamont 2011: 133). However research by Turton (2010) concluded that clergy adopt various strategies to cope with difficulties and rarely consider leaving parish ministry. Career biographical investigations of clergy ordained 1970–2000 conducted by the Church of England's research department (Barley 2009) suggest a best estimate of 6 per cent 'disappearing' clergy (Burgess 1995, 2005), confirming the impression 30 years earlier provided by Towler and Coxon (1979). This compares with a 9 per cent leakage among school teachers in England (Smithers and Robinson 2004). The complexity of clergy transfers in and out of stipendiary/non-stipendiary ministries and work in secular institutions as well as divorce and disciplinary issues, deferred pensions, and early or ill-health retirements make the statistics that are available particularly difficult to interpret. Until recently the Church's database has been unable to extract quantitative data by the range of variables desirable for ministry workforce planning or research purposes. A question in General Synod elicited the following 5-year average from the Clergy Pay Department: clergy who left 'by dismissal/resignation' 62 per year, 'leaving C of E' (6), 'unknown' (36) (Hargrave 2008). The introduction of exit interviews for all clergy making ministry moves would be an additional qualitative way of understanding the clergy population better.

Within the Roman Catholic Church there is a topical concern about 'what priests are for' (O'Collins 2011). A large scale survey of Catholic priests in England and Wales acknowledged difficulties: 'Recruitment and retention of personnel in many professions would appear to be closely linked yet empirical studies of the reciprocal effects of recruitment and retention of priests are nonexistent principally because the data are hard to get and the techniques for testing hypotheses are extremely complex.' The research found that although 'four-fifths of the workforce are content in their vocation and have every intention of staying put . . . an unacceptably high level of priests show the classic signs of burnout as revealed through emotional exhaustion and depersonalization'. Whereas older clergy showed the highest level of commitment in ministry, this affirmation reduced sharply in much younger priests and correlates with the underlying problem of a severe shortage of new vocations and the likelihood that 'up to one fifth of the workforce is feeling unsettled, restless and discontent' (Louden and Francis 2003: 182,186). In Australia McGillion and O'Carroll (2011) found a similar, widely held view among Catholic priests that they are undervalued and taken for granted. Such clergy are unlikely to continue possibly feeling that on reflection ordination was not such a good idea.

While Church of England vocations appear to be holding up better than pessimists predicted (Church of England 2007b), this is largely due to the ordination of women and the expansion of non-stipendiary ministries. For example in the Diocese of Southwell & Nottingham in 1985 there were no women deacons or priests, yet 30 per cent of the clergy in 2010 were female. Nationally there has been a steady decline of male stipendiary candidates from 244 men in 1994 to 173 men in 2010. There may therefore be an argument that a sustained downturn in male ordinations discourages some male clergy, who may take refuge in traditionalist evangelical (Reform 2011) or catholic (Forward in Faith 2011) settings or depart early, and that together these trends may deter further male vocations to ordination. Nesbitt certainly argues so in her feminization thesis which highlights 'the decline and fall of the young male cleric' (1997: 90). Gill (1993) argued similarly that historically, dwindling Protestant congregations in Britain were not only evidence of Church decline, but also a key cause of subsequent decline in adherents and clergy numbers, and, crucially, a decline in churchgoing well in advance of a widespread decline of conventional Christian belief. More recently Francis and Richter (2007) examined laity church-leaving. They found that up to a quarter of leavers were dissatisfied with the clergy and that the 'feminization' of the Church, or incompatible lifestyle issues, were among the reasons for disaffection. The probability is that, as a proportion of all parochial clergy serving in the Church of England, 'leavers' – understood as those who renounce a believing, active priesthood – remain few. For example in Peyton's time as Archdeacon of Newark 1999–2011 with an average of 100 clergy licensed in the archdeaconry just 4 individuals left by these criteria, including a woman who gave up her priesthood to become a Roman Catholic lay catechist (Lamb 2012).

We do not often hear leavers' stories in detail but an Anglican priest gained some media attention for a bitter-sweet account of his departure entitled *Last Rites: The End of the Church of England* (Hampson 2006) in which he describes what went wrong. Clearly it was not just the way the Church of England hierarchy may have related to his sexuality (he has self-identified as a gay priest) but a mounting catalogue of disillusionment with the failures and ineffectiveness of the Church of England as he saw it that encouraged his leaving after 13 years of ordained ministry. Interestingly he describes his present occupation as a 'writer and retreat leader'. His experiences concur with research by Greeley (2004) on Roman Catholic priests in the United States which demonstrated that celibate priests thought to be leaving principally in order to get married rarely leave for that single reason. Greeley established that a more significant explanation for their departure was a high level of dissatisfaction with priesthood and ministry. Celibacy is not a problem for priests engaged in satisfying ministry and few who leave to marry would return if compulsory celibacy was abandoned by the Church. Perhaps therefore because unhappy, permanent departure is counter-vocational among Church of England clergy, research participants are troubled by news of colleagues quitting. Sarah for example 'found this year a very difficult year . . . quite unsettling in that three people I knew quite well have left ministry'. While James did not feel that ordination was a dreadful mistake he nevertheless expressed some anxieties:

> It has never happened, but in the back of my mind is this nightmare that one day I will wake up and say 'I don't believe anything of this anymore' and I have always said to myself if that day happens I couldn't with integrity carry on . . . I am terrified that if that were to happen because I think to myself 'what would I then go and do?' and this is partly having been ordained at 25. I have nothing to fall back on.

This research explores why the vast majority of clergy stay despite the pressures of ministry that overtake their lives and those of their families.

Clergy durability may be partly explained by their ministerial adaptability (Percy 2006) or alternatively, as a few of the research interviewees suggested, there may be a sad and long-suffering hiddenness of clergy in difficulties. This can suddenly become visible in clergy marriage breakdowns or similar 'critical incidents' which we explore in greater detail in Chapter 5.

Managing clergy lives

Our study does not claim to be representative of the entire population of Church of England clergy. Rather, we focus on theoretical consistency and compare the similarities or disparities of participants' experiences with existing literature about clergy lives. Reflecting and theorizing from our data has led to some preliminary observations. The predominant understanding of clergy is largely built either around professional ministry encouragement within a Church struggling against a secularizing tide or, conversely, around a research concern (epitomized in Warren 2002) to discover why clergy become dysfunctional or leave their ministries. Perhaps there is also another story to tell. Through our qualitative interviews, we seek to understand reasons for the apparent high job satisfaction, low clergy drop-out rates and continuing recruitment among Area/Rural Deans in the Church of England. Although our research focuses on these parish clergy – who remain a powerful ministerial paradigm in the Church of England – our findings and reflections make many connections with other patterns of ministry, for example chaplaincy and with other Churches.

Gaining qualitative access to parish clergy we applied complementary approaches in shaping the research, in careful semi-structured interviewing and in evaluating the data. During the research one of us was active in the Church of England's General Synod (Peyton 2006), the other publishing about gender and work (Gatrell 2008), so some participants might have known our views. We have tried to position our values at critical distance to our enquiries, both the interviews and the analysis, and to apply a reflexive curiosity. In so doing, we draw upon a critical management studies tradition which utilizes the critical lenses of socio-political, organizational and ethical/cultural disciplines (Alvesson and Willmott 1992). It constitutes a perspective rather than a precise management technique – a reflexive conversation here between the Church and the academy. Indeed some bishops suggest that management theory and the Church are mutual filters and critical friends (Williams 2004, Croft 2005, Peyton 2009). The reflective practitioner-researcher bridges the two worlds: 'The technically rational world of disciplines and the reflection in action of competent practitioners and researchers who develop a phenomenology of practice' (Schon 1987: 308–9). Achieving critical distance in practice presents particular challenges, in our case recognizing the significance of researching 'down' one's own organization. Anthropologically, Peyton was 'one of the tribe' – an insider with 'street credibility' who already 'understands' (Robson 2002: 382) 'having a depth of understanding of the local context as well as a general understanding of the cultural context essential to qualify for the label ethnography' (Alvesson and Deetz 2000: 200). The contribution of a management sociologist (Gatrell) has enabled the inspection of clergy lives from a perspective that extends beyond the arena of the Church itself. The concept of 'emergent managers' proposed by Watson and Harris (1999) is a helpful parallel to our practical theological proposition that priests are not only 'changed' at ordination but 'become' through their lives.

Research themes

In order to interpret the enduring vocational commitment of contemporary Church of England clergy the research considered five topics:

- The content and morale of their ministry
- Community expectations, recognition and professional status
- Their key relationships and boundaries
- Their work–life balance
- Their priestly authenticity and endurance

These questions explore the daily activities of the clergy and in particular their personal and community identity within the social context of their lives. The key issue of personal agency within the requirements of an ordained life is drawn out within the interview conversations and in analysing the data. We have found illumination in applying a number of theoretical perspectives afresh to the clergy of the Church of England. In particular the disciplinary Panopticon of ordination (Foucault 1977), the self-governed clergy soul (Rose 1996, 1999), clergy identity, embodiment and gender (Giddens 1979, 1991, Shilling 2005, 2008, Howson 2005, Puwar 2004, Gatrell 2008), the emotional labour of priestly ministry (Hochschild 1983) and clergy household practices (Morgan 1996). Arguably, 'prison-like organizational arrangements (Foucault) may be the interpretation searching for empirical material to respond to' (Alvesson and Deetz 2000: 177) and these theoretical perspectives are here worked through as analytical lenses for the data and distilled into the three themes at the heart of our book: obedience, sacrifice and intimacy.

Ministry in the Church of England

Established

The Church of England has the largest following of any denomination or faith in Britain today. Four out of ten people in England regard themselves as belonging to the Church of England with 1.7 million people attending monthly and considerably more for Christmas and family rites of passage. A million pupils are educated in 4700 Church of England schools. English cathedrals are centres of spirituality and service attracting a growing number of worshippers and 9.5 million visitors each year (Church of England 2012).

The two distinctive features of the Church of England's continuing role within the life of the nation are its ubiquitous presence and particular polity. The Church of England comprises two Provinces, Canterbury and York and the country is divided into 42 dioceses (44 including dioceses for the Isle of Man and in Europe). The diocese is the fundamental unit of the Church of England (Podmore 2009: 2) led by a bishop with its own internal organization and strategic priorities for mission, ministry, education and social responsibility. National Church policy is coordinated by bodies based at Church House in London. The Church covers the whole of England through its parish system staffed by clergy, thus providing a Christian presence in varied urban, suburban and rural settings and a Christian contribution to community life. As Hinton (1994) argues, parish and place are synonymous because the Church of England has always been territorial not just in the sense of ecclesiastical and civil parishes originally coinciding, 'but also in its commitment to whole communities beyond its membership, indeed the affairs of the nation as a whole' (Hinton 1994: 139).

The Church of England is established by law with its own rulebook, the Canons (Church of England 2000b), and is designated as the national Church for the people of England (Hill 2007). Often described as 'episcopally led and synodically governed' (Podmore 2009: 9), indicating that bishops, clergy and the laity each have a place in the leadership and management of this traditional organization, the Established Church enjoys certain obligations and privileges. For example (despite recent reform proposals) 26 bishops remain members of the House of Lords and are engaged in debates about legislation and international affairs. Since 1919 the Church of England has had its own national 'parliament' or assembly of bishops, and elected clergy and laity. From 1970 called the General Synod it has power to prepare legislation on ecclesiastical matters (Canons and Measures) which, subject to a reference to the Parliamentary Ecclesiastical Committee, gain the Royal Assent without party political interference. At the most local level the priest and people combine the episcopal and synodical dimensions of governance in the elected Parochial Church Council where the vicar leads the work of the parish.

It is interesting to reflect on just what kind of organization the Church of England is. For example, judged by the typology of organizations suggested by Morgan (1997) the Church of England has the characteristics of both an 'organism' and a 'culture'. As a Christian organism the Church is responding to the challenges of the external environment (secularization, institutional marginalization) and its survival into the 21st century is success. At best this model creates a diversified, reflexive and adaptive organization. As a Christian culture the Established Church emphasizes symbolic activity (worship) and shared meanings (faith, tradition) recently described as 'the faith of the English' (Rooms 2011). The culture understands the socially constructed nature of its existence (Established, national) as well as the avenues of organizational change (gradualist). As Anglican commentators (Podmore 2005, Avis 2007) have noted the restrained approach to continuity and change renders the Church of England a complex organization which neither of Morgan's two types fully captures, while its clergy are a good barometer of how the Church resists what it perceives to be both excessive liberalism and intrusive corporate management. It is perhaps better to look for the cultural aspects of an organization such as the Church, rather than an organizational culture, to ascertain the 'set of meanings and values shared by members of the organization that defines the appropriate ways for people to think and behave' (Watson 2002: 224).

The shape of the workforce

The parish clergy of the Church of England are the subject at the heart of this research. A century ago clergy were more numerous, peaking at 25,235 in 1901 (Hinton 1994: 12) since which time the vocations and finances and membership of the Church have declined amidst a rising population. In 2010 the stipendiary clergy numbered 8,501 together with 3,151 non-stipendiary colleagues. Active retired clergy who still officiate voluntarily account for a further 5,674 priests (Church of England 2012).

Candidature for the priesthood begins when vocational enquirers emerge locally and are processed in dioceses (Church of England 2011a). National selection takes place at 48 hour residential Bishops' Advisory Panels for which there is no pass quota. Candidates are measured against nine criteria: vocation, ministry within the Church of England, spirituality, personality and character, relationships, leadership and collaboration, faith, mission and evangelism and quality of mind. Successful candidates should have a wide range of spiritual, intellectual and interpersonal skills and a robust character suited to public representative ministry in the 21st century Church. Additional ordination criteria are applied to some 'pioneer' and to locally restricted ministries. Ordinands train for 2 or 3 years in residential colleges or on local part-time courses. Those selected for leadership as opposed to supporting priestly roles may already have higher educational qualifications and/or acquire theology degrees and other ministerial awards. Ordination Services are conducted annually by bishops in their diocesan cathedrals and 563 women and men were ordained in 2010 (Church of England 2012), a figure which has remained stable since the millennium.

However the Church recognizes (Barley 2009, Church of England 2012) two urgent realities: an aging workforce and a shift in emphasis from paid to non-stipendiary, 'self-supporting' (Francis and Francis 1998) ministry. Older working is a growing UK phenomenon and McNair (2008a, 2008b) has applied research findings to the Church of England. The average age of stipendiary clergy is now 52, while 20 per cent are over 60 and only 12 per cent are under 40. In 2007 the number of pensioned clergy exceeded the paid for the first time. The average age of female and male ordinands for stipendiary ministry has risen for a decade to over 40, although encouragingly one in six is now under 30, a figure that has seen a sharp rise in the last few years. Just 46 per cent of those ordained in 2009 entered stipendiary ministry compared with 78 per cent in 1994. In contrast the vast majority of Peyton's contemporaries at theological college in the mid-1970s were under 30. It is projected that self-supporting clergy will outnumber stipendiary colleagues by 2021, providing local and voluntary clergy but fewer deployable clergy.

Newly ordained clergy are deacons for their first year, and although there is some interest in also having a permanent or 'distinctive diaconate' (Church of England 2001b) they are then ordained priest. As Assistant Curates new clergy are placed in training posts, with a training incumbent (an experienced priest) for a period of up to 4 years. The training course is designed to cover 3 years after which clergy look to move to their first 'in charge' post in a parish or perhaps chaplaincy ministry. Deployment throughout clergy careers is achieved through a mixture of advertised posts and patronage (by bishops, private patrons and patronage societies). Chaplaincy ministry in secular settings (hospitals, prisons, armed services) follows secular employment practices. Advertising in the church press and on diocesan websites, open competition for parish and diocesan posts is the declared policy of most dioceses backed by human resources advice from Church House in London.

The clergy career structure offers more sideways moves than promotions, traditionally called 'preferment'. Parish appointments of various kinds with more or less responsibility are commonly available, as are a range of chaplaincy posts. Becoming Rector of a Team Ministry or taking on the role of Area/Rural Dean are deemed to be more senior and increasingly demanding, as emerges in this research in which Area/Rural Deans are the clergy sample. Beyond that there are two or three senior preferment routes: cathedrals via residential canonries (100 posts), Dean (44), Archdeacon (116) and Suffragan (assistant) Bishop (61) any of which may presage consideration as a diocesan bishop. There is some cross-fertilization and connections with specialisms such as theological education or advisory roles. The two archbishops are usually appointed from among senior diocesan bishops in England or the Anglican Communion. Overall, the Church of England has a noticeably flat organizational character with modest opportunities for clergy promotion.

Archdeacons and Area/Rural Deans

The clergy interviews were conducted by Peyton in his time as Archdeacon of Newark while studying for his PhD at Lancaster University with Gatrell as supervisor. As senior executives in the Established Church archdeacons are responsible for large geographical regions within dioceses. Archdeacons are balancing mission with maintenance, leading new things and managing old problems and working with appointments and staffing, discipline, pastoral reorganization, church property and finance. Archdeacons remain priests however: 'priest means something crucial about me, about why I do whatever I do', remarked one interviewee about the link between ordination and leadership in an earlier study of archdeacon roles and identities (Peyton 2003: 40).

Area/Rural Deans lead their deanery which is a subdivision of an archdeaconry, a collection of parishes, teams and groups of parishes, often shaped to conform to local authority areas. Together with a Lay Chairperson and the Deanery Synod they provide a characteristic local example of English Anglican governance 'for effective mission and ministry' (Greenwood 2002: 34). The deanery leaders work closely with the archdeacon in an executive leadership team. At the time of our research these 722 'middle managers' formed 8.6 per cent of the total number of stipendiary clergy. Since the late 19th century the role has traditionally involved the pastoral care of clergy colleagues and being 'a channel of communication' between the local church and the bishop (Cross and Livingstone 1997: 1425). As the deanery has become a more strategic unit of the diocesan management of people, money and buildings, the Area/Rural Dean has assumed a greater pro-episcopal leadership role shaping policy and planning in the local church. The Deanery Resource Unit, launched in 1989 (Parish and People 2008) with its conferences and publications is a self-conscious reflection of the deanery's ascendancy in Church life, 'bringing fresh air into the missing link in the Church's structure' (Church of England 2007c: 302). Curiously, empirical qualitative research into this group of clergy appears absent.

Area/Rural Deans have their own parishes but voluntarily undertake additional pastoral and leadership roles over a wider number of deanery parishes and clergy, typically for 5-year terms. The bishop usually appoints after consulting the deanery clergy and deanery standing committee. Although clergy may politely decline the invitation the role is now perceived by some as an opportunity for career advancement (Church of England 2007d: 30) although it normally carries no additional remuneration. Because on average their role requires them to engage in close working relationships with a dozen or so other clergy this places them in an advantageous position to survey a variety of clergy lives and to reflect on their own. Their interview data serves the research objective to explore everyday lives and to discover what clergy are actually doing in relation to the many expectations projected onto them by bishops, parishioners and the media. The research is important because the 8,120 stipendiary and 3,150 non-stipendiary clergy ministering in the Church of England in 2010 form a significant occupational group. They are so regarded by Revenue and Customs for UK taxation purposes and through the English parochial system make an interesting case study of professional lives and wider social issues. Our findings may have relevance for Church policy and provide insights of value to other professions, for example on work–life balance and the blurring of roles and boundaries.

The remuneration package

The 'remuneration package' for Church of England clergy includes four elements: stipend (salary), housing provision, the full reimbursement of approved parochial working expenses and a pension. In the last major review of stipends, *Generosity and Sacrifice*, stipend was described as a hybrid of a salary and a living allowance and the definition accepted by the Church of England explicitly recognized that financial sacrifice is fundamental to following an ordained vocation in a stipendiary capacity:

> The stipend is part of the remuneration package that is paid for the exercise of office. It reflects the level of responsibility held. This package acknowledges the dual demands of Scripture of generosity and sacrifice on both those who receive the stipend and those who raise the necessary funds and this assumption is based on the reasonable expectation of the clergy that any comparisons made with professional secular groups does not in itself imply that comparable remuneration should be paid. (Church of England 2001a: 28)

Table 1.1 *The stipends of the Church of England clergy 2011/12*

National Minimum Stipend = £21,370 (2011/12)
Differentials are calculated by multiplying the NMS as indicated below:

BISHOPS
Archbishops £71,870–61,600 (× 3.50/3.00)
Diocesan Bishops £39,020 (1.90)
Suffragan (assistant) Bishops £31,830 (1.55)

PRIESTS
Cathedral Deans £31,830 (1.55)
Archdeacons £31,110 (1.50)
Cathedral Canons £24,640 (1.20)
Parochial Clergy £22,810 (1.10)
Including
Area/Rural Deans £22,810 (1.10)
Assistant Curates £21,370 (1.00)

Source: *The 38th Report of the Central Stipends Authority* (Church of England 2011b)

A key feature of the stipend structure is the way it reflects the flat organizational structure already noted and in particular offers no financial increments for experience, additional qualifications or length of service and modest differentials for those fewer clergy in senior roles (see Table 1.1 opposite). The egalitarian nature of Christian thinking concerning service and reward has sometimes led to fierce arguments in General Synod about having any differentials at all. More than the clergy the laity generally feel that some modest enhancements are justified.

The radical aspiration in *Generosity and Sacrifice* was to raise the basic stipend by a one-off increase of 17 per cent to pay clergy 80 per cent of the salary equivalent of a primary school head teacher, the discount reflecting the notional value of vicarage housing. Provision of tied accommodation is however often perceived by the clergy as something of a mixed blessing, the value of which is difficult to calculate. The Church has recognized the disadvantages:

> Clergy have no unfettered choice of where to live or the kind of housing provided for them; clergy have concerns about the cost of housing themselves in retirement; the housing is probably larger than clergy would choose for themselves and attracts higher bills for heating; part of the house is used for work purposes, and is effectively not part of the home; there is an expectation of constant availability. (Church of England 2008b: 17)

This explicit acknowledgement by the Church subsequently disappeared when the value of housing for clergy was recalibrated against mortgages and in 2011 was deemed to be £9860. In the early years of the new millennium some incremental stipend increases were introduced but the hope of *Generosity and Sacrifice* was never fulfilled (Church of England 2008b), largely because of increasing fears in dioceses about the rising cost of pensions. In common with secular pay in general, stipend levels are reducing in real terms against cost of living indices and the Church is concerned that stipends are adequate and equitable across the dioceses (Church of England 2011b). The Church of England clergy pension scheme is a noncontributory, fixed benefit, final salary scheme which provides a death in office or retirement lump sum and an annual pension based on years' service paid at two thirds the current stipend and index-linking together with a widow(er) pension. The rapidly rising cost of employers' contributions from the dioceses since 2000 has put a considerable strain on Church finances. Clergy, perhaps reflecting an older workforce, have generally been keen to protect their pension expectations even at the expense of suppressing stipend increases. The research interviews certainly struck a nerve among clergy eager to express their views on financial sacrifices and in Chapter 4 we further explore the opportunity cost of ordination.

The ordination of women

The single biggest change for clergy in the Church of England in centuries has been the entry of women into the priesthood since 1994. For its entire history since the Reformation the Church of England, following Roman Catholic and Orthodox Christendom, ordained only men into its ministerial priesthood. In the last quarter of the 20th century however this gendered approach began to unravel as certain provinces in the Anglican Communion for example North America and New Zealand debated the theological, ecclesiological and social issues and enacted the legal and practical changes to enable the ordination of women. From an ecumenical perspective women had been ordained for some years in Protestant denominations such as the Methodist, Presbyterian and Lutheran Churches in Europe and North America.

Women were first ordained Deacon in the Church of England in 1987 and following emotive General Synod debates culminating in a decision in November 1992, were ordained Priest from March 1994 onwards. At that time the Church of England excluded any change to a solely masculine episcopate, a decision which institutionalized a 'stained glass ceiling' that has arguably held back the Church of England for two decades. The numerous reports and debates in General Synod since 2004 have been edging towards women bishops. The Church of England accommodates a breadth of opinion on many matters as it is in its nature to be 'ancient and modern' at the same time. Speaking in support of opening the episcopate to women Peyton (2006) argued that historically the DNA of the Church of England is characterized by an 'avant-garde conformism' (MacCulloch 2003: 510) which enables theological development and ecclesial change across the centuries. Women's ordination has undoubtedly raised the temperature of Church debate considerably and 42 out of 44 dioceses backed the draft legislation (Beavan 2011) presented to General Synod in July 2012. However further reflection by the House of Bishops was deemed necessary.

Episcopacy and integrity

Following the General Synod's decision in 1992 to ordain women as priests, but not as bishops, legislation and arrangements were put in place to accommodate the opponents of the change. These allowed individual clergy and Parochial Church Councils to exclude women priests and to enjoy extended episcopal oversight from Provincial Episcopal Visitors (PEVs) who cannot accept women priests, as well as the oversight of their diocesan bishop, the majority of whom ordain women. PCCs may pass Resolution A to exclude all women priests celebrating Holy Communion in their parish and/or Resolution B to prevent them having a woman incumbent. Under the Episcopal Ministry Act of Synod (Church of England 1993) they can also petition to have an additional bishop – there are three PEVs covering England – and about 300 parishes have taken advantage of the (some would say over-generous) provision (Kuhrt and Bentley 2001: 238). In addition £19.1m was paid in compensation to 480 male clergy who chose to leave the Church of England in the years immediately following the decision to ordain women under the special (some would say highly contentious) severance arrangements put in place.

The 1998 Lambeth Conference, conscious of the divisions within and between Provinces of the worldwide Anglican Communion on women priests passed a resolution to the effect that both those accepting of women priests and bishops and those opposed have a place in the Church and are to be regarded equally as 'loyal Anglicans' (Anglican Communion 1999: 395). This led to the idea that 'two integrities' might be held together – a characteristically uncomfortable Anglican compromise which for a while enjoyed a currency in local church conversation (Kuhrt and Bentley 2001: 238). Barnes (2001) argued that the Act of Synod was necessary in the period of reception of an innovation, attempting to hold together in one Church those of differing views. Conversely Furlong (1998) dismissed it as a form of ecclesial apartheid and institutionalized schism which is seen as increasingly implausible by both those within the Church and beyond in the wider community. Women and the Church (WATCH 2012) is a pressure group in the Church of England and its synods which has been working for some years for the rescission of the Act of Synod and the admission of women into the episcopate (Harris and Shaw 2002). In a study of first generation women priests in England, Thorne (1999) concluded that the Act of Synod was deeply harmful to women priests on a practical, emotional and spiritual level because it legitimized the exclusion of women from parts of the Church and fostered the idea that ordained women might taint or invalidate a man's ministry.

It remains a concern for 'sacramental assurance' focused on a male-only apostolic episcopal lineage and a male-only celebrant of the Eucharist that concerns traditionalists who until now have felt secure within their separate integrity within the Church of England. In 2010 Pope Benedict established the Ordinariate within the Roman Catholic Church to receive disaffected Anglicans and a number of male clergy (including several PEVs) and laity have taken advantage of these arrangements. Once women are ordained as Bishops, accommodating those who cannot accept female ministry will become a source of impossible tension within the Church.

Two-clergy couples

The advent of the ordination of women in the Church of England in 1994 opened up new possibilities: both members of heterosexual married couples and lesbian partners might be ordained. Some form relationships during the course of their ordination training or during early years in ordained ministry. Others became two-clergy couples when a spouse or partner was ordained at a later time. In the early years women joined clergymen, in a gendered catching-up period. The guidance paper, *Partners in Marriage and Ministry* (Church of England 1995a) and two pioneer studies of the experiences of two-clergy couples, 'Marital Bliss: Ministerial Enigma' (Saint George's House 1998) and 'Double Blessing' (Walrond-Skinner 1998) chart the early progress of this new pattern of ministry evoking a sense of self-conscious innovation. Bentley (2001) found that perhaps 4 per cent (364) of stipendiary clergy were part of such couples while the more recent NADAWM (2008) survey identified 146 clergy couples. Our research included six such couples.

These developments presented the Church with a number of new human resource and deployment issues and for some years it struggled to establish standard terms and conditions. Bentley (2001: 209–10) reported a lack of encouragement and consistency by diocesan managers in employing two-clergy couples: were two-clergy couples entitled to one post or 1.5 or two, one stipend or 1.5 or two, job-share, two curacies in the same or adjacent parishes, even two vicarages or housing allowances? Women clergy often felt unfairly forced into the supporting role, often unpaid or part-time, in an ordained version of 'the clergy wife as unpaid curate' assumptions of earlier years. The erratic treatment of couples persisted across the dioceses as the Church caught up with equal opportunities best practice and a new generation of clergy emerged more willing to stand up for their legal entitlements. Archdeacons shaping two-clergy appointments appreciate how upset and uncomfortable such couples can feel when placed in a position where they have to challenge bishops within a Christian organization assumed to be built on respect and generosity, risking being labelled as 'difficult' or as demanding 'designer ministry' – with potentially negative career consequences. Over the past decade, due to an increase in more professional human resource practices in the Church, together with more realistic expectations among two-clergy couples, there has been a growing appreciation that clergy should apply for posts that the diocese seeks to fill and that posts are not artificially created simply because clergy happen to be married to each other. Our research takes the opportunity to capture the particular way in which ordained vocations are sometimes embodied in each gender within two-clergy marriages by incorporating a number of two-clergy couples as one Area/Rural Dean household variable among many within the research sample.

Feminization

Nesbitt's North American research suggests that the feminization of the clergy, as in some other recently feminized secular occupations, paradoxically has had adverse effects on women clergy careers: either male paradigms and authority structures remain dominant or 'by the time substantial numbers of women gained access, the occupations not only had lost their attractiveness to men but were offering tangibly fewer advantages to women' (Nesbitt 1997: 162). In the Church of England increasing numbers of women have reached the seniority available to them – of a total of 352 dignitaries in 2010, 37 were women. But as the National Association of Diocesan Advisors in Women's Ministry warns (NADAWM 2008) gendered career stratification persists through differential training and deployment patterns. Nevertheless Nesbitt believes that significantly, unlike secular work, female advancement in organized religion holds the prospect of ideological influence over large sectors of women, indicating that 'the clergy becomes strategically more critical as a battleground for occupational feminization and its implications' (Nesbitt 1997: 162).

Church Statistics produced by the Church of England (2012) shows that 21 per cent of stipendiary clergy and 18 per cent of incumbents are female. A higher proportion of women, 53 per cent, served as self-supporting clergy. In 1994 just 26 per cent of all ordinations were of women, rising to 51 per cent in 2010, a period in which the average annual number of men and women ordained was 488 candidates. Significant evidence points to a decreasing availability of male clergy and stipendiary clergy of both genders in the coming years in which the number of stipendiary entrants does not increase and a large number of existing clergy approach retirement. In contrast, 70 per cent of part-time paid posts are thought to be occupied by women (NADAWM 2008) and the number of non-stipendiary clergy over half of whom are female continues to increase.

The delay in accepting women bishops in the Church of England appears to be not the only 'stained-glass ceiling'. As the Group for Rescinding the Act of Synod (GRAS) reports, the Church of England is only 'a third of the way to reaching gender equality' (Beavan 2011). Their annual Furlong Table (named after an early advocate of gendered statistics, Furlong 1998) indicates that in 2011 on average dioceses achieved 35 per cent gender equality, calculated by combining the number of full-time stipendiary women clergy and the number of women senior post-holders, up from 26 per cent in 2005. A perfect score of 100 per cent would indicate the half-feminization of clergy in a diocese. However there are at present 4 female cathedral deans and 16 women archdeacons from a possible 116, while our research found that women priests accounted for 10 per cent of the 722 Area/Rural Deans in the Church of England. Whether this amounts to a feminization of the clergy in the Church of England parallel to the North American experience reported by Nesbitt (1997) or a gradualist and 'culturally normalizing' gendered evolution within the clergy 'species' (Percy 2006: 104) is open to debate. Bagilhole (2006) argues that women are still pioneering their way through not so much a glass ceiling as a lead roof. As Anglican woman priest Green (2009, 2011) suggests, although we are past the point of no return as a maturing priesthood of both sexes honouring sexual difference in mediating the divine and shaping a more effective Church in the world, 'women need to encounter not just passive tolerance but positive acknowledgement and active, practical affirmation' (Green 2011: 44). If bishops are gatekeepers to preferment, a positive vote by General Synod for women bishops may accelerate progress for women in English ministry although some Anglican provinces that allow women bishops, the Scottish Episcopal Church for example, have not so far chosen them. In New Zealand, Penny Jamieson, the first woman to become a diocesan bishop in the Anglican Communion, describes the anticipation which surrounded her appointment:

> Ordination always changes people – that is what the Holy Spirit is about – but for me it has been a sea-change. My consecration precipitated me into a realm of activity, publicity and spiritual turmoil for which, despite my best efforts, I was totally unprepared. The ordinal itself is quite terrifying in the expectations it gives rise to, but these pale into insignificance against the expectations people had of me. I hardly knew who or what I was. (Jamieson 1997: 2)

Faith in research

Sociology and the sacred

Our 'search for priesthood' is focused on empirical research, listening to Church of England clergy talking about their experiences, and on sociological and theological reflection about the embodiment of priesthood. We therefore close this introductory chapter by locating our contribution within social theory and practical theology. In late modernity the relationship between theology and the social sciences has ranged from antipathy to absorption and can be observed in the growth of biblically fundamentalist Christianity, a more liberal interpretation of Christianity and in the development of the academic discourse of Practical Theology. From a Christian perspective for some academics postmodernity marks the end of theology while for others it marks a new beginning. Essentially a contested concept, postmodernity 'is perhaps best construed as an "exodus" from the constraints of modernity' (Vanhoozer 2003: xiv). Some have doubted whether the engagement of theology with the sociology of religion can prevail. Milbank in *Theology and Social Theory: Beyond Secular Reason* (1990) developed a critique that came to be termed 'radical orthodoxy': 'secular reason claims that there is a "social" vantage point from which it can locate and survey various "religious" phenomena. But it is has turned out that assumptions about the nature of religion themselves help to define the perspective of this social vantage' (Milbank 1990: 139). Shakespeare (2000) accused Milbank of romanticizing and deifying the Church and its classical doctrines while

Roberts (2005) argues that Milbank is positing an abstract opposition in which theology and social theory are reduced to rhetoric disconnected from their academic roots. Our fruitful empirical research into 21st century clergy lives concurs with the view that 'the tasks of theology and sociology are mutual in at least as much as they address the human condition in exploratory and interpretive terms . . . [which embrace] ethnography, that is, the effective representation and interpretation of what is actually happening in human lives' (Roberts 2005: 381). In relation to our clergy lives project this highlights an important distinction:

> Whereas the sociologist, in general, may tend to concentrate on the 'is' rather than the 'could be', that is, on the empirical rather than the speculative, the sociologist working within applied theology may be encouraged to give equal attention to both. Provided that he [sic] does not confuse the 'could be' with the 'ought to be', his [sic] task remains properly sociological. (Gill 1977: 118)

Gill, an academic theologian, served for many years as a non-stipendiary Anglican priest in parishes and particularly appreciates the capacity of the social sciences to provide explanatory insight which 'entails a critical evaluation of faith upon action and of action upon faith . . . sociology can perform a crucial function in highlighting the social consequences of belief in general and theology in particular' (1977: 119). More recently Gill has revisited his earlier work on the relationship of theology with social context and structure (1977) arguing strongly against Milbank for a more appreciative engagement with sociological perspectives which 'can perform an important function in discerning the social context which theologians need to take into consideration if they are to communicate effectively . . . sociology is of central importance to theologians and the latter ignore it at their peril' (Gill 2012: 22–3). Indeed, within multi-cultural 21st century Britain there has been a renewed interest in religious topics within sociology and at the same time a fresh confidence in the application of the social sciences to faith subjects, epitomized in the wide-ranging Religion & Society Programme (Woodhead and Catto 2012) whose findings are informing policy-makers and cultural commentary. It is this spirit of collaborative and critical enquiry which energizes the authors of this book.

Within our research (as for Gill and Woodhead) the 20th century sociologist Berger stands out as a prescient contributor to current debates about the place of religion in society. In *The Sacred Canopy* (1967) and *A Rumour of Angels* (1969) he described religion as the human enterprise in which 'the purpose of religion is to construct a sacred cosmos . . . religion offers a protective canopy of transcendent legitimacy, meaning, and order to the precarious constructions that society calls "reality". The fate of any social order is therefore inevitably bound up with the fate of religion' (Dorrien 2001: 32). Woodhead (2001) highlighted Berger's key idea that growing pluralism undermined stable belief systems and encouraged secularization. It is this process set against residual religious expectations that forms the social context for the clergy studied here. Berger argued that Christianity is socially constructed and as open to critique as any other belief system. Methodologically he perceived theology as a universe of discourse, but existentially as a living people in a social location with a social biography. A conversation between sociology and theology therefore is an open partnership which we have applied to clergy lives. Berger wrote from a self-confessed Christian perspective and at one time considered a ministry vocation (Berger 1967, 1990 edition: xvi, Dorrien 2001: 27). He did not address the issue of religious professionals in detail but recognized that the 20th century bureaucratization of both Catholic and Protestant Church traditions 'corroded the identity' of clergy and religious leaders (Berger 1967: 140). Later in Chapter 4 we develop the idea of 'the sacrificial embrace' as an explanatory metaphor for the continuing plausibility of an enduring vocational commitment to priesthood in the 21st century.

In our research the juxtaposing demands of God and the Church are centred in a discussion about obedient bodies (Foucault 1977, 1979, 1988; Shilling 1993, 2005, 2008) and governed souls (Rose 1999, Hochschild 1983) in clergy lives and the consequences for intimate relationships (Giddens 1992). We describe the complex relationships between personal belief and professional belonging to the Church and between the structural context of parish ministry in the Church of England, the role of gender (Howson 2005, Puwar 2004, Gatrell 2008) and the agency and identity of individuals (Giddens 1979, 1991). Given the context of postmodernity's challenge to theology, our interest lies in how clergy beliefs, ministerial practices and personal lifestyles absorb or resist postmodernity's radical instincts. There is an ongoing debate about precisely what bodies can be recovered and studied in research, theoretically and empirically. Methodologically there are issues of theological and philosophical perspective in the context of lived priestly bodies as socially and personally constructed. Our clergy research has analogies in health research and management studies. For example there is a tension noted by Gatrell (2008) between 'the created bodies of particular societies' which may often be considered in the theoretical abstract (Evans and Lee 2002) and the 'real materiality of bodies' which may experience fatigue and pain (Thomas 2002). Further tensions exist between the ideal of a professionally socialized 'emergent manager' (Watson and Harris 1999) who is seen to be in control of body and mind, and the everyday challenges faced by professional employees who are experiencing embodied changes which are difficult to contain such as pregnancy or ill-health (Haynes 2011). The religious dimension is explored by Shilling (2008) in his work on 'believing bodies' which indicates that practising religious believers, especially the clergy, will over time 'become the religious subjects they seek to be' (Shilling 2008: 166 original italics). The argument of 'priestly becoming' over the years since ordination developed in this research is that clergy authenticity is expressed materially and culturally in the congruent self which lies at the heart of enduring vocational commitment.

We therefore explored embodied and obedient vocational souls within the personal and social constructs shaping their lives, their behaviour, attitudes and feelings, both disclosed and hidden in a 'relational conceptualization of the self' (Denzin and Lincoln 2000: 1042). The principal researcher was a senior Christian leader researching a Christian institution. The Christian discourse – theology – is essentially embodied and relational and our approach has a Christian ontological basis in a belief in God, and also reflects the philosophical environment of the research sample of Church of England clergy. These add up to a coherent theological construction of reality for an embodied individual who 'commits himself [*sic*] in a comprehensive way to the new reality . . . to the faith . . . with what is subjectively the whole of his life . . . the readiness to sacrifice oneself is, of course, the final consequence of this kind of socialization' (Berger and Luckmann 1967: 145). This faithful socialization in a religious community, which lies at the heart of the research question, is embodied in the Church and its clergy.

Practical theology and theological reflection

The location for the open conversation and partnership between sociology and theology harnessed in our research is what the Church and the academy have termed 'Practical Theology'. The extent of practical theology in terms of academic maturity and professional reach is well rehearsed by Ballard (2000) and Woodward and Pattison (2000). Until the late 20th century Practical Theology in British theological faculties and seminaries was largely regarded as an a-theoretical 'second order' discipline, uninformed by the human sciences and professional skills, simply concerned with the practice of Christian ministry and discipleship, exclusively focussed on (largely male) ordained professional practice – rather than as the arena for broader critical reflection it has now become, aided by the ascendancy of religious studies over traditional academic theology subjects. More recent work has explored the relationship between theology and the social sciences specifically as it relates to the use of qualitative empirical research methods in the process of theological reflection starting from the assumption that 'human beings by definition are interpretative creatures' (Swinton and Mowatt 2006: 29). They argue that qualitative research is one way in which we can 'look behind the veil of "normality" and see what is actually going on within situations' (2006: vi). It is this interpretive journey into the stories of clergy lives that we have made in search of an account of 21st century Church of England priesthood.

We previously pointed to an overemphasis on the need for pastoral care for failing clergy to the detriment of broader insights. Our project seeks to redress the research imbalance exploring with the clergy participants their experience and understanding of priestly ordination and its enduring vocational command over the discipline and loyalty of individuals. Graham (1996) noted approvingly that the dominance of therapeutic models of care was being replaced by a wider range of pastoral practices. The shifting paradigms of practical theology have witnessed a move beyond individualistic, clinical models to a more communal horizon within the life of the Church, better equipped to tackle the challenges of postmodernity:

> Practice emerges as something which mediates between structure and agency, seeing culture as a human creation which nonetheless persists over time; and of the norms of practice as in some sense rule-governed and institutional but still dependent on individual and collective agency for their maintenance. Such a focus avoids rooting the values of hope and obligation in a meta-physical extra-cultural realm, but rather allows us to plot the dynamics of the ways in which purposeful practices are the implicit bearers of ultimate truth claims. (Graham 1996: 97)

The primary mode of enquiry for pastoral theology is phenomenological, respecting the reflexivity of gender and contextuality of individuals. Within this framework 'theological reflection' is the method deployed (Graham, Walton and Ward 2005) constituting a continuing conversation generating many ways of knowing, a 'pluridoxy' (Graham 1996: 200). Roberts argued that this is more than critical reflexivity: 'theological reflection . . . can do little without the un-predetermined gift, the charisma that goes with vocation' (Roberts 2002: 211). The clergy in our research are products of social construction but each individual's identity and story are not predefined. Our interviews with 46 Area/Rural Deans form, in William James's terms, living human documents in which 'private and personal phenomena . . . realities in the completest sense of the term' (James 1902: 498) are brought to the surface. This approach is central to our argument that the disciplined bodies (Foucault 1977) and obedient souls (Rose 1999) of the priest participants are both the theoretical basis and the empirical finding which can explain the enduring vocational commitment of the parish clergy. Our perspective is that theology and sociology are mutually tasked to explore and interpret the human condition and provide a plausible explanatory framework for why clergy are who they are and do what they do – how they embody the priesthood.

2

Describing Clergy Lives

In his poem 'Blame the Vicar' John Betjeman (*Church Poems* 1982) praises the virtuous Vicar with a collar the wrong way round who keeps the faithful flock bright and undismayed. As a humorous and affectionate portrayal of the priest's role in the lives of parishioners it captures something of the romantic and residual religious expectations that secularized society has of the religious professionals of the Church of England. The recent popularity of television's fictional *Rev* featuring a hapless but ultimately admirable east London vicar dealing with 21st-century issues confirms a critical appreciation of the sincerity of the clergy role which 'does not win prizes for all the things done unnoticed' (BBC 2010, 2011). Under the headline 'airwaves to heaven' the Roman Catholic weekly *The Tablet* described the BBC2 television sitcom *Rev* as a good religious programme which 'successfully captured a curious audience' (*The Tablet* 2010). For some the local vicar is a figure of fun whose work cannot quite be fathomed, a person on whom others project their own frustrations, yet without whom, as our interviewee Julian put it, something would be missing: 'clergy are handling the moments in people's lives that nobody else knows how to deal with'. This chapter introduces how we identified our research participants and the research process. It offers an overview of who Church of England priests think they are, what they do and what they believe.

The interviews

Contemporary clergy in the Established Church pursue a particular kind of Christian vocational role which is unfashionable and counter-cultural and an essential aim of our *Managing Clergy Lives* research (Peyton 2009) has been to allow the clergy to record their own experiences and explanations of their vocational commitment. The data gathered from the clergy interviews provides the conversational references which illustrate the 'analytical story' (Strauss and Corbin 1990: 230) in relation to previous scholarly work and the impressions generated by Church of England's own literature and the media.

Our empirical study of Area/Rural Deans takes up Warren's suggestion that we need to know more about how the clergy understand their priesthood and their relationships with other clergy in the deanery setting (Warren 2002) but with key differences. Firstly, Warren was concerned with 'the psychotherapeutic needs of Anglican parochial clergy today' and 'about reparation' (2002: 219, 17) whereas this study is concerned to understand the enduring vocational commitment of Church of England clergy. Secondly, Warren focuses on what clergy lack and need as vulnerable people, whereas our approach is positively focused on what the clergy already have, their daily strategies and inner understandings which contribute to their determination to remain effective, contented clergy. Warren concluded that her hypothesis – that many parochial clergy have in recent decades suffered a severe loss of confidence because of societal and intra-Church change – has some basis in reality. This indicates however that many others remain more secure in their ministries. Our approach followed up the notion that clergy who succeed evidence 'greater ego integration' (Warren 2002: 18) and generated data supporting the alternative view that Church of England clergy remain largely confident in their faith and committed to ministry. Although two or three clergy we interviewed mentioned the value of counselling support in dealing with professional or personal issues, stories of stress-related illness were few. Indeed the Area/Rural Deans responded to burn-out warning signs in colleagues and themselves. This is consonant with Percy (2006) who argues that across denominations clergy have historically been an adaptive species rather than the dislocated, endangered workforce described by Warren.

Participating clergy

The Area/Rural Deans participating in this study covered a 30-year age range (from 36–66 years old) and a similar range for the number of years ordained (8–41 years). However a typical Area/Rural Dean in this research sample is male and married with children at home. Only three single men emerged from the 32 male clergy interviewed, while among the 14 women in the sample only three married women had children at home. A woman Area/Rural Dean is thus likely to be older and/or single and because women have only been ordained to the priesthood in the Church of England since 1994 some have achieved Area/Rural Dean status with just 8 years priestly ordained experience. The youngest male research participant was 36 years old, ordained 9 years, the youngest female was 40, ordained 8 years. It was reported that some dioceses in metropolitan areas welcome younger appointments to the role of Area/Rural Dean. Participants confirmed that the process for becoming an Area/Rural Dean is largely standardized across dioceses: the bishop appoints after taking soundings among the clergy of the deanery and its standing committee. Appointments are usually for a 5-year period and can be resigned without leaving the particular parish in which the priest serves. Most participants welcomed the additional responsibility and interest it gave to their ministries. They frequently commented on the burden of extra meetings and conflict resolution in the parishes of the deanery but equally these Area/Rural Deans clearly put a great deal of pastoral effort into supporting their clergy colleagues some of whom are challenging characters for others to relate to, or who are in difficulties with professional ministry or their personal lives. Richard based in a market town summed up the changing shape of the Area/Rural Dean role from a pastoral one to a strategic one:

> The role has changed from being a shop steward into being, without this being misunderstood, that quasi-episcopal managerial role.

The interviews also confirmed the diversity of Anglican theological and ecclesiastical traditions within the Church of England as the Area/Rural Deans demonstrated differing perspectives on the nature and practice of ministry. Indeed the Church tradition labels which the clergy were invited to give themselves at the outset of each interview – Evangelical, Catholic, liberal, traditional and so forth – were often no stereotypical guide to their explanations of the ordained life or their opinions about particular issues. Personal journeys of maturing faith and changing preferences over the years in many cases enabled participants to understand other theological viewpoints only too well, enhancing their reliability and interest as informants and probably explaining their Bishop's and local colleagues' confidence in their appointment as Area/Rural Dean. Indeed the particular finding which emerged across the sample was the diligent aspirations of most of the Area/ Rural Deans' ministries which is discussed in Chapter 6 where the concept of clergy authenticity is explored.

Bryman recommends 'purposive sampling' in which there is a correspondence between the research question and the sample, the saturation point for variables and the ability 'to support convincing conclusions' (2004: 333–5). The initial selection criteria were therefore: geographical spread across each mainland diocese in England, gender, age and training institution – these were designed to provide breadth of ministerial experience and theological perspective within the sample. Subsequent criteria were ethnic origin, marital status, number of years ordained, number of years as an Area/Rural dean – these were designed to gain wider cultural, household and professional contributions. Further variables only came to light during interviews, for example divorce, sexuality, partners' occupations and household circumstances. A few variables proved elusive, particularly minority ethnicity (Church of England 2007e, 2007f) and disability (as noted by Thomas 2002 and Church of England 2007g) and Area/Rural Deans of either gender under 40 years old.

The research sample of those Area/Rural Deans who participated is shown (with pseudonyms) in Table 2.1 linked to occupation prior to ordination illustrating the extent to which priesthood has been the main life's work or a second career.

Table 2.1 *Interviewee pseudonyms and previous occupation*

Keith	Student
Malcolm	Music teacher
Philip	Chartered accountant
Sarah	Social worker
Robert	Local government
Linda	Nursing
Beryl	Physiotherapist
Matthew	Student
Richard	Student
Daniel	Social worker
Benjamin	Banking
Nicholas	Linguist
Adam	Solicitor
Kevin	Health service administrator
Tony	Student
Mark	Missionary overseas
Kenneth	Teacher
Derek	Musician
Geoffrey	Student
Jonathan	Teacher
Trevor	Manufacturing
Alistair	Painter and decorator
Neil	Student
Liz	Teacher
Julian	Merchant Navy
Colin	Teacher
Pauline	Chartered accountant

Table 2.1 *Continued*

Roger	Industrial salesman
Roy	Teacher
Jacqui	Musician
Fiona	Administrator
James	Ecologist
Patricia	Teacher
Janet	Senior nurse tutor
Simon	Student
Carole	Librarian
Laurence	Teacher
Penny	Insurance services
Charles	Teacher
Irene	Psychiatric nurse
Jean	Civil servant
Ralph	Student
John	Banking
Jeremy	Horticulture management
Fred	Printer
Angela	Accountant

Those whose previous occupation is given as 'student' entered the ordained ministry without pursuing a career or significant work prior to becoming an ordinand, usually in their mid-twenties. The clear finding here is a gendered picture reflecting the entry of women into the full-time stipendiary priesthood in the Church of England from 1994. Hence the significant preordination careers of now maturing first-generation ordained women compared to a more balanced male sample. The first wave of women pursuing a life-long ordained vocation has yet to make its way into Area/Rural Dean posts in significant numbers. However as noted in Chapter 1 the increasing age at ordination is steadily reducing the number of life-long clergy, both women and men.

Table 2.2 illustrates the geographical and diocesan location of the clergy interviewed. For some administrative purposes the Church of England groups dioceses geographically in line with the Government's regional template. We are unspecific about which dioceses provided which participants, especially by gender, to disguise identification. Women were however interviewed in each region.

Table 2.2 *Geographical and diocesan location of clergy interviewed*

English regions Church of England Dioceses	Clergy interviewed
North West Carlisle, Blackburn, Liverpool, Manchester, Chester	5
North East Newcastle, Durham	2
Yorkshire York, Ripon & Leeds, Bradford, Wakefield, Sheffield	5
West Midlands Lichfield, Birmingham, Coventry, Worcester, Hereford	5
East Midlands Lincoln, Southwell & Nottingham, Derby, Leicester, Peterborough	6
Eastern Norwich, Ely, St Edmundsbury & Ipswich, Chelmsford, St Albans	6
London London, Southwark	3
South East Canterbury, Rochester, Guildford, Chichester, Portsmouth, Winchester, Oxford	8
South West Truro, Exeter, Salisbury, Bath & Wells, Bristol, Gloucester	6
TOTALS 42 Dioceses used for interviews (NB. Diocese of Sodor & Man and Diocese in Europe excluded)	46 Interviews (14 women) (32 men)

The following three Tables provide more details about the age, gender and professional maturity encompassed within the research sample.

As noted previously, clergy gender is a recurring topic throughout this research. The balance within the sample was not predetermined and as we started to select and contact clergy we realized that an age band approach to the sample would deliver a suitable sample of women and men across the other variables in which we were interested.

The availability since 1994 of Church of England ordination for women clearly influenced the shape of Table 2.3 and a similar framework applied to the careers of the clergy interviewed as shown in Tables 2.4 and 2.5 illustrates the point sharply.

Table 2.3 *Age and gender of clergy interviewed*

Age bands Years old	Male clergy interviewed	Female clergy interviewed	Total clergy Interviewed
35–39	6	0	6
40–49	8	6	14
50–59	13	6	19
60–66	5	2	7
TOTALS	32 (69.6%)	14 (30.4%)	46 (100%)

Table 2.4 *Number of years ordained of clergy interviewed*

Number of years ordained	Male clergy interviewed	Female clergy interviewed	Total clergy interviewed
Under 10	3	3	6
10–14	8	4	12
15–19	2	4	6
20–24	7	3	10
25–29	5	0	5
30–34	6	0	6
35 and over	1	0	1
TOTALS	32	14	46

Clergy take on the role of Area/Rural Dean voluntarily and are licensed by the bishop for a limited period, usually 5 years. As Table 2.5 shows a significant number (9) of women in the sample were 2 years or less in post. Three experienced male priests had fulfilled the role for longer than one period.

Finally there follow Tables 2.6 and 2.7 illustrating the ordination training institutions and church traditions of the female and male participants. These were ascertained from *Crockford's Clerical Directory* (2007) and checked in the interview preliminaries. We were able to achieve a breadth and balance enhancing our analysis.

During each interview the priest was invited to describe their 'churchmanship' [*sic*] or church tradition and Table 2.7 shows the descriptions given.

Clergy are familiar with these terms which are also used by the Clergy Appointments Adviser (2012) to compile standardized CVs for clergy seeking a ministry move. The particular relevance of information about personal church tradition is that it potentially locates individual clergy on a

Table 2.5 *Number of years as Area/Rural Dean of clergy interviewed*

Number of years as Area / Rural Dean	Male clergy Interviewed	Female clergy Interviewed	Number of Area / Rural Deans interviewed
Under a year	4	1	5
1 year	3	5	8
2	8	3	11
3	4	3	7
4	3	1	4
5	1	1	2
6	6	0	6
7	0	0	0
8	0	0	0
9	0	0	0
10	1	0	1
11	1	0	1
12	1	0	1
TOTALS	32	14	46

Table 2.6 *Theological colleges and training courses of interviewees*

THEOLOGICAL COLLEGE / TRAINING COURSE	NUMBER OF INTERVIEWEES
Cranmer Hall Durham	3 (2 male 1 female)
College of the Resurrection, Mirfield	3 (3 male)
Oak Hill Theological College	2 (2 male)
Queen's College Birmingham	2 (2 male)
Ridley Hall, Cambridge	4 (4 male)
Ripon College Cuddesdon, Oxford	3 (2 male 1 female)
St John's College, Nottingham	6 (3male 3 female)
St Stephen's House, Oxford	2 (1 male 1 female)
Trinity College, Bristol	3 (2 male 1 female)
Westcott House, Cambridge	4 (3 male 1 female)
Wycliffe Hall, Oxford	2 (1 male 1 female)
Chichester Theological College	1 (1 male)
Lincoln Theological College	2 (1 male 1 female)
Salisbury & Wells Theological College	1 (1 male)
East Anglian Ministerial Training Course (EAMTC)	2 (2 male)
Northern Ordination Course (NOC)	1 (1 female)
Southern Theological Education & Training Scheme (STETS)	1 (1 female)
West of England Ministerial Training Course (WEMTC)	1 (1 female)
Lampeter Theological College	1 (1 male)
St Deniol's College, Hawarden	1 (1 female)
Overseas Anglican training institution	1 (1 male)

Table 2.7 *Church traditions of interviewees*

Conservative Evangelical 2 (2 men, 0 women)
Open Evangelical 9 (4 men, 5 women)
Central / Evangelical 11 (8 men, 3 women)
Central / Catholic 9 (6 men, 3 women)
Liberal Catholic 11 (8 men, 3 women)
Traditional Catholic 4 (3 men, 1 woman)

TOTAL 46

Additional influences mentioned:
Charismatic Renewal 5 (2 men, 3 women)
Ecumenical 2 (2 men, 0 women)

---

spectrum of theological and ecclesial standpoints with regard to the nature of Anglican ordination and the practice of ministry in the Church of England of some importance to self-perceptions reported in the interviews.

Ethnography at the vicarage

Potential participants were contacted by telephone, anticipating the research interview in allowing clergy to make a more personal assessment of the researcher. Most were pleased to be approached, a few were cautious. Background information and a paper of discussion topics were provided to help clergy prepare for the interview. These were held in the clergyperson's vicarage at their convenience. The home setting was important because of our interest in the work–life, public–private boundaries of clergy lives. As suggested by Bryman (2004) additional information is gained from observing other interactions as many of the interviews were punctuated by interruptions and incidents, some mundane, others quite dramatic. Interviews were taped and designed to last up to two hours, an optimum length for a qualitative interview beyond which the discussion and research relationship can change (Elliott 2005: 32) inappropriately mutating into counselling (Brannen and Collard 1982) or compounding the problems of researching one's own organization.

The interviews generated good discussions and data across the research topics and questions within this framework. Overall the clergy were relaxed and talkative about their work and open to discussing sensitivities, difficulties and vulnerabilities. Thoughtful pauses were common, as well as humour and a certain earthiness, perhaps because interviewees thought that an experienced archdeacon was pretty unshockable and would understand. A few participants were slower to contribute or appeared tired or perhaps even depressed. Body language, throw away or tangential remarks and reactions to vicarage interruptions gave ethnographic clues about the comfort zone or preoccupations of each interviewee.

Each interview discussed the five research topics introduced in the previous chapter: the nature of your current ministry, professional identity, relationships and boundaries, work–life balance and priestly vocation. Suitable informant questions were designed to encourage conversations into the research topic area, for example, 'how would you describe your morale?' or 'when are you most priestly?' Over the interviews a lexicon of prompting words or topics emerged, available to the researcher to stimulate a flagging interview. The semi-structured format allowed the clergy to cover the topics in their preferred way and for interesting enthusiasms and digressions to emerge naturally.

Previous researchers (Collinson 1992, Coffey 1999, Watson 2001 and Bryman 2004) have shown how an ethnographic dimension to interviewing and participant observation can make a useful contribution to qualitative research. The vicarage carries significance: because clergy are required to live in a property they cannot own, how they embody their lives in the vicarage is particularly interesting. While undertaking the face to face interviews observations in field notes about the locality, the interview setting and about the interviewee were recorded. Contextual awareness – 'reading' how the vicarage is being used and its atmosphere – added to the experience of conducting the actual interviews because it provided visual clues about the contentment or otherwise of each clergyperson in their particular situation. Liz, a busy incumbent whose vicarage showed all the signs of embedded family occupation was nevertheless clear about the transient nature of ministry: 'If this is home it isn't permanent'. Each appointment brings a new home.

How much of the house was open to the public or kept very private, which room was used for the interview and the overall 'signs of occupation' as a home were revealing to the trained eye of an archdeacon-researcher used to visiting clergy and clergy families in their vicarages. The clues are more subtle than house pride or differing personal standards of tidiness. About half the interviews took place in clergy studies, the other half in living rooms (all downstairs, excepting one upstairs study) each suggesting varied patterns of working and living. Nearly all the studies appeared busy and organized, even the more untidy or cramped ones, although in one case the researcher squeezed in among the vicar's sporting equipment! Living rooms were usually comfortable and welcoming, often evidencing the normal chaos of family life and probably not much extra housework was put in for the interviewer's benefit. The issue of clergy keeping up appearances is an interesting one. In a few households the residents seemed not really *at home* – 'camping on the surface' as one Diocesan Buildings Surveyor has described it from his visiting experiences. Equally, tidy vicarages may disguise discontentment or trouble in the lives of the occupants and in this respect there were hints of mismatches in the interviews confirming Warren's 'immaculate house and well groomed priest' who was 'very stressed and talked about the pressure of life constantly' (Warren 2002: 109).

The interviews were in daytime on weekdays when some spouses were at work and children at school. In two-thirds of the research visits no person was in the vicarage other than the interviewee. However the ghost-like absence of, or lack of references to, an existing spouse or children occurred more often than we might have expected. This may confirm the often expressed frustration in clergy households that vicars, despite working from home, dissociate from their families (Meyrick 1998, Warren 2002, Burton and Burton 2009). When asked about this issue Jonathan spoke almost managerially of the hectic family teatimes in his vicarage as 'being like one big diary meeting'.

The research participants not only gave the impression of willing engagement with the interview but did in fact talk readily about ministry issues and their lives and the time invariably passed quickly. The few interviews that were harder to sustain (perhaps three or four) were so because the participant appeared to be tired or depressed, confused or in difficulties about their work or life. This made it more difficult to develop a coherent conversation. However even the more conventional or slower interviews had their surprises (illuminating interruptions, surprising personal information) and the interviewer learned to keep his researcher's wits about him. Every research interview was interrupted, most commonly by the telephone ringing. Very few calls were answered by the interviewee unless urgent or expected and the answering machines fulfilled their function as essential vicarage tools. During several interviews the doorbell rang and was answered by the interviewee with interesting consequences. The tape was left running and when we settled down again the interviewee explained who the visitor was, the reason for the visit, and fascinating accounts of fussy parishioners, stormy Parochial Church Council meetings and the fire-bombing of one rectory (the paint did smell fresh) emerged in ways they might not otherwise have done. Other interruptions came from spouses needing some urgent word or from children looking for their tea or a 'peek' at the visitor: vicarage children handle adult visitors as a normal feature of their embodied yet porous home territory.

It was impressive that the clergy really did block out a couple of hours in their busy diaries for the research visit. Indeed some participants said that they were keen to tell their stories and to make an interesting contribution to the project. Malcolm's query towards the end of the interview, 'has any of that been helpful?' was typical. Some may also have welcomed a researcher as a 'willing ear' (Robson 2002: 273) for their personal concerns. The interviews were restricted to no more than 2 hours, and about 90 minutes emerged as the mean length. Some clergy were very engaged in the conversation and would have continued longer while a few became distracted towards the end as they perhaps began to consider their next diary task or family demands.

Qualitative, familiar, truthful?

Peyton being an insider-researcher, sharing a common language and understandings certainly played its part in eliciting informative responses in a time-efficient manner. There was a priest-colleague character to each of the conversations and openness about ministry matters. Some participants had prepared loosely for the interview and had to hand the background papers, sometimes with a few notes scribbled. Exceptionally two interviewees relied in the early stages of the conversation on reading material which they had carefully written out in advance. Most however were content to begin apparently unprepared and to simply talk.

A critical caveat for qualitative research based on interviews however is that as individuals we are not always the most reliable witnesses of our own behaviours and motives. Thus the question arises, were the participants more or less truthful in their accounts when talking to a researcher, especially one from within their own organization? Interviews do not provide a precise mirror image or account of the social world but they do provide empirical data and access to the meanings people attach to their experiences and social worlds. The ability of interviews to reflect broader reality or the subjective world of the interviewee is limited because statements are liable to reflect the interview context itself and 'cultural scripts about how one should normally express oneself on particular topics'; a research interview is a social situation and is 'better viewed as the scene for a conversation rather than a simple tool for collection of data' (Alvesson and Deetz 2000: 71–2).

Undertaking 'insider' research we are especially aware that the clergy stories were told to a particular person which may have influenced the 'truthfulness' of the data forthcoming from participating Area/Rural Deans. On a few occasions, respondents strayed into using the interview for counselling or career advice, or one sensed that there may have been an element of impression management at work. In accordance with Gatrell's (2005) experience when interviewing fathers, the interviewer resisted these distractions but did find himself emotionally drawn into the accounts in all their variety that clergy gave of their ministries.

As in previous research interviewing archdeacons (Peyton 2003), oscillating between insider ('we're both priests') and critical researcher ('I'm doing research at Lancaster') was experienced but the positive gain was that colleagues did readily participate. Certainly the interviews contained elements of the 'heroic account' familiar in workplace management research (Collinson 1992, 2003, Watson 2001) as the Area/Rural Deans explained what they were up against and what they were achieving. Balancing this, almost without exception, the interviews also volunteered personal material, not always self-complimentary, that could have remained hidden as clergy spoke readily about their personal failings and professional struggles. Respondents also volunteered information on some intimate topics without direct probing for it, for example about domestic and marriage difficulties, sexuality and relationships, financial anxieties, radical interests, erosion of belief and fears for the future. Platt (1981: 82) found that confessional honesty is increased when interviewing one's peers and the clergy transparency and self-deprecation in this data probably reflected an implicit trust in the confidential nature of the research interview familiar to them in their pastoral work. They presumably trusted that the Archdeacon would not carry unhelpful messages back to any bishop – however as Chapter 4 notes, ambitious clergy might be pleased if positive recommendations did reach the right ears! Many clergy at the end of the interview said how valuable they had found the opportunity to take time to reflect on what it really meant to them to be a Church of England priest at this time. When asked, 'how often do you have conversations like this interview?' the reply was invariably, 'hardly ever' or in some cases 'never'. It seems that, for some participating clergy at least the interview provided a safe place to open up about priesthood which was qualitatively different from other professional opportunities such as the diocesan scheme for Ministerial Development Review (Church of England 2008c), spiritual direction or a conversation with their bishop.

We certainly completed the interviews bearing a sense of responsibility for the anonymity of our informants. The ethical principles we used in response to these legitimate concerns are respect for autonomy, doing good, doing no harm, and justice. Discussed by Holloway and Wheeler (1996: 39) in relation to qualitative research in the health services and applied by Gatrell (2005) to management research we incorporated them into the information sent prior to each interview in which we assured participants of our sensitivity to the issues of informed consent, voluntary participation, confidentiality and anonymity, dignity and self-respect, and protection from harm. In researching individuals it is crucial to offer reassurance that their names and locations will be anonymized and that participation will not disrupt or jeopardize their careers or personal lives.

We have attempted to make interpretive readings of the data to construct arguments and to reach conclusions. However as researchers we are 'inextricably implicated in the data generation and interpretation processes' and therefore we are also making a reflexive reading of the data, recognizing our role and perspective in the project (Mason 2002: 149). Following Holloway and Wheeler (1996) we have applied four goals as the criteria for achieving a trustworthy research report: credibility, transferability, dependability and confirmability. There is a research tension in preserving individual participants' voices while generating the broader analytical picture. As far as possible we have tried to remain faithful to the words and meanings captured in the tape transcriptions. In particular, quotations used are not taken out of their original context, nor used simply to make a point. We have attempted not to fragment interviewees' narratives and stories, allowing them to make their own meaning although this sometimes leads to longer quotations. We have also sought to shape an 'ethnographic story' (Watson 1995, 2000) of a conversation as well as the accurate recording of an interview which in any case cannot easily translate voice intonation and mood, let alone body language.

Lights still burn in vicarage windows

One Christmas Eve a national daily newspaper carried a feature about Church of England clergy working in socio-economically deprived areas of the country – in Birmingham, East London and on a grim housing estate in Nottingham. Entitled 'Faith under fire' it recounted the pressures local clergy are under from needy and socially excluded people, difficult community relationships and the threat of personal violence. Their parishes are described as,

> places that almost no one who could choose where to live would select a home. The one exception is often the Church of England vicar. When night falls the professional who work in such areas – teachers, social workers and others – head for more salubrious neighbourhoods, lights still burn in vicarage windows. And in these areas the vicar's influence reaches far beyond the usually tiny Sunday congregations. While many faith leaders take responsibility just for their own, a vicar's writ extends uniquely to all who live within the parish. Vicars remain widely accepted as community leaders. (Chesshyre 2005)

This admiring view of the Established Church at work begs the question why an interest in the lives of clergy persists – especially given the widely recognized marginalization of institutional religion in secularized English society (Brown 2001) sometimes characterized as 'believing without belonging' (Davie 1994), or as empty detraditionalization (Woodhead and Heelas 2000). Revelations about the periodic misconduct of vicars titillate tabloid readers because of shared assumptions that standards set for clergy are differentiated from other groups. The caricatures in *The Vicar of Dibley* series (BBC TV 1994) were a mixed blessing for the first generation of women priests and it was only a matter of time before a 'Priest Idol' version of the popular show graced television screens (Channel Four 2005).

Serious critical consideration however of the continuing role of the Church of England and its clergy within national life in the wider press and broadcast media bears further reflection and explanation. Our research finding is that parish clergy are faithful pastors, responding to residual expectations. In recent years exemplars are not hard to find. When tragedy overtook their communities the personable and responsive ministries of Tim Alban-Jones, Vicar of Soham at the time of the infamous child murders, and Christine Musser, Vicar of flood devastated Boscastle, caught the imagination and admiration of many through the media. A sensitive documentary, 'Gay Vicars', brought to attention a much needed insight into the Church's view of homosexuality (Channel Four 2006). In many ways the fictional TV *Rev*, soldiering away in his dysfunctional parish, accurately embodies the community servant of last resort pictured by the Christmas Eve journalist, working at the margins yet not entirely marginalized. TV's *Rev* has his crises, doubts and scruples but rises to the big moments, admitting to a parishioner, 'no, I don't know what heaven is like, but I will accompany you until you get there' (BBC TV 2010, 2011).

Managing expectations

In broad terms the Church of England has spent the last 30 years going through a process of modernization involving its theology and liturgy, its structures and personnel. The pace of change is accelerating partly because of internal Church problems but importantly in response to changing expectations in a changing society. In particular the Church of England has to face up to an increasingly secularized British society in which the Church is marginalized with a declining membership, fewer clergy and considerable financial and organizational implications. Urgent warnings are periodically delivered about the evidence of (Brierley 2000), reasons for (Norman 2004) and solutions to (Jackson 2002, 2005, Croft 2006) the alleged demise of the Church of England.

However this area of the sociology of religion is contested with complex evidence both for the pervasive secularization of society (Brown 2001) and the dogged persistence of religion (Davie 1994). The secularization process identified by Martin (1978) is not universal and, informed by empirical enquiry, continues to evolve with considerable regional variation (Martin 2011). Revisiting the secularization debate more recently Gill asserts that in Britain a cultural paradigm best explains the social transmission of religious beliefs and values and that although Christian socializing does appear to be declining it may not always be replaced simply with secularism (Gill 2012: 168, 184–5). Voas and Bruce (2004) perceived a 'fuzzy fidelity' attitude towards religion in the 2001 Census returns while Woodhead and Heelas (2005), Barley (2006) and Woodhead (2005, 2007) point to the variety of spiritual and sacred commitments in contemporary British society which contribute towards a complex picture – not simply religion versus atheism or secularism (Pigott 2007). Findings from the Religion & Society Programme, the largest ever research project on religion in the United Kingdom, characterize the emergence of new holistic spiritualities and faith identities as a time of 're-enchantment' (Woodhead and Catto 2012). There is therefore a somewhat opaque relationship between belief, belonging and attending, itself affected by the plurality of politics, religions and cultures now found in 21st century Britain.

Contemporary theology, like other critical theory, has been influenced by the insights of postmodernism. Vanhoozer (2003) argues that theology has a mission to challenge postmodern incredulity with a Gospel that shapes human living in an engaging way: 'the condition of postmodernity is neither simply philosophical nor simply socio-political, but *spiritual*, a condition in which belief and behaviour come together in the shape of an embodied spirit' (2003: 23). Indeed one of the paradoxical outcomes of secularization in late modern society is the emergence of postmodern spirituality – a 'new openness in religious expression' (Fisher 1999: 27) which Griffin (1998) characterizes as a global melting pot of plural religious and cultural experiences. Drane (2000) reinforced this view, applying Ritzer's 'McDonaldization' theory to the Christian Church and observing the failure of prepackaged religion and spirituality to make headway in a sceptical Britain.

In response to these challenges the Church is trying to become more 'mission-shaped' (Church of England 2004b) and 'multiplex' (Francis and Richter 2007) with a more 'pioneering' or 're-imagined missional' style of ministry (Church of England 2011a, Heywood 2011) and a 'deep listening, missionary anthropology' (Rooms 2012). Meanwhile others question whether Christian activism can succeed without authentic spiritual leadership (Dorr 2006) or whether the current enthusiasm for 'fresh expressions of church' is an effective missional response to postmodern culture (Davison and Milbank 2010). Some theologians believe that appropriating the classical Anglican inheritance (Chapman 2010) provides greater hope for the Church's future. The clergy interviewed here certainly felt the weight of expectations to grow Church membership and outreach but experienced anxieties about what they might achieve in practice, and how they might manage this.

The occupational survival of the clergy on the margins of 21st century English society is therefore an interesting Darwinian phenomenon which Percy (2006) argues is evidence of an adaptable and effective species. The task of our empirical research was to ascertain how contemporary clergy interpret their vocational role and it appears that the Church of England and its clergy may still retain some social significance, reflecting perhaps the residual expectations of the surprising 71.6 per cent of the population who avowed to be Christian in the UK 2001 Census (Office for National Statistics 2003). Although the 2011 Census results are awaited with some apprehension national surveys continue to endorse the role of the Church of England within the pluralistic life of the nation. In October 2007 a national survey conducted by Opinion Research Business revealed that approaching half the adult population regards itself as Anglican and that 86 per cent of adults had visited a local church in the previous year for a wide range of activities alongside attendance at worship. A quarter of weddings in England each year are still conducted by Church of England clergy (Church of England 2012). In two recent initiatives the Church relaxed its rules to allow couples to marry in a wider variety of churches with which they might be connected and launched a Weddings Project to enhance outcomes (Meyrick 2008).

How are Church of England clergy managing these expectations of their continuing professional roles? What does it mean to be a vicar at the start of the 21st century – from the perspectives of the clergy themselves, or the Church as an institution, or popular perception? Are clergy lives interesting because they really are so different from those of other professionals or because they highlight in a particular (or exemplary) way common and topical issues facing many occupational groups in society? An Area/Rural Dean outside the sample summarized his perceptions for us: 'we're mostly in the same boat; some bereavement symptoms about what has been lost, confusion about what to do about it; doubtful about the Church as a pastoral resource for a secular society, yet unclear about styles of evangelism to such a society which feels rather sectarian'.

From a parochial viewpoint Greenwood undertook a brief qualitative survey and challenging theological reflection about the future priorities for the work and life of the parish priest. He asked 45 clergy an appreciative enquiry question about what energized them or inhibited them in their work and concluded that parish priests are called to a 'navigator leadership' role: 'the unique timbre of the work of the ordained . . . called to be at the interface between every dimension of human existence, parish clergy inevitably absorb and carry some very deep emotion and aspirations for the entire community' (Greenwood 2009: 50).

Another issue is how clergy manage the work–life balance in their professional and personal lives. On a spectrum with work–life differentiation at one pole and work–life integration at the other, are Church of England clergy an extreme example of total vocational integration or unhealthy dysfunction? The advisory network for women in ministry describes work–life issues as 'significant . . . clearly demonstrating that demands and expectations are not in proportion to the time available' (NADAWM 2008). Similarly, 'women clergy, in particular, felt family circumstances hindered their employment and even their vocation' (Barley 2009: 10). Clergy undoubtedly have both public and private personae, blurred role boundaries and restricted choices which may lead to their living confused or even contradictory lives. Nevertheless clergy persevere, navigating difficulties as pictured by R S Thomas in his poem 'The Priest'.

Russell (1980) argued that the clergy of the Church of England, unlike other vocational careers in law and medicine, never became fully professionalized and the continuing ramifications of this are particularly explored in Chapter 4. In the new millennium however three initiatives mark significant moves towards a belated professionalization. First, the Clergy Discipline Measure (Church of England 2003a, 2006b) now provides a transparent framework for modern professional practice which should have the confidence of the clergy, church members and the general public. Secondly, the *Guidelines for the Professional Conduct of the Clergy* (Church of England 2003b) produced by the clergy themselves and based on the *Ordination Services* (Church of England 2007a) exhibits all the characteristics of a professionals' foundation document. Thirdly, under pressure from the government to include all religious bodies within employment legislation, the Church of England has implemented a fresh human resources strategy and a framework for Clergy Terms of Service (Church of England 2004a, 2005b). Since 2011 clergy remain (as traditionally) 'office holders' but with the new security of common tenure, terms and conditions, ministerial review, capability and grievance procedures and protection under secular employment legislation. These new arrangements aim to improve clergy professional accountability and the human resources support they receive. There is a recognition that some clergy working practices are not always effective, healthy or wise, and that without undermining vocational freedoms, clergy would benefit from a clearer professional working framework and regular ministerial review by the diocese (Church of England 2008c). Percy (2006: 175) observes that the ordained ministry is predominantly 'a public matter rather than a private affair' and a matter of public interest, while Rooms and Steen (2008: 26) argue that this makes it 'entirely appropriate that clergy are transparently accountable and properly supported'. A Sunday newspaper commended the Church of England's progressive adoption of clergy ministry review, indicating that clergy exhibit the inherent challenges in many performance management situations (Caulkin 2005). It would be a mistake however to assume that Church of England clergy will embrace such a fundamental shift from covenant to contractual arrangements, from ordination promises to paperwork and appraisal, without critical comment – as the research interviews and current clergy feedback demonstrate.

Enough decent priests

An internal survey of Church of England Bishops about quality and quantity in ministry revealed that though the vast majority were confident in the skills of those being ordained, the bishops were anxious about some clergy not coping with fast-changing ministry demands. The findings of the survey which were leaked to the press also indicated a concern that pay and post-retirement housing provision might be deterring recruits (Church of England 2007b). An editorial in the *Church Times* sought to balance the picture by pointing out that had the bishops been asked slightly different questions they would probably have reported that their parish clergy are in the main multiskilled and hardworking, highly committed and fulfilled. There was no evidence of 'a systems failure . . . there are enough decent priests in the right posts to stop the Church from despairing just now' (Church Times 2008).

This exchange of views reflects an underlying tension within the Church of England about the quality and effectiveness of its ordained ministry: are its priests fundamentally in difficulties finding their way in ministry in 21st century contexts and conditions and is their vocational integrity intact? This underlines the importance of our central research question about enduring priestly commitment while our findings demonstrate two fundamentals in ministry. First, that ordained lives are constructed and constrained in ways which make intrusive demands on individual clergy and their households which would simply not be allowed or tolerated in other working worlds. Our participants speak frankly on a range of ministry, family and personal problems that routinely arise. Secondly, however the same clergy with few exceptions unequivocally confirm an impressive faithfulness and loyalty to their ordination promises and their life-long implications including limited room for manouvre in personal matters. The findings in this research appear to indicate that once ordained clergy are powerfully motivated to maintain their commitment within a personal identity and a way of life that has overtaken and embraced them.

Among the research participants Linda reflected that ordination 10 years ago had enclosed her in a new way of life, permanently: 'I will never not be a priest . . . that began to really make me realize how much part of my personhood it is'. She found the sense of vocational separation unnerving: 'It's quite a unique sense . . . I have, you know, quite frequently in my ministry felt set apart, not in terms of being somehow being special or wonderful or holy . . . but that sense of being not quite as others are and I found that quite frightening in some ways and quite lonely. And people don't necessarily understand that until they're ordained themselves. I didn't understand it until I was ordained'.

Jonathan similarly declared that after 20 years in ministry, 'No I am not a quitter' and felt a conviction about his original vocation which countered any notions of giving up the priesthood: 'I think it is being authentic to what you believe God has called you . . . I suppose it is about conviction . . . yes, you could give up but I would be unhappy giving up. I mean before I became ordained I was always thinking, "what should I do?" I taught – drifted into this and that – feeling, you know, moderately fulfilled . . . what I actually wanted was to be ordained . . . I have always felt wonderful about it'. While there can be a thin line between R. S. Thomas's limping or laughing priest there is a distinctive positivity among our clergy participants that suggests an embodiment of priesthood that effectively governs body and soul.

Clergy optimism

Despite the secularizing cultural challenges there was a great deal more optimism in the interviews about the future prospects for the Church of England than might have been expected. Perhaps the broader perspective enjoyed by Area/Rural Deans kept their morale high. Julian, ordained in the 1970s, encapsulated a number of optimistic responses:

It seems to me that we are in the midst of huge change and rightly so, but I have a firm trust and belief in the robustness of the Church of England and that I suppose . . . we work out the Christian faith in the light of the flawed human institutions and that no human institution is going to be exempt from societal pressures but that the fact that we do connect robustly to our local communities is of huge significance when it comes to looking at our future. And I think it is important to me that we don't lose confidence that what we are, sort of who we are and what we stand for and actually the expertise and abilities that we have.

Many participants made a link between competence, morale and realism. There was feeling among the majority of Area/Rural Deans interviewed, like Richard in East Anglia, that the pastoral excellence of the parochial ministry of the Established Church is now 'spread thinly'. For Fred who has served three decades in the same part of the diocese the reduction of available stipendiary clergy amounted 'to trying to change the Church by the death of a thousand cuts'. Roger urged the Church 'to think outside the box'. Notwithstanding this, even Neil, a radical voice among our respondents, who in the opening minute of his interview said emphatically, 'I think the future is terminal' also believed that 'it's still a job that's worth doing . . .' The Church of England clergy interviewed illustrated the variety of ways in which their vocations endure despite personal cost. Whether they always feel it or not their ministries are sustained lifelong because they remain loyal to their original commitment and leaving the ordained ministry is rarely considered an option, as Penny in rural ministry described, 'I press on because we can't just, I mean there is something about it in all of us, about ordination, that we have somehow committed to the fact that we don't live lives for our own benefit and then we are there for others' to which Roger added, 'I couldn't get God off my back'.

What emerged across the entire sample was a powerful collective appreciation of ordination as an occasion, the vocational moment that the Ordination Service represented once and for all time in an individual's life. Many participants recalled the overwhelming or life-changing significance of the event, intellectually, emotionally and physically, recollecting the force of the vocational commitments:

I felt remarkably restored when I was ordained . . . I think ordination recognises what you have become . . . (Jonathan). My ordination . . . was just incredible . . . I felt that something had happened and that I would never be the same again . . . (Carole). I can remember coming around the cathedral, going through that door and totally unable to sing, just this huge lump in my throat . . . a very proud moment . . . (Fred). The one thing I remember is hands being anointed . . . being given authority and hence confidence in a way to go out and be a priest . . . (Penny)

These observations underline a key theme that is developed throughout this book, that ordination, whether regarded as imparting an abiding character or simply entrusting a leadership function, has an enduring influence over clergy lives that powerfully and permanently changes them.

Because Area/Rural Deans have a voluntary leadership role that is endorsed both by the bishop and their local clergy colleagues it might be possible that they represent a happier sample of the clergy population. However this does not entirely account for their confidence as the majority of our interviewees voluntarily expressed professional concerns and personal weaknesses. They recognize the pressures and determinedly struggle not to be overwhelmed by them. Essentially the role of Area/Rural Dean is a transient undertaking and among the 46 research participants, 30 per cent (12 men 2 women) had been in their parish for over 10 years, that is, longer than their time as Area/ Rural Dean. Their willingness to share considerable professional and personal concerns, arising from overall responsibilities over time, suggests that our sample is not so different from the clergy interviewed by Warren (2002). Indeed their relationships in a typical Deanery with a dozen or so fellow clergy means that they understand clergy lives in a broader context helping us to explain the enduring vocational commitment of contemporary Church of England clergy.

Faithful community pastors

As outlined in our opening chapter the research interviews focused on five core themes and related topics designed to elicit from respondents data that could shed light on the research question. These were explored through a number of informant questions which proved to be productive lines of enquiry, allowing clergy to move between fairly mundane descriptions and more sensitive accounts of what was in their view really going on in their ministries and lives, emotionally how they felt about it and intellectually the meanings they attached. Initial findings in relation to the five core themes are summarized as follows:

- *What are clergy doing in their ministry?*

I had a week where we had a couple of funerals in the church; we had a wedding on the Saturday; we came to the Eucharist on the Sunday and there were baptisms after that service as well and I just had a moment, and every now and then I have these moments, and I can be doing absolutely anything, when I stood there and looked out from behind the altar, I looked at out the congregation and thought, yes, I am a priest and I am here. (Fiona)

The Church of England clergy we interviewed embody the provision of worship, pastoral care and community leadership in their parishes. In particular priests alone can preside over the celebration of the Eucharist in the local congregation. Many of the clergy avowed that a residual English Christendom still exists despite the erosion of church membership. For Roger, surveying his 1950s housing estate, 'the Church of England at the moment . . . is still maintaining its parish profile in the land'. The majority of the research participants demonstrated a firm personal faith in God and Church values and a continuing energy for mission and ministry within their parishes. Simon like many relishes the sheer daily variety that the ordained ministry brings:

> What I enjoy most is the variety that I have . . . that incredible variety of things that I do every day and every week and every month that it is never the same and I would be absolutely bored to tears if I was in a job where I left home at quarter to eight or seven thirty in the morning and then returned home in the evening having done the same sort of thing every day, that would drive me nuts.

However participants also indicated a 'darker side' noted by Savage (2006) where clergy are continually dealing with conflict and difficult people, trying to operate consensually while balancing competing expectations in the parish. Understandably where intra-church life is overstressful some clergy find fulfilment elsewhere in community involvement or personal pursuits.

- *What recognition do clergy gain for their ministry?*

> Although there is a population of 10,000 it is still called a village, yes, there are some in the village who regard the vicar . . . with respect, you know, as an important figure. I am surprised actually sometimes about how many people do continue to hold the vicar as . . . some kind of recognized person . . . I am involved in the community in various ways so I kind of chair the school governors at one of the schools. I am on various sorts of charities and village organisation and groups and in some of those I can do it wearing my hat as the vicar, which can be very useful because it means I am a kind of neutral figure. I have a kind of a special status. (Simon)

In one diocese 93 per cent clergy reported significant affirmation from their parish churchwardens (Liverpool 2011) and almost without exception the clergy we interviewed still gain considerable fulfilment simply by an effective local presence. They continue to receive community recognition for their pastoral care, schools work and involvement in local life. As has been pictured, clergy bring peace and foot-washing service into a noisy and acquisitive world (Winkett 2010: 137). Where clergy respond astutely to latent Christian expectations they may gain considerable approval. Remarkably, Jacqui reckoned that some clergy were still 'revered' in her northern urban context. Clergy are particularly appreciated as articulators of God in important family and community moments. Roy recalls visiting a family at their dying teenage son's hospital bedside and the mother saying, 'Come on, it's time for you to do your stuff'. Roy knew that she expected her vicar to pray the right words, comforting them through their pain and anguish. In contrast Simon and a number of respondents commented however that respect from local people was no longer bestowed automatically. Warren (2002: 66) claims that negative recognition is never far away and some participants reported aggressive or unenthusiastic responses among church members and parishioners. Trevor watched out for 'the black cloud that always spoiled the silver lining of ministry'. Rather gloomily, Richard noted that his predecessors went unremembered in local life and he expected similar treatment: 'I know that I am going to be forgotten as soon as I go'.

Nevertheless clergy enjoy acknowledgement from the Church hierarchy and professional colleagues that they are appreciated and this was certainly true of the Area/Rural Deans in the research sample whose appointment helped them feel rewarded for their talents and efforts in ministry. The wider issues of ambition and preferment did surface more explicitly with six respondents and these are discussed further in Chapter 4. Ultimately clergy regard God's recognition, whether judgmental or approving, as determinative, though it is hard for them to be sure sometimes: 'I guess I'm answerable to God but he hasn't told me much lately!' said Robert at the start of his sixth parochial appointment towards the close of a long and fruitful ministry.

- *What relationships and boundaries are of key importance for clergy lives?*

I think for me, it is the relationship in the role that you have, rather than the relationship fully with me as a person being myself, and some of those relationships therefore are quite dependent upon you. Last year we took somebody into our home for three months whose children had been taken away and . . . we had a very, very close relationship, but it was absolutely wearing and was totally dependent. That is an extreme example and it is one that we have had to back off from but, in terms of relationships in the village and getting on with people, a lot of them are people who still want to some extent to be dependent on you and it is not an equality in the relationship . . . you forget sometimes what it is just to have a relationship when . . . you lean on the other . . . there needs to be more of an equality in that relationship for me to be satisfied. (Liz)

Clergy share some similar issues with other public professions and those whose work is based at home but finding the right public/private boundary in ministry is particularly difficult for all clergy and no clergy in our sample had found a perfect solution. Clergy are sensitive to local church and public intrusions into their private spaces: some are more defended and consistent, others are tactical from day to day. The public presence of the vicarage and church buildings, especially when adjacent, signals clergy availability.

In the research interviews many Area/Rural Deans indicated confidence about their relationships with Bishops and Archdeacons in contrast to the nervousness sometimes found among the parish clergy in the local deanery. Area/Rural Deans, particularly the older, long-ordained men, enjoyed a healthy and robust 'critical friend' approach towards the hierarchy. Clearly the quality of local working relationships with colleagues and lay leaders makes a considerable difference for good or for ill. Competitive ministries and power struggles on the Parochial Church Council can over time sap clergy self-confidence and morale.

Likewise, marriage, the family and friendships are most important for personal happiness. However the boundary between professional and intimate relations is challenging for clergy. Interpersonal distancing, discord and loneliness were not uncommon in the experiences related within the sample. The priest's experience of an intimate spiritual relationship with God through their prayers and an articulate and confident faith are clearly crucial for personal stability and ministry performance. Indeed, if any of these three relational areas – colleagues, family, God – are in a poor state, especially simultaneously, the research indicates that clergy may find themselves in serious difficulties in terms of spirituality, functionality and health.

- *What work–life balance do clergy achieve?*

  I'm always vigilant about taking a day off. I've got no time for clergy who say they never have time to take a day off and I just have to say 'well, who are you fooling?', it's just an act of self-justification. I feel it's my duty to take a day off duty as a husband, a father, as a priest as well because I'm not going to be at my best if I don't have that kind of space, so on that score there is a boundary there and although the day off inevitably gets eaten into on occasion I do my best for it not to be. (Keith)

Because the vicarage is both workplace and home the challenge to achieve a *work–home* balance has a sharper meaning for Church of England clergy than the work–life balance more generally discussed in contemporary debate. Single and married clergy struggle equally in the matter of healthy lifestyle, while clergy married to clergy face particular issues about work, children and domestic arrangements. Many clergy attempt precariously to maintain regular quality time off, especially when remaining at home. Like many clergy interviewed, Julian, tinkering with his vintage car on the vicarage drive, is exasperated by church members who wander in knowing that it is his day off and finds himself 'struggling for the polite way of saying "sod off then"'. Those reporting as most relaxed usually managed to put physical and emotional distance between themselves and the parish, through family and friendships, activities, hobbies, and imaginative holidays. For example, John is 'writing a historical biography . . . getting into the last stages of that . . . it emerged out of the sabbatical . . . I spend a lot of time closeted away in libraries'. Although Beryl always feels in role in her Urban Priority Area parish she escapes through overseas adventures: 'I travel a lot into wild and holy places and I love experiencing new cultures . . . I went to Thailand last year and I have travelled wildly and widely and that's a huge source of energy and perspective. It puts everything back in place, and it will do when I go to Nepal. And I enjoy that, and that's how I tend to use holidays. I will take a big block of holiday. I'm going for three weeks'.

- *Where do clergy find priestly authenticity and endurance?*

I suppose I am at the altar really presiding, but also when some people are dying, when I have been called to be with people who are dying. I pray with them and anoint them but it is the sacramental stuff I think really. Those kinds of moments when I suppose heaven and earth meet in a very profound and present way.

Jacqui went on to talk of the transformational possibilities of the ordained ministry: 'I believe in it. I believe being a priest is hugely worthwhile. If you see faith as being something transformative, that changes people's lives and changes the lives of congregations and communities . . . I can't see anything more worthwhile doing really'.

The clergy interviewed almost without exception believed that their ordination had been the right thing to do and that over the years they were living out their original vocational commitment. Equally however they articulated the subtle difference between choosing and being chosen. With God there can be no going back, clergy are captives of their faith and cannot escape the consequences of their ordination. Many participants conveyed ambivalence about this at least some of the time. However when pressed whether they had ever considered quitting the ministry the answer was invariably less about, 'well, I couldn't or shouldn't' and more an affirmation of genuinely not wishing to leave. They find authenticity in their core activities: presiding at the Eucharist, preaching and teaching, marking rites of passage, caring for the needy and bringing people into a Christian faith. They find authenticity in community involvement and appreciation and in accepting the 'until death' cost of such a commitment, in the personal restrictions (as well as the demanding possibilities) that pastoral embodiedness brings. As Fiona said, echoing a number of similar remarks by interviewees, 'I don't ever feel "not priest". I can't say that I ever switch off'. This research indicates that clergy who willingly embrace vocational sacrifices, negotiating changing challenges over the years are those who will endure.

Summary

This chapter has introduced the Church of England clergy lives at the heart of the research project and provided some first-hand data about their perceptions together with some initial findings, in particular that despite their struggles the majority of clergy interviewed shared a more optimistic view of their current and prospective ministries than is often portrayed. They aim for a vocational equilibrium which has been described by Oliver (2012) as 'ministry without madness'. It is clear that their pastoral embodiedness is a key characteristic arising from the particular work–life setting of these clergy physically rooted in their vicarages and parishes. They know that although parishioners might forget what their vicar said, folk do remember and appreciate that the clerical collar visited their home. As some interviewees recognized, clergy are not unique in their professional working arrangements, nevertheless the 'disciplinary reach' of ordination in the Established Church gives rise to a particular form of personal pastoral embodiment. This concedes a low value of the earthly body in which faithful ministry contributes to a worthwhile parochial life now and earns a deferred reward in eternity. The intensity of Church of England clergy embodiment has not been fully understood – both in its empowering and disempowering aspects. The findings from this research sample provide fresh out-workings for the theories of Foucault (1977) and Shilling (2005) on disciplined and obedient bodies to which we now turn.

3

Obedient clergy bodies

You don't stop being a priest when you're off duty.
BERYL

I am the only one handcuffed here.
ADAM

The Panopticon of ordination

The ordination of a priest disciplines and governs body and soul during every waking hour from the moment of ordination, until death. Throughout this life, clergy believe that their physical, intellectual and emotional selves are permanently claimed for the service of God. Ordination is thus life-changing for all priests because it entails an enduring commitment to promises made to God. These promises require life-long and whole-hearted personal and embodied obedience in God's service, as well as an adherence to the doctrine and governance of the Church. Put simply, in the words of parish priest Linda, ordination offers no 'opt out clause'.

For priests who took part in our research, ordination initiated a lifetime engagement with the rules of an entire supervisory system, always under God's watchful eye. Once ordained, priests accepted and embraced their obedience to God, an immortal and all-powerful being who is entitled to judge their earthly behaviour. Priests regarded themselves as under God's continual and continuous surveillance. In keeping with the observation made by 20th century-French philosopher Michel Foucault, they believed God to be capable of seeing, and knowing, everything: 'the perfect eye that nothing would escape' (Foucault 1977: 173).

In this chapter, drawing upon our research evidence, we show how parish priests feel obliged to govern and self-regulate their bodies in accordance with what they believe is expected of them by God. We also demonstrate how priests grapple with determining the relationship between the obedience they owe to God, and the extent of their obligations towards Church, parish and family. In the context of their parish and family lives, we evidence ways in which clergy accept or resist encroachments on body and soul imposed through a range of working practices and lifestyle arrangements which extend beyond the remit of 'vicar' and may intrude upon intimate corners of priestly lives. Family compete with God for the vicar's attention. We conclude that parish priests consider it a privilege to be ordained and to serve God. However, we also observe how priests who accept this honour pay a high and very personal price.

The concept of the disciplined body and soul confirms the indelible character of vocational obedience. Once ordained, and throughout the remainder of their earthly lives, clergy challenge themselves to be exemplary in keeping their ordination promises both in lifestyle, and in the performance of their duties. This is not merely a theoretical expectation but an obligation which is central to priestly identity. It extends beyond what may be observed in public and intrudes upon the most private of thoughts and actions. The implications of the oaths, declarations and promises made by clergy on the day of ordination, with regard to self-discipline and the priestly body, are complex. This is partly because priests tend to differentiate between their duty to God (which they regarded as an incontestable priority) and their duty to their employing body the Church, about which they are less clear because of its being an institution directed by imperfect human beings. Similarly, priests may be ambivalent about the nature and extent of their duties to parishioners. This is because, while the vicar is appointed to serve the parish, she or he might expect a level of 'give and take' on the part of local people. The boundaries between priestly obligation and parishioners' respect of priests' right to a private personal life are blurred, an uncertainty which can cause misunderstandings and resentment on both sides.

Priestly responses to ordination promises are further complicated because parish priests within the Church of England hail from a range of theological backgrounds. Those who took part in this research demonstrated how Anglican priestly views and understandings of Christianity range across broad catholic and evangelical, traditional and liberal perspectives. Where priestly views converge, however, is on the impact of ordination on the priestly body and soul. No matter what their theological standpoint, virtually all priests who took part in the research for this book – regardless of age, gender or liturgical preference – professed a deep and enduring commitment to the belief that the priesthood is forever. Once ordination vows have been taken, there is no 'going back'. In accordance with the explanation of vocational obedience provided by the German theologian Pannenberg, priests believe the character of ordination to be 'abiding'. The 'lasting marking of ordinands in terms of the . . . promise and sending that constantly govern the ordained and claim them for Christ's service' are authentic (Pannenberg 1998: 398). Clergy therefore expect to live their lives under self-surveillance as obedient servants of God. The indelible character of their clerical orders, like baptism, is permanent, unrepeatable and life-long. Priests' commitment to obedience requires them to be exemplary in keeping their ordination promises both in lifestyle and in the performance of their duties.

The concept of being bound for life was accepted – only one interviewee explicitly denied it – regardless of whether they found compliance to be challenging or whether they appeared to have the 'gift' of obedience. This was the case through good times and bad. Some priests who felt affirmation in their faith expressed joy at the notion of being Christ's obedient servant on earth, and this joy extended beyond the service of God to encompass parishioners and the Church. Others were struggling – with challenging parishioners, with specific aspects of their jobs or simply with the daily grind of attempting, consistently to be an obedient body and soul. Struggling priests described the lack of 'get out clause' in terms of feeling 'trapped'. Some felt so constrained by their commitment to God and their role as parish priest that they represented themselves as captives – imprisoned by, and shackled to, the ordinal promises they had made and the places they were called to serve. However, none of this made any difference to the binding nature of ordination. Priests expressed the belief that they had made promises which could not be broken. They regarded their promises as deeply ontological in character. For better or for worse, all had committed to the priesthood and the obligations which this entailed at all times, for the duration of their earthly lives.

In what follows, we consider in depth the centrality of priestly obedience to ordained lives. We examine how our interviewees attempted to fulfil what they regard as the obligations of ordination. We illuminate the concept of divine surveillance and the disciplined body and soul drawing upon the perspectives of scholarship on governance and the body, with particular reference to Michel Foucault's theoretical perspectives on self-discipline. We go on to consider how some priestly bodies may be treated as 'different' and 'out of place', making the notion of obedience, compliance and 'fitting in' with what is expected more challenging for this group than for others. As examples we analyse the case of Liz and priestly pregnancy, and Daniel, a black male priest.

The complexity of the relationship between powerful presiding regimes, and the corresponding obedience or resistance of individual subjects within such regimes, was central to the scholarship of Michel Foucault. He was preoccupied with how, and why, individual subjects may be persuaded to engage in disciplining their own bodies so as to satisfy and obey the requirements of ruling entities such as the state, institutions and God (Foucault 1977, 1978, 1979, 1980a, 1980b, 1988). Our observations regarding the enduring vocational commitment of Church of England clergy led us to the work of Foucault, as a means of understanding how priests interpret and achieve the obedience they believe they owe to God and how far these obligations extend to the Church, and the parishioners whom they serve. Gutting (2003: 16) describes Foucault as an impressive theoretician who gifted his 'scaffolding of ideas' to the imaginative application by others. Specifically we draw upon the Foucauldian metaphor of the 'Panopticon' to crystallize our interpretation of priestly obedience. The Panopticon was an architectural design for a prison building created by the 18th-century utilitarian philosopher Jeremy Bentham. The Panoptical prison was designed to allow the observation of inmates' behaviour from one central point at all times. This idea behind such continuous surveillance was to impel captives to be obedient bodies in the most literal sense. It was intended that inmates under surveillance would engage with prison rules and self-regulate their own embodied behaviours in accordance with these rules. Inmates' physical compliance with prison rules was predicted on the basis that they were stripped of all right to privacy, and felt under the constantly watchful eye of prison guards. This is graphically illustrated in the picture below by N. Harou-Romain: in the plan for a penitentiary, 1840, a prisoner in his cell kneels at prayer before the central inspection tower.

The physiology of the Panopticon prison design was interpreted by Foucault as a theoretical metaphor for subjectivized power. In this view, an individual who is subject to constant surveillance under a given power regime or institution will internalize and engage with what is required to achieve obedient behaviour (Foucault 1977). In response to unrelenting surveillance, compliant individuals thus accept responsibility for self-regulation and self-discipline in accordance with what they believe is required by surveillance regimes.

According to Foucault's interpretation, 'the Panopticon must be understood as a generalizable model of functioning; a way of defining power relations in terms of the everyday life of [sic] men' (Foucault 1977: 205). His metaphor resonates with the manner in which parish priests describe the self-imposed and embodied obedience to which they commit themselves following ordination. While clergy may consider themselves as having relative autonomy regarding how they manage their roles as parish priests, they believe themselves to be continually under the powerful gaze of a panopticon of vocational obedience: that they are unremittingly surveyed by an all-seeing God from whom they cannot hide. God is entitled to judge their embodied and emotional behaviour on earth and he demands and deserves faith, loyalty and obedience at all times until death. This belief promotes and requires a large degree of self-discipline and professional identity in keeping with Foucault's observation that on the walls of the prison cell, are written the words 'God sees you' (Foucault 1977: 294).

Clergy are not of course the only Christians under scrutiny. Since the 15th century the consciences of all the faithful have been stirred at the opening of the Eucharistic Liturgy with a 'surveillance prayer' (Stoddart 2011: 41), more commonly known as the Collect for Purity:

> Almighty God, to whom all hearts are open, all desires known, and from whom no secrets are hidden, cleanse the thoughts of our hearts.

Under these circumstances, it is easy to see how Foucault's concern with obedient bodies and outward embodied behaviours could be extended to encompass Godly surveillance of the soul. The management sociologist Burrell (1988) has previously suggested how 'complete and austere institutions' (Foucault 1977: 231) become 'panoptical locations of correction and control, not only of the body but also the "soul", the mind and the will . . . *the* metaphor for the disciplinary mode of domination within organizations' (Burrell 1988: 225–6, *original emphasis*). Similarly, Staples (1997) has observed a postmodern shift from 'big brother' surveillance in which individuals are seen, literally to be under a watchful eye, to Foucauldian micro-techniques of disciplinary power. These techniques are seen to target the soul as well as the body as an object to be watched, assessed and manipulated. The boundaries between the comportment of the body and the inner beliefs and thoughts of the souls become confused. This approach is more personal and intimate, a shift from public to private, to reforming people from the inside out and subtly masking examination, domination and docility as social humanitarianism. The application by earthly power regimes of micro-techniques to invoke disciplinary behaviour on the part of individual subjects may be applied to clergy to explain how priests measure personal performance and maintain priestly identity – in relation both to God and to earthly institutions, the Church and the parish.

The belief among almost all parish priests in *Managing Clergy Lives* is that they were bound to their ordination promises, and that this included innermost thoughts and attitudes, suggesting that their determination to achieve embodied self-discipline extends to an enduring governmentality of the soul, as described by Foucault and also by Rose (1999). In Foucauldian terms, therefore, ordination appears to provide an invisible but ever present framework for an ordered, and ordained, life's work. This raises questions about agency. To what extent do ordained parish clergy remain, in a Foucauldian sense, obedient bodies, captives of what they understand to be the expectations of God's panoptical vision? Are clergy bodies simply subjugated to what they believe is God's will? And if so, how far are they obedient to the earthly requirements of Church and parish? Or do priests retain critical agency, exercising choices about whether and in what manner to comply with or to contest the constraints of ordination?

Promise and praxis

We have already shown how the meaning of priesthood and priestly durability is embedded in the meaning of ordination. Metaphorically, within the scriptural notions of bodily obedience and descriptions of the Church as the Body of Christ are core themes which define the lifestyle of the priest and the organizing principle of the parish. The gathered Body of believers within the Church of England are each and all embodied agents and vessels of incarnation and salvation (1 Corinthians 12; 2 Corinthians 4). On their vocational journey as ordinands and during the early years of ordained ministry clergy are accepting an individual spiritual calling and submitting to professional incorporation and socialization, 'formation' within the communal life of the priesthood of the Church.

Theologically – and in practice – clergy embody their work identity as vicars in ordination and priestly ministry in the Church. Here the theology and sociology of the body and the management of vocational professional lives converge to reveal the central theoretical paradox of ordination: the voluntary imprisonment of the body by an obedient vocational soul. Based on the historical incarnation of Jesus Christ (John 1:14) this ministry is typified in the biblical (and notably male) image of the priest as 'Good Shepherd' (John 10) who faithfully watches over a dispersed flock. Thus enfleshed and embodied priests provide a professional pastoral presence that is rooted locally in geographically defined parishes covering the whole of England. Priests must physically appear in churches because their ordained embodied presence guarantees the celebration of the Sacraments and the authorized preaching of the Word.

Guidelines for priestly obedience embedded in the English Ordinal date back to the 6th century *Rule of St Benedict* which became a pattern for monastic order and piety. Benedict's *Rule* is characterized by the idea that obedience is fundamental to ordained identity, following the biblical pattern of Jesus Christ and his obedience to God. Such foregrounding of obedience is designed to promote trust, individual respect and community life, exhorting members of the Christian Church to 'outdo each other in mutual obedience' (Benedict 2003: chapter 96). The *Rule* has directed governance and discipline in the life of the Church for centuries and continues to influence priestly behaviour into the 21st century. As parish priest Richard explained, 'that almost Benedictine pattern of Anglican spirituality' offered him an influential template upon which he relied in establishing 'the stabilitas and rootedness' of what daily priestly behaviour should be.

The Benedictine model of discipline and priestly obedience is formalized today at heart of the priesthood within the Church of England. Benedictine obedience is enshrined within the vows made by priests on the day of their ordination. As shown in below, ordinands are required to declare a belief in their calling by God, to accept the revelation in Holy Scripture, to accept the doctrine of the Church of England and the discipline of the Church. All promise to give due respect to those in authority, and to be diligent in prayer, study and Christian lifestyle, and to devote their earthly bodies to the service of God – until death. Ordination marks an entry, an embodiment into the socially constructed framework of the Church's ministry.

FROM ORDINATION SERVICES (CHURCH OF ENGLAND 2007A)

Will you accept the discipline of this Church, and give due respect to those in authority?

From *Guidelines for the Professional Conduct of the Clergy* (Church of England 2003a)

The clergy swear an oath of canonical obedience to the bishop.

The clergy should participate fully in the life and work of deanery, archdeaconry, diocese and province, giving support and respect to those given the responsibility of leadership and oversight.

The clergy should know how canon and ecclesiastical law shape their exercise of office and ministry, and should respect such regulations as are put in place by the Church.

In this respect, the need for priests to regulate their own behaviour is represented as paramount. While bishops wield considerable power to deploy their clergy, day-to-day responsibility for governing the priestly body and soul lies with clergy themselves as a form of self-discipline. Avis (2007: 15) argues that it is a matter of grace rather than law: 'Clergy are required to adhere to tradition through loyalty, respect and gratitude, rather than through juridical intimidation'. Parish priest Irene echoes these sentiments explaining: 'It is the job of those in senior posts to make sure that their clergy are self-disciplined'. Archdeacons respond to this contradiction in terms with a paradox of their own: how to simultaneously pastor and police their clergy. Perhaps Area/ Rural Deans are better placed to mentor their local colleagues.

For parish priests, ordination often means a life-long struggle to interpret how the asymmetric relations between obedience and self-identity may be resolved. Our research shows how parish priests in contemporary England are prepared to accept the principle of obedience to God's will throughout this life, and many have a reasonably clear idea of what the idea of 'God's will' means to them on a personal basis. For some, however, the balance between obedience and the self is difficult to determine and maintain on an everyday basis. Our research demonstrates that such difficulties arise because the promises of ordination extend beyond practising the 'day job' to the point where a priest's body, their home and family, lifestyle and behaviour are all subject to embodied discipline imposed by ordination. Priestly bodies and bodily comportment are seen, by parish priests, to be under surveillance by God, which all accept as a nonnegotiable element of the ordinal promise. In addition, however, priests regard their bodies as routinely and 'officially' under the control of the diocesan employing authority. They further interpret obedience as including a responsibility to those living in the parish. Many, however, were ambivalent about how to interpret – and to consistently maintain – the balance between obedience and the self on earth, on an everyday basis, and in relation to human surveillance. Assumptions that priestly behaviour may be judged by parishioners correlate with the views expressed in the media when priests' lives fail to comply with standards set by ordination promises. For example, when a senior cleric left his wife for a relationship with another woman, he was described in the national press as a 'disgrace to the ministry' who should be 'setting a better example' (Russell 2010). All priests who took part in this research were acutely aware of the obligations associated with being Christ's servants on earth, and the pressures under which this placed them. Janet, for example, explained how she found the demanding ambassadorial challenge of being an embodied and embedded Christian presence in her parish to be quite overwhelming:

> I find it actually quite daunting that God has in some way called me as his ambassador in the community in which I live and work – 'to be his hands, his mouth, his feet' (you know the prayer) in the place where he

has set me. That is daunting, that is scary, that is when I see His presence because I think why, why me?

The incarnational passage, familiar among Christians which Janet refers to is attributed to the spiritual writings of St Teresa of Avila (1515–1582) and illustrates very aptly how the theoretical promises of ordination must be interpreted by priests in the practice of their daily lives:

> Christ has no body on earth but ours,
> No hands but ours, no feet but ours,
> Ours are the eyes through which to look out
> Christ's compassion to the world.
> Ours are the feet which he is to go about
> doing good.
> And ours are the hands with which he is to bless
> men and women now.

In practical terms, the notion of the obedient, self-disciplined and surveyed body was demonstrated in a literal sense through priests' discussion of two obligations relating to the role of parish priest which, they felt, reinforced their embodied visibility and rendered them open to intrusive behaviour on the part of both parishioners and strangers. The first of these related to the Church of England obligation upon parish priests to reside within the vicarage, or 'tied house', the second to the wearing of clerical collars in workplace and social contexts. In what follows we consider the everyday implications and experiences of being an 'obedient body' within the parish priesthood by considering first what it means in practice to live in a tied house, and second, what impact the wearing of 'dog' collars (i.e. being 'on a lead') has on clergy lives. We then observe how there are some priestly bodies which appear to be more visible and under greater surveillance than others because they are different from the traditional image of the white middle class male commonly associated with the role of priest. Such differences made it more difficult for some individuals to appear compliant and obedient since, according to the cultural sociologist Puwar (2004), they found it impossible to 'blend in' with white male colleagues. To illustrate this notion of 'blending in', we provide an example of the experiences of a pregnant woman, and a black male priest. We then conclude Chapter 3 with a discussion of what it means to be obedient until death.

Life in the vicarage

We begin with a discussion of the vicarage as a location of surveillance. While priests may believe they are surveyed by God who sees everything, both priest *and* family are obliged to live under the eagle eye of the local congregation, in the vicarage. This residence, which is often situated close to the church, is a nonnegotiable part of the job of parish priest. Traditionally priest and family are 'tied' to the vicarage (as leasehold occupants) for the duration of the priest's appointment until resignation, death in service or retirement. Within such an organizational regime the Church of England requires its clergy to have the bishop's licence to minister in a particular parish and to live in the vicarage provided in that parish, whether it is particularly desirable or not. As Sarah explained, parish clergy are expected to be resident in person and available not only to the local congregation but to the wider parish: 'It is about being a visible presence'.

While it might be imagined that the provision of a house could be seen as a 'perk' of the job, the vicarage is in practice regarded by many clergy as a 'mixed blessing' (Meyrick 1998: 94). This is partly because anxiety around obtaining a mortgage and affording a house for retirement hangs over many clergy, and we explore the economic sacrifices and concerns of the ordained life in the Church of England in Chapter 4. However, the vicarage is often also a source of worry and strain among clergy because such properties may be larger than priests would choose, with running costs and the standards of care varying in different dioceses. Adam, tied through his job to the vicarage within his rather prosperous parish, expressed a degree of envy in relation to his professionally mobile neighbours. He found himself living among parishioners whose lifestyles were well beyond his own financial capacity. Conversely, some clergy in poorer areas are troubled if vicarages are higher quality than surrounding properties.

The tied house may also be seen as a source of resentment and dissatisfaction because the notion of visibility and availability as described by Sarah imposes an embodied domestic constraint which controls whole families as well as individual vicars. Living in the vicarage may limit schooling options as well as social and employment opportunities for partners and dependents. It signifies pastoral embodiment in a place that one might be rather happier commuting to in order to work – as a teacher or social worker might well do – and 'going home after work' (Meyrick 1998: 103). However, taking up the parochial appointment without living in the vicarage has been not permitted, whatever shortcomings parish living arrangements may inflict upon vicars and their families. From 2011 within Clergy Terms of Service (Church of England 2004a, 2005b) residence is explicitly defined in the 'statement of particulars' – the equivalent to an employment contract for clergy as office holders. Thus, all 46 Area/Rural Deans participating in this research obediently conformed to the principle of residential presence. Even though it might in theory be possible for those clergy who reported owning a property elsewhere to deceive the diocese, they were not even contemplating living there and travelling in for work purposes. Instead properties with or without a mortgage were rented out or used for holidays. At the start of the 21st century the vicarage as much as the parish church thus continues to symbolize the commitment of the

Established Church through its clergy to the whole population, regardless of the socio-economic status of different communities. As Hinton argued in his historical account of the English parish clergy, the bodily presence of the priest-in-residence is crucial: 'the church and parsonage are emptied of meaning if no priest inhabits them' (1994: 142).

Pastoral presence is however never permanent. Clergy and their spouses sometimes comment to archdeacons that they feel unable to personalize the vicarage as their home 'because it's not really ours' (Meyrick 1998: 96). Liz had noticed that 'all the places we have lived in have very different attitudes towards clergy . . . I mean, clergy come and go'. She recognized that while clergy are rooted for a while in and for their community, they remain essentially incomers, and not of their community. Despite this the findings suggest that parish clergy endure vocationally not only because they accept that the Established Church's pastoral presence has embodied implications, but also because in their heart and soul they have accepted ordination as a way of life for themselves and their families in the vicarage. Although nowadays tempered by concerns about children's schooling or spouses' career, most clergy, and certainly all the research participants, still understand their fundamental calling to present themselves where God and the Church needs them and are aware of the sheer variety of potential locations. Extra-parochial clergy are of course no less embodied – indeed their public and representative commitment as chaplains in schools and universities, in prisons and hospitals and the armed services is similarly intense regardless of housing arrangements. Likewise, as Francis and Francis (1998) illustrate, self-supporting clergy with a secular day job (sometimes called 'ministers in secular employment') equally embody the priesthood.

Nevertheless the parochial paradigm has deep roots. In their late Victorian and Edwardian ascendency when Church of England clergy numbers were at their zenith and twice the present workforce (Sowerby 2001: 94), vicarages were often substantial residences with servants. The local clergy and community shared expectations that the vicarage was the place where certain meetings and events took place (Russell 1980). Dioceses 'officially' encourage 21st-century clergy to use their smaller, less pretentious vicarages primarily as a home and not as the parish office or substitute church hall. Nevertheless, some clergy inherit local arrangements or intrusive assumptions from their predecessor's time that can be hard to challenge even when the archdeacon has emphasized the vicar's domestic privacy to the Parochial Church Council during the vacancy process prior to appointment. The findings in this research (and in the clergy family interviews conducted by Burton and Burton 2009) showed how, in many everyday ways a Church of England vicarage functions as a domestic 'panopticon' around the clergy who are under surveillance from all angles by parishioners, the diocese and God. A key feature of this panopticism is the total blurring of the distinctions between work and home, public and private, body and soul; vocational endurance is based on acceptance that this is so for parish clergy in the Church of England.

In our research, clergy responses to keeping an 'open house' or retaining privacy varied. Some like Philip in his rural rectory and Roger on his Midlands housing estate were keen to establish a welcoming regime at the vicarage, using it for church meetings and social events. Liz also explained: 'When we came we inherited a history of people not being allowed in here which we weren't happy with and we were a bit more flexible about.' Conversely, other clergy appeared almost desperate to reclaim private space at home as they sought to protect themselves from prevailing intrusive assumptions. For example the not uncommon possession of vicarage keys by church officers can be a difficult emotional frontier for vicarage households. Perhaps the most extraordinary experience cited was the 'woefully inappropriate' location of the church photocopier in an upstairs bedroom in Julian's vicarage. Vicarage design and safeguarding policies (Church of England 1998, 2004c) should have already eradicated such arrangements but in some parishes there is probably room for further improvements.

A particularly high price can be paid by the vicarage family if the parish office and secretary is located in the vicarage. This may explain why only four interviewees tolerated such an arrangement which exposed the clergy household to intimate surveillance. Foucault explained the efficiency of such panoptical observance as 'the greater the risk for the inmate being surprised and the greater his [sic] anxious awareness of being observed' (Foucault 1977: 202). Richard, an experienced town centre incumbent expressed palpable relief about a recent change: 'One of the difficulties is that until last week the parish office was in the house and that was horrendous. Because actually having a day off at home was a complete impossibility because she [the secretary] was just, you know, in and out'. Ironically this priest subsequently became an archdeacon only to inherit a similar arrangement again!

Two clergy in the research lived in village vicarages where a parish room was physically part of the house. Both these clergy, Pauline, a single woman, and Penny, married and without children, admitted that these arrangements were less than ideal as they blurred public and private boundaries and gave rise to some security issues. More generally because the vicarage is where anybody can contact the vicar, within or outside 'working hours', parishioners and the bishop, funeral directors and the local newspaper potentially have the clergy under surveillance.

As demonstrated above, living in tied accommodation added to a sense of vulnerability and of feeling 'beholden'. Many clergy interviewed commented on the erosion of privacy and how difficult it was to protect their day off when people knew where the vicarage was. Most vicarages visited as part of this research were within the environs of the parish church. Locked churches often point visitors to 'seek God at the vicarage' (Nash 1990). For most clergy, taking time off at home was difficult if not impossible because some parishioners viewed the vicarage and its depersonalized occupants as though in a fish-bowl. The transition for families when a parent is ordained in mid-life is particularly abrupt as Roy, previously a teacher recalled:

> For the family . . . suddenly they weren't just my wife, son and daughter they were, 'oh, that is the vicar's wife and the children you know' and they began to feel some pressures there and we lost our privacy to a great extent, we became public property.

As indicated here, although only the parish priest has taken ordination vows, the role of the vicar and vicarage is nevertheless projected onto other family members. Theirs is a typically embodied experience transforming a family's previous domestic self-understanding of what it means to be at home. Clergy sometimes adopt deceptive strategies to avoid surveillance. Colin and his wife felt under such pressure that they deliberately put down the shutters and pretended to be away from home on Bank Holidays:

> We will put the car in the garage and drop the blind in the living room and if we want to sit in the garden and read a book or something like that we shall do it and probably in front of the television as well, because otherwise people even ring on Bank Holidays won't they? So I have never had to be short with anybody about that but I think you have got to be a bit inventive.

Sometimes in the interviews clergy echoed the sentiment that under God's guidance they ended up going to parishes where they once thought they could not. This was not merely a social or class distinction but recognition that, church life being so different across England, clergy must learn new contexts, live in affluent or hard places and perhaps never really feel that they belong. Sarah spoke of 'a cross-cultural experience in my own country', in which she reinvented her ministerial and social personality in order to fit in with white male late-industrial cultural customs and expectations. Fiona explored her new parish by going incognito to a local pub: 'I wanted to find out what sort of community I was coming to and the local people'. Derek discovered that his preferred Anglo-Catholic spirituality didn't suit his rural village parishes where preserving a broader tradition for all-comers carried more weight. In a sense he was not his real self, nor at home in his own church. Kenneth and his wife Marjorie have now lived for over a decade in a northern coalfield parish where it appeared they were not entirely comfortable and felt unsupported by the bishop:

> No . . . I have looked back and reflected, but never thought I am in the wrong place. When I was in my previous parish we came over on occasions to this area and the further we came . . . the more depressed we

felt, Marjorie and I, so we turned the car round and went back. That was enough . . . but here I am!

Clergy in theory have discretion about how to use the vicarage but in practice it requires determination and consistency to manage expectations and boundaries. Both more open and more closed policies can have unexpected consequences. For example, when Philip opened his vicarage for regular charity 'hunger lunches', some parishioners took advantage and Philip found it stressful trying to cope with parishioners who roamed around his house without asking, partly because his wife Debbie (occupied in full time work teaching) found this so upsetting and it caused marital tensions:

> People come in; they don't knock, they just come straight in. They'll rifle through the kitchen cupboards to get the stuff ready for lunch without asking . . . I suppose because I'm too easy going really, maybe I should be more protective. But I'm just pleased to encourage the fellowship that comes with it that I don't want to come across as a reluctant host I suppose. In some ways I see it as a compliment that they feel at home, but there is that downside that it is our home first and foremost, and they wouldn't be too pleased if I went in their home and started wandering through cupboards.

At times the uncertainty between the public and the private within clergy homes extends beyond inconvenience and intrusion, to the point of physical danger. A freshly redecorated vicarage provided a clue at one interview as Malcolm, working in a pleasant seaside town, reported the unexpected arson at his rectory by a schoolchild living very nearby:

> We actually had a firework, a rocket through the letter box a year ago on November 5th and we caught fire, and it was pretty horrific. We had a really nasty fire which was put out, and engines came and police came and everything, and we know who did it. There was a short while where we were pretty unnerved.

As Kuhrt and Bentley (2001) have observed, the arrival of single women clergy in vicarages has probably stimulated awareness about security issues for all clergy. A protective attitude by the diocese and her neighbours was reported by Sarah from her 19th-century urban home, but it appeared that such protection was afforded at the price of an increased 'public gaze' (Foucault 1977):

> One of my concerns about moving into this house was security. I was really very anxious about moving in, it's an old house, it's not particularly secure, it's quite isolated, it's set back, it's next to the church yard and I was worried about my security. I haven't had any worries . . . the diocese

have been quite supportive in that and have helped me clear the garden because I had a visit with the crime prevention people and they said I needed clear sightlines from the garden, but I think part of feeling safe is actually the local people saying in unspoken ways, 'we're going to make sure you're OK . . . and we know that you're a woman and you're on your own'.

The sense of its being 'public knowledge' that Sarah was alone in her vicarage is not entirely reassuring because, arguably, the 'wrong' kind of neighbour might have more intimidating ideas. During 2007 a priest in Cornwall was driven from her vicarage by a series of increasingly threatening letters and two arson attacks from a mystery stalker (Gledhill 2007). The letters expressed anger that the vicar was a female priest. For her personal safety she agreed with the Bishop to take leave from parish duties. Criminal behaviour beyond her control removed her from the vicarage and hence doing her job. Months later she returned to public ministry only to receive a written death threat (Beavan 2008).

In recent years dioceses and parish clergy have become more aware of the need for personal and domestic safety. *Knocking at Heaven's Door: Challenges and Opportunities Presented by the Casual Caller in the Parish* (CARIS 1996) opened up the issue and a number of high profile assaults and murders of UK clergy at their vicarages, most recently in Gloucestershire early in 2012, have encouraged better risk assessment by dioceses. One self-help organization, National Churchwatch, advocates that signs saying 'Vicarage' be removed from Church property. Yet parish priests resist this approach fearing that it undermines the traditionally accepted degree of surveillance integral to a visible ministry. In almost all cases in this research vicarage signage was conspicuously present – Wakefield Diocese providing an attractive standard design – arguably an example of panoptical branding. The majority of clergy seem to be resisting any watering down of their interpretation of obedient bodies and souls, governed by a vocational conviction of the need to remain present, identifiable and available.

Collared: visible and vulnerable

The public nature of a priestly vocation lived in the vicarage points to significant challenges that the clergy face in being available, visible and vulnerable in terms of where they live. The same might be said of the clerical collar, indeed a book on Christian vocation often given to potential ordinands, *Called or Collared?* (Dewar 2000) reminds its readers of the public representative reality of ministry. The clergy we interviewed were aware that some clergy, both men and women, can look scruffy and carry an unsure body language while others have a smart and professional ministerial appearance. Perhaps clergy forget that the public may take them at their own estimation? Some express their individualism through brightly coloured clerical shirts and blouses and others prefer a more uniform black. Very few of our respondents deliberately eschewed wearing the 'dog collar', most valuing it functionally as opening doors, conversations and relationships regardless of what might happen as a result. Nicholas, typical of many positive comments, believes it 'a wasted opportunity not to wear it' when 'on duty'. Removing the clerical collar periodically is more usually a signal that the vicar is off duty, as Keith clearly expressed it: 'It's dog collar unless it's my day off'. The design of modern clerical blouses and shirts with white plastic slip-in collars makes slipping in and out of role remarkably easy in public. The BBC2 TV character 'Rev' Adam Smallbone infamously removed his collar in order to swear at neighbouring builders who were annoying him with their anti-clerical jibes, leaving them speechless. Across all Church traditions most clergy in the sample took much the same view, although for many the person and the role were not purely defined by the clerical collar. James for example found it

> very blurred between being in role and out of role. I don't think I sort of put a dog collar on and I become a different person. I think what you see is what you get really . . . I'm Yorkshire . . . sometimes yes, you are much more in a role, I can see that . . . but generally I am who I am.

Similarly, Jacqui and Fiona both drew the line at the supermarket where they wanted to be out of role:

> I do feel a slight awkwardness going out shopping with a dog collar on but . . . I am usually on a time limit and I really don't want to have to be pastoral for very long which is actually not very good because that is where you do meet people . . . I can remain completely anonymous and sometimes you don't want everybody knowing what is in your trolley thank you very much!

Roy was particularly embarrassed to be caught speeding by the police while wearing his collar and it certainly did not gain him preferential treatment. A few interviewees however seemed less assured in their daily practice or in the rationale behind it. Linda for example explained her 'policy' as follows:

> What's my policy? I don't wear a dog collar most of the time. I choose to when I wear it though. I wear it for all services and professional things in that sense. I wear it to any house I'm visiting where I'm not known or any funeral visits and things like that. I will wear it for certain media events or if I'm going to visit as a clergy person in role as it were like an interfacing I would do that. A lot of the time it would set me apart in a way that would be unhelpful in terms of being able to get alongside somebody in compassion in a way that they might feel accepted. They

would see me sometimes as being sitting in moral judgment I think. And I think that's part of the battle of trying to change the way in which people view vicars.

Perhaps Linda's inner city ministry context has something to do with her concern not to be misunderstood but her pastoral exceptions for wearing the clerical collar seemed to make the same case for compassion and accessibility as her pastoral argument for routinely not wearing it. Tony expressed a more general worry that a strict adherence to Church of England uniforms may be counter-productive:

> You know there are situations where to wear a dog collar is to put people off . . . I am not keen on Anglican robes and forms of service necessarily . . . I think they can be barriers rather than gateways.

Benjamin, working in a monochrome new town parish agreed that habitually not wearing a clerical collar when working was really his 'disguise' and seemed strangely reassured by this approach to public ministry. Was he being idiosyncratic or simply matching his role anonymity to the contextual community anonymity, 'fitting in' like everyone else? It may be that routinely ceasing to wear a clerical collar is an indicator of vocational discomfort and interestingly Hampson's account of his departure from the Church of England recognized that 'the establishment image was also a burden: halfway through my time in the parish I realized I was wearing the clerical collar less and less' (2006: 31–2).

The extent to which clergy lives are 'called or collared' – in the sense of being shaped by obedient embodiment through pastoral presence and residence – raises the question of personal agency. Our bodies do not exist in isolation but in relationship with other bodies, affected by the social influences of the contexts of our lives. Since Turner's *The Body and Society* (1984) ideas about the body and embodiment have grown in significance across a number of academic discourses. Turner advanced a sociology of the body in which he viewed Foucauldian panopticism as the regulatory, and arguably oppressive tool of the government of the body by social institutions and organizations. More optimistically, the process of structuration, identified by Giddens (1979) describes the reciprocal influences and interactions between individuals and their social worlds. In Giddens' view, people are shaped by the values and norms of the groups to which we belong, but equally have 'agency' to make personal changes to these norms over time. From a feminist–medical perspective Nettleton identifies the 'lived and performative body' (2006: 114). In relation to clergy obedience, the question remains as to how far priestly bodies are subjugated by their ordination promises and how far they retain critical agency and could thus be seen to be obedient by choice.

Corporeal realism (Shilling 2005, 2008) offers a further framework for understanding the embodiment of priesthood in Church of England clergy in terms of how vocational endurance may be seen to be a calling and how far obedient priests may be seen to be 'collared'. Corporeal realism helps illuminate the competing influences of structure and agency in that it examines the relationship between socially embedded structures within the Church, and the relative freedom of individual priests to exercise personal choice. In our research clergy generally persisted with the clerical collar, presenting themselves to the public at large as Christ's representative on earth and displaying their role as parish priest through the wearing of a dog collar. For some, particularly in more volatile urban communities, this brought accompanying risks. For example Mark was attacked when wearing his dog collar when he visited his local bank at the start of his curacy: 'This guy came up and punched me on the face . . . and he was not well, but I remember going straight back to the vicarage door . . . and saying to my vicar, "well, if this is day one, what is the rest of it going to be like?" . . . but thankfully that has been a one-off experience'. Mark still wears a clerical collar in the high street where his present church is prominent.

Bodies out of place?

The interpretation of what is meant by obedience, however, remains complex. While priests like Mark may develop their own understanding of what it means to be a 'good' priestly body in terms of his relationship with God, fitting in with the expectations of the Church and other human subjects such as local parishioners can be challenging. This, we argue, may mean that some priests experience social exclusion and discrimination as they attempt to follow their vocation and become 'obedient'. In what follows we illustrate, through the narratives of pregnant priest Liz and black priest Daniel, how issues of obedience and compliance are experienced in the context of gender and race. For women and black priests while all humans may seem to be equal in the sight of God, unfair treatment on earth appears to be all too common.

Reverend mother: the baby in the priest's body

We begin by considering Liz's experience of being a pregnant ordinand. Since 1994 priestly ordination in the Church of England has inhabited female bodies as well as traditional male ones. The inclusion of women in the priesthood is in keeping with the increasing presence of women in the labour market, a phenomenon which has prompted a growing and innovative research field on bodies and work (e.g. Puwar 2004, Wolkowitz 2006, Gatrell 2008). Nevertheless, questions about how women manage their reproductive bodies within their workplaces remain unanswered.

The relationship between women's reproductive, and women's paid, or productive work, in the context of the priesthood has proved complex both for individual women priests and within the Church more broadly. This is reflected both formally in that women are precluded from promotion to Bishop (the so-called 'stained glass ceiling') and more subtly. As Puwar suggests in her research on racialized and feminine exclusion: 'the most archaic of rules and ritual, wrapped up in an apparent language of gender neutrality, can be utilised to differentiate the prescribed from the proscribed . . . so we see how rituals, working practices and performative genders coalesce in the accomplishment of specific institutional scripts that take specific [i.e. white male] types of bodies as the norm' (Puwar 2004: 88).

Once opportunities for women to be ordained were in place, most boundaries constraining women's progress could have been described as invisible until they reached senior levels – with one particular exception. The ordination of women introduced an additional biological possibility within the ministry of the Church of England – pregnancy. Just as Puwar observed in Parliament that a breastfeeding MP was seen as disruptive so too the Established Church has for centuries 'been a male space unaccustomed to giving women's issues serious consideration. So talk of female bodies can create bizarre reactions' (2004: 88). Puwar's point was sharply illustrated in the research in a disturbing personal story recalled by Liz whose ordination to the priesthood in the mid-1990s was delayed because she was pregnant. Painful memories and angry dismay pervaded the interview as Liz recalled how she was first informed that her stipendiary post as an Assistant Curate would not be open to her following her return from maternity leave:

> We hit a series of huge issues during that period . . . when we got here our first child was five months old. And we discovered I was pregnant again which wasn't planned, and was difficult to come to terms with at the time. And it was made clear to us at that point that when the next child was due there would not be a job for me to return to. So that was the first thing that happened.

Liz's experiences accord with those observed by Gatrell (2005, 2007a, 2007b) who found that pregnant maternal professionals frequently feel side-lined, stigmatized and downgraded. Liz's predicament coincided with the first ordinations of women into the priesthood of the Church of England, before clergy maternity leave policies were required to conform to employment law. Liz had imagined that she would be a part of this historic occasion and had prepared herself spiritually and emotionally. Unfortunately, she discovered that this opportunity was to be closed to her:

> That was at the same point as women were going to be priested. There was a huge issue about my involvement in that service because the baby was due . . . with the end result that I was forbidden priesthood at that

point . . . And my child was premature because I was so distressed . . . in fact he was born four weeks before the ordination . . . so by the time all of this had happened I found myself not priested, without a job and with a new baby.

It was unclear whether the prohibition by the diocese was justified to Liz on theological or medical grounds. Was there an unspoken concern that the unborn baby would also be ordained within the womb? Did the diocese believe that being pregnant might render the mother unwell or unfit to be ordained and therefore require a caring pastoral response? Alternatively, was this evidence of a deeper patriarchal anxiety linking women's biological functions – menstruation and childbirth – with a disruption and diversification of traditional assumptions about religious purity, religious authority and divine immanence, as argued by Nesbitt (1997: 176) in her illuminating North American analysis of the feminization of the clergy? Howson (2005: 75) also is critical of the excessive regulatory processes that hinder the body as the site of women's endeavours and empowerment. The impression gained from Liz's account was that the authorities found the position just too novel and threatening to handle sensibly and that what ensued amounted to the misuse of 'pastoral power' (Foucault 1988: 68– 90) in the gendered way identified by Cassell (1998) and Pringle (1998). Liz, like some of Gatrell's research informants, briefly considered quitting her employment as a result of her experience, but felt unable to ignore her calling to serve God on the basis of Diocesan discipline: 'I think it there were very serious times when I was ready to jack it in and jack the Anglican Church in . . . but for me to even think about chucking that in, for me, was a very big issue'. Looking back Liz recalled her pragmatic resilience as she coped with a difficult pregnancy and a sense of disappointment: 'I was in hospital . . . four weeks before the birth but it was very touch and go at a number of points, but he is fine and as it was things have sort of worked out. But I do look back and I think there is a part of me that wishes to have had the experience and a joyful priesthood but in the end I did it because I knew I needed to do it to get on to the next step so there we go.'

Eventually, once the baby had been born, Liz was permitted to be ordained. She recalls some backpedalling on the part of her diocese which attempted to accommodate her maternity postnatally. 'I was then priested in the summer, eventually, when nothing was too much trouble and this child of course could come on the Ordination Retreat . . . nothing was too much trouble and the thing was a nonsense really'.

It is unclear why the diocese changed their attitude towards Liz: perhaps a sense of guilt that it had made a mistake, contributing to a premature birth. Maybe they were relieved and pleased to see a healthy baby safely delivered? Possibly they were fearful of a discrimination case? Or maybe the child, once born, was no longer an objection to ordination and it was the notion of the pregnant priest which caused the Church to refuse Liz's ordination. In retrospect Liz wished she had made much more of a fuss at the time, protesting the injustice and insisting her right to be ordained:

> I think looking back now I wish I had had more of the courage that I have now, which I probably have because of what we went through . . . so that is the irony of it . . . to actually have brought it out into the open and not hidden what was going on . . . the way we were being treated.

However the experience undoubtedly left Liz cautious about authority in the leadership of the Church:

> I want to be obedient to hierarchy so one of the things that I really knocked me for six was the fact that it was the hierarchy who messed up . . . I am probably a little bit more cautious and more sceptical than I was and I need to be convinced through a period of time that the person can be trusted whereas I would probably have been somebody who just accepted that because they were in that role they could be.

In Liz's story we have a threefold embodied disruption of traditional Church spaces: the female body in the priesthood, the baby in the priest's body and the pregnant priest in the body of the Church. As Gatrell (2008: 281) has argued, women embodying both productive and reproductive work challenge power relations in organizations. In 1994 the male leadership of the Church of England found it hard to accommodate maternity in the clergy workforce. Since then, as the proportion of ordained women engaged in full-time stipendiary ministry has steadily increased to 29 per cent in 2010 the Church has (as Liz herself acknowledged) made significant strides towards achieving justice and family-friendly practices for all clergy, promptly effecting statutory maternity/paternity/adoption leave entitlements and pastorally flexible arrangements for individuals. In 2011 most dioceses still retained a female Dean or Advisor for Women's Ministry and their national network has done much to improve the treatment of women clergy (Kuhrt and Bentley 2001). Nevertheless many years beyond Liz's experience, it seems that the pregnant body is still perceived as occupationally awkward in professional settings (Haynes 2011). As Anglican priest Green suggests, there remains a subversive character to her role: 'a woman's calling to the priesthood has required her to enter into an overwhelming male clerical caste, an alien culture at times hostile to her presence' (Green 2009: 155). A recent female priestly contribution to our research indicates that even now physical appearance may attract negativity:

> In the parish I have received very barbed comments about my hair colour or even the practice of dying it at all . . . by people in leadership here, in front of other parishioners and among the deanery clergy . . . consequently, I am conscious of having it toned down for church.

We conclude that for some human subjects the notion of the obedient body remains inextricably bound up with notions of 'fitting in' and being the type of body traditionally associated with the priesthood in the UK – typically a white, male body.

Daniel: embodying race

Just as women priests may be faced with practices of exclusion and unfair treatment, so are some black priests. As Puwar acknowledges: 'formally, today, women and racialised minorities can enter positions that they were previously excluded from' (2004: 8). In Britain, despite the growth of the United Kingdom as a multiracial society with an increased number of ethnic minority Christians, and despite an increased awareness in the Established Church (Lawrence 2001, Churches' Commission for Racial Justice 2003, Church of England 2000a, 2006c, 2007e), there is (with the exception of the Archbishop of York) a clear underrepresentation of minority ethnic people – just 2.2 per cent – within the priesthood of the Church of England, against 8.7 per cent in the UK population as a whole (UK Government 2008). At the time of writing no English diocese has an Area/Rural Dean with such a racial background.

Daniel, the sole ethnic minority priest in our research group, had experienced – even in a metropolitan setting – how a black person wearing a clerical collar can generate the bodily dissonance in 'reserved occupational spaces' (Puwar 2004: 32). In keeping with Puwar's observations, Daniel's experience shows how 'the entry of a black female, or male, figure is, however, received quite differently. This presence is still capable of inducing a state of ontological anxiety. It disturbs a particular look' (2004: 39). Daniel vividly recalled his early experiences in the Church of England as a Black African priest and

> people who felt a little uncomfortable, a black person being a vicar, because it is a contradiction in terms . . . and a dog collar denotes power and authority but then it had black face which actually is against that.

Puwar describes how black professionals come up against the exclusive and differentiated hierarchies in which 'racialised minorities have to prove themselves . . . in a place where they are largely invisible as automatically capable' (2004: 59–60). Daniel came to the Church of England with over two decades of ordained Anglican ministerial experience in Africa but immediately felt downgraded:

> I came to be a Parish Evangelist and I used to wake up in the morning and say to my wife what are we doing here? Literally what are we doing here? And I found my experience was, I was wasting time, really wasting time

having done all that I had done . . . I had to start all over really because
they could just not think that a black person had anything to offer . . . but
eventually again I built up relationships.

Daniel's ministry exhibited considerable resilience and maturity. In fact,
across the research sample, Daniel appeared to be one of those clergy most
strongly secure in his vocation to the priesthood, his marriage and family
life. He spoke warmly about serving the needs of his inner city community
and confidently about his role as Area/Rural Dean. Approaching retirement
Daniel would seem an excellent role model for any Anglican Christian
considering ordination. Daniel is also a reminder of just how much still
remains to be done to improve ethnic minority embodiment in the Established
Church. The July 2007 General Synod debated the topic of the participation
of ethnic minority Christians. Rose Hudson-Wilkin, a black Anglican priest
and chairperson of the Committee for Minority Ethnic Anglican Concerns
in the Church of England, acknowledged our research when commenting on
the continuing underrepresentation of black clergy among Area/Rural Deans
(Church of England 2007f: 230). In the same year a General Synod report on
promoted posts in the Church recommended that 'bishops should be asked
positively to look for minority ethnic clergy who might either be qualified
for inclusion on the Preferment List or might be developed in a way that
they might be qualified later on' (Church of England 2007d: 37). As already
noted, in relation to women clergy, undertaking the role of Area/Rural
Dean can be a route towards further promotion so the continuing rarity of
appointments like Daniel is disturbing. The Church has policies in place but
as Gatrell and Swan (2008) note, many organizations find that successfully
embracing equality and diversity is elusive and marginal in effecting change.
Furthermore the lack of any other ethnic minority clergy holding the role
of Area/Rural Dean places some limitations on how representative data
from his interview might be. However, given the very small numbers of such
clergy within the overall Church of England workforce Daniel's experience
of the white 'undeclared corporeal norm' (Puwar 2004: 55) is probably a
reliable and uncomfortable reflection of attitudes in the early 1990s when
he arrived in England and of the continuing situation. Interestingly no other
clergy in our research sample raised the issues of race or the problems of the
Church of England better reflecting national ethnic diversity. The challenge
it seems remains persistently invisible as Puwar contends.

Getting to the finishing line

Clergy often remark that ministry is always unfinished and without end.
Having accepted that their ordination is permanent and irrevocable, clergy
are somehow trapped in the ministry of the Church by their choice – almost
as though the life-changing decision to 'go into the Church' becomes akin to

a life sentence. As the TV character Rev accurately expressed it in an episode focusing on his frustrations and doubts: 'It's alright for you but I can't be un-called for the day' (BBC TV 2010). More than one of our interviewees reflected on this, for example Linda:

> I was quite shocked, you know. It wasn't that long after I was ordained that I suddenly realized: well, this is it for life – I have no 'opt out' clause! Even when I retired, that wasn't the end of it – I was always going to be a priest now!

The limitation of freedoms described by Linda were accentuated even more strongly by some clergy who, reflecting perhaps on their years in priestly ministry, used darker Foucauldian images of discipline and captivity. For example Keith, ordained in the 1970s, and moving to his seventh and final post before retirement, used the imagery of public gaze and execution described by Foucault as 'the spectacle of the scaffold' (1977: chapter 2): 'On ordination . . . you do become a visible focus for a particular lifestyle and ethos and all the rest of it. And you do in a sense put your head on the block'. Sarah wonders, 'Why am I flogging myself for this parish?' Adam, ordained 9 years, a vicar working in a southern commuter parish, 'becomes the principle of his own subjection' (Foucault 1977: 203) constrained by 'A sense of feeling trapped, that (not that you are the only one who belongs), but that you are the only one who is handcuffed here'.

In recent years the sense of ordination in the Church of England as an enduring life sentence governed by disciplinary surveillance has been made explicit in the Clergy Discipline Measure (Church of England 2003a, 2006b) which carries the force of English Law. The Measure covers all clergy, paid or voluntary, licensed or retired and clergy cannot escape the supervisory gaze of its rules and tribunals this side of the grave. For example the first tribunal under the Measure concerned the alleged adultery of a priest whose personal relationships and embodied behaviour remained under scrutiny well into retirement. Disciplinary proceedings held in York reiterated the Canonical requirement that, 'at all times a priest shall be diligent to frame and fashion his [sic] life . . . according to the doctrine of Christ' (Church of England 2000b, Herbert, S. 2008).

The majority of the clergy in this research recognize that the constraints and opportunities imposed by their faith are precisely what embodying a lifetime's authentic priesthood means. For example, Ralph described his priesthood as an accepting, growing relationship, an explanation clearly more in line with governmentality of the soul (Rose 1999) than Foucauldian austerity:

> I am not imprisoned by it; I am here because this is what I choose. I don't know if I could choose any other, mind you, but there is an element from the moment in a sense you say 'yes' to the vocation you say 'yes' to something and it develops and grows.

Simon, who neither expected nor rushed to follow in his father's footsteps as a vicar expressed his embodiment of priesthood in very clear terms:

> I saw ordination as becoming who I wanted to be and I continue to see that. I am being who I ought to be and I am discovering more about myself by being it. So it is not it is certainly not a job I do and it is not a robe I put on although sometimes I can be the vicar but that is self-consciously playing at it. I really see it as who I am. I exercise my ministry by being who I am.

Simon, like many of the priests who took part in this research, felt secure in his vocation and sense of self, inhabiting the priesthood in a way that functions and has meaning for him.

Despite a usually robust pastoral approach to the life and death issues of parishioners and a firm belief in the Christian resurrection to eternal life, when thinking about themselves the clergy interviewed revealed a greater anxiety about the mixed blessings of ministry in this world rather than an interest in deferred benefits in the next. These may have been assumed though none of the clergy interviewed expressed a willingness to work themselves to death simply to gain a reward in heaven. Nevertheless they do work extremely hard in the service of God. Colin recalled being described 'by a parishioner as a prayerful, jovial workaholic'. Roy who was interviewed at the point of his early ill-health retirement regretted his manic ministry style of little delegation and even less sleep which had contributed to a series of life-threatening heart attacks:

> And people could see what I couldn't see, that I wasn't well . . . I indicated that I was taking early retirement . . . that I planned to go because I knew that I just didn't have anything more to give. I was virtually burnt out. I have already been burnt out once in ministry and I tried desperately not to do it again . . . and people could say, 'Oh you have been looking so tired for so long' and so you know they had seen it. I think one or two people might even have had a guilty conscience, you know, some of the pressures that they put me under.

The clergy know that sacrificing the earthly body in 'Good Friday experiences' are part of the mirroring of Christ-like ministry and some, like Colin and Roy, find it hard to separate priestly dedication from self-harm. This is because spiritual values are lived out in the body and the experiences of the clergy reported in these research interviews illustrate the pervasiveness of the 'spiritual corporality' paradigm identified in Foucault's work on religion Carrette (2000: 4). Because ordination is life-changing and life-long ministry never really ceases, only death intervenes to discharge clergy of their embodied obligations and the extent to which respondents casually used life and death language was surprising. There is a recurring theme in several interviews where clergy describe death, imagined or real, as the only way out of embodied demands. For example at a very mundane level Geoffrey, a busy Team Rector, regards his telephone answering machine is essential because: 'for one's own sanity one needs to back off from time to time and play "honorary dead" for a while'. With a touch of dark humour Derek pointed to the annual village Harvest Supper where 'my absence might just be excused if I was dead or in Intensive Care'. More poignantly, Trevor recounted his experience of very serious personal illness, explaining how 'clergy absence can paradoxically have transformative power because parishioners are forced to discover ways of managing . . . the most effective ministry I did here was the three months being laid up in bed'. Nevertheless it appears that while 'nearly dead' may be an acceptable excuse the clergy body is expected by parishioners to re-present itself, visible and contactable, without delay. Regular churchgoers may take a remarkably unsympathetic approach to the extended absence of their clergy, particularly when clergy attend to family crises or their illness is unpredictable or imprecisely defined as 'stress related'.

It seems that most clergy work long hours, believing in the need to devote their bodies to God's service, seeking little rest from their embodied duties as a priest. Our research confirms the findings of Meyrick (1998: 67) and Warren (2002: 12) that there is for Church of England clergy a tension between total vocational commitment and quality time off. Long hours can be an acute issue for many parish clergy who work a six day week and who simply do not follow the 48 hour week in European Working Time directives (Department of Health 2008) nor Church guidelines which commend 'sufficient time off for rest' (Church of England 2003b: 10) and an uninterrupted 24 hours off within a 7 day period. According to their terms of service clergy are entitled to 41 days annual leave including national Bank Holidays and six Sundays, adjusted for Holy Days of Obligation, for example Good Friday and Christmas Day.

A common theme across our participants was a sense of failure at the end of the week of the many uncompleted tasks. Several clergy were confident that they often worked 12/14 hour days and 60 hour weeks. The reality is that most clergy in this research are already fully extended, working long hours and trimming days off and holidays with some regularity. Kenneth's report is typical:

> Holidays? Yes, usually half of the holidays are spent outside of the parish, half of them usually spent inside the parish and in that respect the parish is good if they know that I am off they don't normally come knocking at the door. The telephone doesn't stop of course, that continues. Day off? Maybe I get one out of three.

Strictly speaking their terms of service now require clergy to account for hours worked and time off. Clergy like Jonathan occasionally admitted in our research that their spouses would be more critical of their partner's working habits and explanations if it was they who were being interviewed: 'It may be unhappy (if my wife is watching) but . . . the most I feel is tired because I have long hours but . . . I don't feel worn out'. What do you mean by long hours we asked? 'Well, 6 a.m. till midnight'. Jonathan, 16 years in his present parish, devotes his earthly body to his ministerial work, accepting that tiredness is part of the job, but presumably won't be worn out until his body literally can go on no more and he dies. In the third millennium there is an increased research, public concern and media interest about the work–life balance in everyday lives (Houston 2005, Moynagh and Worsley 2005, House of Lords 2006, Fleetwood 2007, Gatrell 2005, 2008, Gatrell and Cooper 2007b). Clergy are not the only professionals selflessly overfocused on their work and blind to the selfishness they may impose on their families. However, as vocational professionals working from their vicarage home, the parochial clergy offer a particular forum for a work/home debate. Interestingly among the research interviewees Jonathan's wife was a hospital chaplain and another parish priest interviewed, Beryl, enjoyed a preordination career in health services. They shared an interesting perception about contrasting clergy working arrangements illustrating an urgent issue. Health care chaplains, unlike their parochial counterparts, are contracted to a number of core working hours each week. Although our respondents understand the 'good practice' this indicates they instinctively questioned whether this is sacrificially embodied priesthood. Nor is this attitude simply envy at better pay and conditions – in their hearts, like Beryl, they just cannot see that kind of ordained ministry as right or workable for themselves:

Where the Church of England looks to be more professional, we bring in more contractual arrangements and that's good because it protects. It makes you more accountable which I think we should be. But there is a huge grey area over the two because nor do I want to become entirely contractual. As friends who have worked in the health service in chaplaincy, have said to me, 'it's fantastic! I just work 37 hours a week,' and you know . . . to me it's also about who you are and not what you do, and we all know that. What does that make of you as a priest when you're off duty? You don't stop being a priest when you're off duty.

In terms of priestly obedience we can now explain the kinds of self-imposed, embodied obedience practised among clergy such as Jonathan and Beryl. This vocational diligence has consequences in later life. In the sense that priesthood is life-long clergy don't really retire after leaving stipendiary ministry and continue to do occasional duty covering colleagues' Sundays off, conducting weddings and midweek funerals. Some attempt to continue in this fashion as they become extremely frail and elderly until death finally intervenes. Although 70 years of age is the upper limit for licensed ministry in the Church of England research by Barley (2009) indicates a complex picture: 18 per cent of stipendiary clergy leave before they reach 60, a further 29 per cent leave aged 60–64; only 28 per cent of clergy retire at the normal pensionable age of 65 while 25 per cent continue until 66–70. While the number of ill-health retirements has remained stable for a decade it seems the proportion of all early retirements due to stress, anxiety and depression is increasing as the pressures of ministry take their toll. The Welsh Anglican priest-poet R S Thomas whose poem 'The Priest' opens our book wrote a number of poems touching upon the darker side of clergy lives. The following extract from 'The Minister' develops the theme of cynical parishioners' disregard for the bodily limitations of their pastor. In Foucauldian terms they are 'flogging a dead horse':

THE MINISTER

They chose their pastors as they chose their horses
For hard work. But the last one died
Sooner than they expected; nothing sinister,
You understand, but just the natural
Breaking of the heart beneath a load unfit for horses. 'Ay, he's a good 'un,'
Job Davies had said; and Job was a master
Hand at choosing a nag or a pastor.

And Job was right, but he forgot,
They all forgot that even a pastor
Is a man first and a minister after.

R S Thomas *An Acre of Land* (1952)

Everyday death

In this chapter we have endeavoured to describe obedient clergy bodies in terms of the panopticon of ordination and its everyday consequences. Although Foucault does not offer a critique of the Church or its clergy his work on Christian governmentality with its emphasis on obedience and self-sacrifice offers a challenging theoretical framework for exploring ordination and vocation commitment among contemporary Church of England clergy. Foucault proposes a spiritual corporality which informs self-discipline:

It is a renunciation of this world and of oneself: a kind of everyday death. A death which is supposed to provide life in another world . . . it is not a sacrifice for the city; Christian mortification is a kind of relation from oneself to oneself . . . a constituent part of the Christian self-identity . . . the Christian pastorship has introduced . . . a strange game whose elements are life, death, truth, obedience, individuals, self-identity. (Foucault 1988: 70–1)

Our research explores how ordination is an 'everyday death' experienced by Church of England clergy and how the asymmetric relations between obedience and self-identity are resolved.

Shilling has observed how the body and embodiment remain contested concepts within the context of both personal decisions and constraints imposed on individuals by wider social structures. In his concept 'corporeal realism' Shilling (2005) foregrounds the significance of self-imposed, embodied discipline. He identifies how the body may be associated, over time, with social structures and institutions – and how such institutions, in their turn, influence bodily actions, behaviour and habits. The notion of 'corporeal realism' may be drawn upon to track how embodied subjects interact with powerful social structures as they either comply with, or resist and transform, social institutions. At the close of this chapter, we suggest that his ideas illuminate an understanding of the priestly desire to put God first.

This does not mean that there are no resistances to the imposed order of the parish priesthood. Some clergy take more time out from clerical collared visibility and question the idea that long hours should be the norm. Nevertheless, our key finding is clergy are less likely to resist the demands of their job and decline to compromise their interpretation of obedient presence, identity and availability. Parish priests accept the blurring of the distinctions between work and home, public and private, body and soul as a commitment to their vocational faithfulness. Applying Shilling's theoretical framework on believing bodies (2008: chapter 9) and echoing William James' classic *The Varieties of Religious Experience* we argue that Ordination is a critical incident akin to the 'self-surrender' inherent in religious conversion (James 1902: 208), an example of a creative crisis in embodiment in which the divine calling changes embodied behaviour forever: 'the body is continually controlled and organized by a religious discourse in the creation of religious technologies of the body' (Carette 2000: 116). Power and control are not just in organizations and structures, but also in individual minds, bodies and souls. Although control may appear to be imposed by power from outside (e.g. diocesan discipline imposed by archdeacons on clergy) personal conviction is fundamental.

However, our findings suggest that priests are not 'docile bodies' in the sense indicated by Foucault when he considers the control of individuals by the state. Rather priests draw upon personal and agential resources to maintain interior self-discipline because it is their personal sense of 'being ordained' in the service of God, which is the source of order. There is nothing temporary or negotiated about the priestly desire to be obedient. Priesthood is seen by parish clergy to be life-long and clergy do not 'hang up their cassocks' but reinvent themselves as retired priests until death alone intervenes. The clear focus of the clergy research participants indicates an invisible and enduring governmentality of the soul. Clergy therefore endure (as opposed to exiting the priesthood when things get tough) because, for the remainder of their lives on earth, they seek a convergent authenticity of Christian belief, professional belonging and personal development – *becoming* – across the years.

4

The Sacrificial Embrace

Teach us, good Lord, to serve thee as thou deservest;
to give and not to count the cost;
to fight and not to heed the wounds;
to toil and not to seek for rest;
to labour and not to ask for any reward,
save that of knowing that we do thy will.

Ignatius Loyola 1491–1556 Founder of the Society of Jesus (COLQUHOUN 1967: 194)

Sacrificial agency: governing the soul

In this chapter, we extend Foucault's metaphor of bodily self-discipline to encompass the notion of personal vocational sacrifice: not only the invisible but enduring self-regulation of the priestly body, but the subservient dedication of the soul. Sacrificial embrace as envisioned within Loyola's prayer above is proposed as a conceptual theme in which the relative agency of clergy to embrace a sacrificial lifestyle on earth is interrogated. This is for two reasons. The first is because for many priests, it is through making earthly sacrifices that they resolve the asymmetric relations between obedience and self-identity. The second reason links to the concept of Godly surveillance as panoptical (discussed in the previous chapter). The metaphorical Panopticon described by Foucault may be interpreted as a technology for the oppression of the body via the constant gaze of the watching guard. The panoptical guard in Bentham's prison, however, could have jurisdiction only over inmates' bodies. He could know nothing of their innermost thoughts. The panoptical gaze of God by contrast, is believed by priests to see into the reaches of their very souls. If priests' sacrifice on earth is not authentic, this could be potentially hidden from the Church, parishioners and family. Priests believe however, in an all-seeing, all-knowing God who will see past the apparently obedient body and will discern instances where sacrifice and service are not genuine. Keeping up the outward appearance of priestly and professional obedience is not enough.

For these reasons, sacrificial requirements engaging both the body and the soul are signaled as fundamental to the priesthood at the very start of ordained ministry. In the *Ordination Services* itself, each candidate is challenged by the bishop 'to devote yourself wholly to [God's] service' and reminded of 'the greatness of trust committed to your charge' (Church of England 2007a: 37–9). Those who choose parish ministry as a vocational career are likely to face heavy costs, both in relation to their personal behaviour and their financial circumstances. Such costs are complex, but usually involve an assumption that clergy should rank the fulfilment of their own ambitions, desires and needs below the requirements of their role as priest. The notion of personal sacrifice was attested to by all the priests who participated in this research: the idea of the sacrificial body and soul was linked inextricably to the enduring commitment of priests to their ordination vows. Alistair, looking back over 30 years as a parish priest explained his understanding of vocational life as one which he had experienced as personally costly but also self-authenticating:

> Yes, I think I have made the right choices in terms of what I believe priesthood to be, but the downside of that is, I suppose, what one would call sacrifice and again, my Archdeacon said to me last week, 'you've done a wonderful job here, you will be very difficult to replace, but we are aware that it is at a great personal cost' . . . I think part of that is to do with my nature. I think the three jobs that I have done I have done well, but I am aware that it is at a personal cost.

That these interrelated related themes of sacrifice and personal cost are intrinsic to lives of all priests is made plain to all by the Church of England at the start of the journey towards ordination. From the outset, those who enquire about becoming clergy are left in no doubt as to the sacrifices required of Church of England clergy. To such vocational enquirers Archbishop Rowan Williams writes:

> You'll probably have begun to face the potential cost of it. At the very heart of this calling is God's invitation just to be there, in the middle of the Church, holding it in prayer, seeking God's will for the Church's future, trying to put yourself completely at the disposal of God for that future. It isn't a role that lends itself to self-congratulation, a nice clear sense that you've done the job, because there's always more to discover of God and God's purposes for the future. (Church of England 2011a)

The *Ordination Services* locate the particular sacrifices made by the ordained within the broader spiritual offering of the whole people of God in life and worship. The clergy proclaim Christ's absolutions, blessings and victory over darkness so that 'a people made whole in Christ offer spiritual sacrifices acceptable to you' (Church of England 2007a: 43). Throughout the *Ordination Services* there are a significant number of biblical references reinforcing the sacrificial life and death of Christ as the pattern for an exemplary lifestyle which those with a vocation to ordination must follow. They emphasize personal frailty and vocational humility, busy-ness, and availability for the task, recognizing the years of pondering and the determination of candidates to reach their ordination day, the heavy weight of their calling and the need for God's grace and power to sustain the role over the years.

While notions of personal sacrifice and cost are generally understood to be part of the role of priest, however, precision regarding what form these costs will take is lacking. Arguably, the ecclesiastical notion that clergy are at the disposal of God is ambiguous. In practice, our research shows how clergy grapple with establishing how far surrender to 'God's will' might be also assumed to include accommodation of the various needs and desires of the Church, parish, and parishioners. While most priests indicated a desire to place the will of God before their own needs, many were less certain about placing themselves completely at the disposal of earthly beings with whom they worked on a daily basis. Furthermore, where financial sacrifices had been made with regard to housing and retirement plans, some clergy remained unconvinced about the benefits or justice of these situations, especially if the lifestyle of family members had been adversely affected.

Priestly sacrifice is made all the more complex by the knowledge that ordination is not enforced, but sought. Here, we attempt to unravel the relationship between sacrifice and the 'potential cost' of priestly calling by examining the extent to which clergy, having chosen ordination, may be seen as self-governed souls and obedient bodies who have chosen to embrace sacrifice within a vocational professionalism. We consider in which respects parish clergy perceive themselves as retaining agency to embrace or reject sacrifice, contrasted with the ways they feel enslaved by the requirements of Church and parish. In so doing, we draw upon Rose's sociological notion of the self-governed soul which is closely intertwined with the concept of the disciplined body (Rose 1999). We go on to develop our own ideas around corporeal realism and embodiment drawing upon the sociological work of Shilling (1993, 2005, 2008) as we apply his work on religiously believing bodies to our clergy research participants. At the heart of this discussion is an examination of the shifting balance between clergy conformity with God and the Church, and priestly agency to choose how far ideas of obedience, sacrifice and compliance might be embraced on an individual and daily basis. We also consider how embracing a sacrificial lifestyle on earth might anticipate the Christian promise of eternity.

Central to our discussion is the need to understand why, if the personal cost of ordination is so demanding and increasingly difficult in contemporary society, do most clergy endure rather than give up over the years? Almost without exception the 46 clergy interviewed reported an enthusiasm to embrace sacrifice. The personal and social consequences however of such a lifestyle are a neglected dimension in the limited number of clergy studies undertaken over the years and here we focus on the accumulative opportunity cost of 'going into the Church' as described by the clergy themselves and their theological and personal rationales.

Sacrificial embrace: a conceptual theme

The term 'sacred canopy' was proposed by Berger (1967), as a metaphor for the inter-relationships between religion, the individual and society. In a similar vein we propose the concept of the 'sacrificial embrace' as an explanatory metaphor for the inter-relationships between ordination, priests and the Church. Berger was a Christian and introduced the notion that individuals find their identity through personal and professional relationships, and among the competing possibilities and constraints which they perceive to be available to them. Subsequent sociology has debated how Berger's 'precarious vision' of religious belief is constructed (Woodhead 2001: 2) and has survived the 'secularizing relativizers' of the late 20th century 'who proclaimed the death of the supernatural' (Dorrien 2001: 33). In the 21st century, the embracing of personal sacrifice, and the governance of body and soul, remain an overarching narrative by which clergy live their lives. This narrative is underpinned by a theological and ministerial rationale, and ultimately an eternal dimension. Clergy place themselves, body and soul, at God's disposal. In our research, ordination was interpreted by all as requiring a self-sacrificial life concluded by death and the embrace of sacrifice in relation to body and soul was seen to govern all aspects of priestly lives: personal belief, ministerial work, social life, marriage, family and intimate relationships.

The sacrificial embrace of the clergy through ordination could therefore be interpreted as an extended type of pastoral 'governmentality' as proposed by Foucault (1979, 1988). It is explicitly articulated in a Christian setting among Church of England clergy who believe that they are called and motivated to imitate Christ the Good Shepherd (John 10) as the pattern of their calling. This life-long vocational commitment is announced in the *Ordination Services* and forms the opening section of the Church's guidelines for clergy professional conduct.

The self-governmental alliance between an individual and an organization (in our argument applied to the Church) is described by Rose as a choice in which governing the soul depends on a plausible understanding of who we are meant to be in life: 'The government of the soul depends upon our recognition of ourselves as ideally and potentially certain sorts of person' (Rose 1999: 11). Clergy in this research are positive about the challenge

FROM *ORDINATION SERVICES* (CHURCH OF ENGLAND 2007A)

They must set the Good Shepherd always before them as the pattern of their calling.

From *Guidelines for the Professional Conduct of the Clergy* (Church of England 2003a)

The clergy are entrusted with the privilege and responsibility of being servants and leaders in the ministry of the Church.

Response to a vocation to serve as an ordained minister signifies the voluntary undertaking of obligations of sacrificial self-discipline above and beyond the requirements of secular and ecclesiastical law.

to embody such plausibility and Janet articulated the views of many interviewees when she said,

> As a priest I believe – for some reason only known to God – he has called me out and set me apart . . . and that is part of the Ordinal isn't it? A sense of being called out and set apart to lead and to be a shepherd . . . and that image of the shepherd who goes not just in front but also when necessary from behind as well.

In these terms the sacrificially embodied embrace of the clergy lifestyle is thus an elective imprisonment of the self-governed soul in a Foucauldian 'house of certainty' (Foucault 1977: 202) rendered all the more powerful by the accompanying theological metanarrative of an all-knowing, all-seeing God and the rules of the ecclesiastical institution in which there is no hiding place. Foucault's interest was the interaction of religion and culture (Carrette 1999) and in particular the 'politics of religious experience' (Bernauer and Carrette 2004) – the link between the self, sexuality and Christian spirituality. The key insight for Foucault was that Christianity promoted the paradoxical self (echoing Mark 8: 35), losing life in order to save it:

> We have to sacrifice the self in order to discover the truth about ourselves and we have to discover the truth about ourselves in order to sacrifice ourselves. Truth and sacrifice, the truth about ourselves and the sacrifice of ourselves, are deeply and closely connected. (Foucault 1980b: 179)

As Carrette (2004: 224) indicates, Foucault anchored a positive 'notion of a coherent self' in sexual identity and theological belief. The clergy interviewed in this research suggest that the sacrificial self lies at the heart of priestly identity – body and soul – lived out in an enduring vocational commitment in the Church.

Sacrificial selves

The relationship between body, soul and the agency of individuals to shape their own lives has been considered by sociologist of the body Shilling (2008), who observes 'how people's embodied appearances, identities and capacities are shaped by various combinations of habit, crisis and creativity' (Shilling 2008: 1). Shilling proposes the possibilities of a dynamic relationship between the external and internal environments of human action, a notion which he terms 'pragmatism' and which is helpful in our context of trying to understand notions of sacrificial agency versus social enslavement in relation to the priesthood (Shilling 2008: 3). For Shilling, the embodiment of identity and the development of personal moral character is a pragmatic process over time, 'more concerned with conceptualizing human identity or character in terms of how individuals *adjust* to and achieve *integration* with their surroundings, accomplishments associated with the human capacity to engage in an intelligent responsiveness'. The emotional experience associated with creativity is at its height during sudden experiences – crises – of revelation when someone is gripped by the realization that their relationship with the environment could be radically different (Shilling 2008: 18–21). The realization that God had called a person to priestly ordination was frequently described by our clergy interviewees as a crisis, a personal epiphany.

In his discussion about religion and believing bodies Shilling notes how the obedient body and compliant soul are central to the Christian faith. He suggests that believing bodies evidence an intellectual and emotional commitment to religious belief expressed in symbolic significance and bodily techniques and an immersion in a collectivity. The bodies of individual Christians are incorporated into the body of the Church through the sacred celebration of the Eucharist. The Body of Christ in the eucharistic meal and the individual body are shared in a socially generative ritual. In his reflections on the character of religiously believing bodies Shilling proposes 'the crucial significance of socially sanctioned embodied habits in developing the huge variety of religious identities that exist in the world today' (2008: 153).

Within the Christian tradition sacrifice and body are central theological motifs. Sacrificial behaviour is central to an understanding of the Church's public representative ministers, while the body denotes the corporate and corporeal reality of the Church community founded as the living body of Christ in the world through history. The Bible's New Testament speaks of Christian bodies as 'a living sacrifice' (Romans 12: 1) and at the liturgical centre of the Church's life is the sacramental body and blood of Christ in the bread and wine of the Eucharist (1 Corinthians 10). At the heart of the *Ordination Services* for Bishops, Priests and Deacons, in the Church of England (2007a) is the Jesus who lives and dies a unique sacrificial biography and calls his disciples to follow him in doing likewise: 'the Son of Man did not come to be served but to serve, and to give his life as a ransom for many' (Mark 10: 45). Within the New Testament there is one passage which refers to embodied sacrifice more explicitly than other allusions. St Paul, writing to the Christian community in Rome *c.* 55 AD, exhorts members of the local church to live a sacrificial lifestyle as the obedient ethical consequence of receiving and believing the Christian gospel:

> I appeal to you therefore, brothers and sisters, by the mercies of God, *to present your bodies as a living sacrifice, holy and acceptable to God,* which is your spiritual worship. Do not be conformed to this world, but be transformed by the renewing of your minds, so that you may discern what is the will of God – what is good and acceptable and perfect. (Romans 12: 1–2, our italics)

Reviewing recent Biblical theology Davison (2010: 71–6) suggests that the body and 'incorporation into Christ' are central to Paul's thought and that 'body' means the whole person, corporeal, mental and spiritual – and social. Sacrifice is communal and ecclesial rather than simply individual and embracing the Christian life demands obedience and belonging, but in a thankful and reasoned way rather than an unwilling or ritual way. Diaconal ministry is foundational as all Christians including clergy serve one another in a redeemed humility.

Shilling's approach thus offers an important way of looking at the life-changing choice of ordination and the vocational journey of priestly ministry in the Church as incorporating both obedience and agency. Applying theories of corporeal realism and the embodiment of pragmatic change to clergy bodies allows the exploration of the body as a location for ordination and the priestly life. Although priestly ordination governs clergy bodies from without through traditional Church discipline, they retain from within personal agency to shape their vocation and the contemporary Church. Research participants recalled both their ordination to the priesthood as a crisis moment of obedient responsiveness and their life-long journey of 'becoming priest' and achieving a degree of personal authenticity. Shilling perceived individuals as uncompromising in undertaking action consistent with their particular religious identity regardless of the consequences: 'it is by engaging in repetitive physical rites over a long period of time that people *become* the religious subjects they seek to be, possessed of distinctive dispositions to themselves and their external environment' (Shilling 2008: 166).

The motif of self-sacrifice – of putting what they perceived to be God's needs before their own – was common to both male and female clergy in our research. The notion that clergy had elected to embrace sacrifice during their earthly lives provided a plausible explanation as to why, and how, they continued as parish priests in the face of a range of difficulties. Looking at a theology of Anglican priesthood through a feminist lens, Green (2009) critiques the unhealthy and nonredemptive forms of female self-denial and subservience and concludes that women should today be able to enter into self-sacrifice as a chosen option, alongside men, as free and responsible agents:

> The nature of priestly vocation is shaped around obedience, humility and spiritual poverty, borne of the *kenosis* [self-emptying] in the imitation of Christ. The priestly role necessarily involves a degree of self-sacrifice in the form of special training, personal discipline and self-giving to others. At the same time, priesthood carries a level of public authority, traditionally the usual domain of men and exercised in leadership, in worship, in preaching and so on.

However the self-sacrifice remains gendered because

> a woman's calling to the priesthood has required her to enter into an overwhelmingly male clerical caste, an alien culture at times hostile to her presence. And, in order to fulfil her vocation, she has been called to take up that authority which is still very novel for women in the long history of the Church, and still not wholly accepted, even by her own male fellow ministers. Here is an example of self-sacrifice that, at least until the last decade, has been innovative and counter-cultural, and which continues to subvert the male-dominated culture of the clerical establishment. (Green 2009: 155)

Feminist theology (Furlong 1984) acknowledges that self-sacrifice is often expected of women and Linda for example would affirm Green's analysis. She pinpointed the defining sacrificial edge for the formation of the priestly life and the tone of her narrative is one of personal agency in relation to having chosen the path of sacrifice:

> I don't want to lose the concept of sacrifice because I do feel that in giving my life in this way it is a recognition of how Christ gave his life for us . . . that does limit my choices and my freedom for the future in a positive way hopefully; but you know I can't just decide I will do my own thing now . . . I've got to be obedient to God.

Linda regarded notions of sacrifice as gendered, but positive in relation to women's position in the Church – sacrifice and the priesthood were available as a choice for women in a manner which had not been the case prior to the ordination of women in 1994 and certainly not available in her conservative, patriarchal Christian upbringing:

> I probably had a hang up with sacrifice as a child because it was very much the theology on which my Christian early life was built; and I think again this is perhaps a gender issue too that women have always had this sacrifice thing . . . I've had to work at that to actually not see, not to

allow myself to have a wrong view of what that meant; to actually see self-identity as being part of that sacrifice and the growth of that too.

For John the distinctions between work, sacrifice and vocation are finely balanced:

> The sacrifice of leadership can sometimes be lonely but I think there are lots of other professions in the same position. I think one can beat our breasts about this as clergy and I think we are not alone in this. There are lots of other people who work incredibly hard, probably a lot harder than I do . . . I mean teachers and doctors.

For John the integrity of individuals, including the clergy, lies as much in their commitment to their life's work as in a particularly godly type of self-sacrifice:

> There are sacrifices but I guess that is part of life in most ways. You commit yourself to a particular profession and that commitment, if you are going to take something seriously, or a particular job, it is sacrificial.

Janet's views of embracing sacrifice however, implied less certainty around notions of agency:

> Well I guess it is . . . an unswerving belief that in my darkest moments, that for some peculiar reason known only to him, God has called me . . . called to a place of servant-hood, of sacrifice, and to believe in a faith however stumbling . . . yet living that faith out. I am constantly surprised at being called to be a priest. I think it is quite a hoot actually I think God has got a wonderful sense of humour . . . I am convinced of it . . . in fact I am quite scared of his sense of humour.

Janet's belief that she was serving God in response to a personal calling suggests that she views the idea of sacrifice in a more constraining light – she perceives God to be revered, but also to be feared. As she describes God's 'sense of humour' in apparently calling her to follow difficult paths, she refers to herself as 'scared'. Janet's fears that God might find it amusing to command her service in difficult circumstances implies her view of Him as capricious – and capable of binding her to the darkest of situations like 'a pit' – the grim urban ring road parish where she ended up as vicar, and survived.

Vocational professionalism

Clergy are concerned with questions of embodied and emotional value – birth and personal relationships, mortality and salvation – and our research participants evidenced a variety of perceptions about their status in contemporary society. As Mark described, clergy are religious professionals with a number of interrelated roles:

> I am a Christian and okay, I am a full time 'professional' Christian . . . I think I am more conscious of the hats I am wearing or not wearing and I am also conscious of the funny-shaped hat which is kind of the blurred one between the different roles.

Over the centuries the Church has articulated a vocation of the ministerial priesthood as a particular commitment to a life-style which goes further than simply doing a job. This sacrificial professionalism has been characterized as the 'unique timbre' of the ordained (Greenwood 2009: 50). When clergy are licensed in the Church of England to parochial ministry the congregation is charged 'to respect those who labour among you, and have charge of you in the Lord and admonish you; esteem them very highly in love because of their work' (1 Thessalonians 5: 12–13). This suggests a mutually obedient, covenantal as well as contractual arrangement, according with the view of many research participants, for example Beryl:

> There's the issue of contract and covenant . . . because we're ordained we have a stipend, we don't get paid for so many hours. That's the deal, that's the promise, that's the covenant.

Professional identity

Given the advance of secularizing perspectives in late-modern Britain this covenant is open to question. It is unsurprising that the role of clergy, like those of doctors, teachers and other professional groups, is being questioned (Macdonald 1995) and this is reflected in the shifting focus of literature about Church of England clergy. A generation ago attention was directed at Anglican clerical formation (Ramsey 1972), Church of England careers (Towler and Coxon 1979) and compared clergy denominationally (Ranson et al. 1977). There followed Tiller's radical ideas about ministerial organization (Church of England 1983) and an assertive theology of the laity (Church of England 1985). Goode (1969) identified the 'semi-profession' and Russell (1980) described the historical emergence of a semi-professionalized clergy (contrasted with law and medicine) while Moody in *Eccentric Ministry* (1992) later questioned the desirability of aping secular professionalism. Freidson noted the autonomy, power and epistemological status of professionals (including the clergy) and the imputed, exclusive expertise among those in 'occupationally *ordained* positions' (Freidson 1994: 64–7, our italics). It is noteworthy that clergy continue to earn significantly less than their professional peers and have never formed a professional organization.

Some writers searched for suitable managerial models of ministry (Bunting 1993, Nelson 1996) while Roberts (2002) scathingly questioned the uncritical assimilation of 'managerialism' into the Church of England. Roberts is suspicious that an essentialist view of the embodiment of clerical authority has transmuted into an equally illiberal postmodern abuse of managerial power. The instrumental effects of this can be observed, he argues, in the Church's increasing emphasis on restructuring the organization, managing the performance of its clergy and leadership through programmed vision which demands followership. Greenwood (1994, 2002, 2009) and Croft (1999) recast the public representative minister's presiding and navigating roles within a theology of mission and ministry rooted in a contemporary Trinitarian theology of relationships in the Church. Green (2009, 2011) has contributed an important feminist theology of priesthood, contrasting male and female identities. Reports have examined episcopal leadership (Church of England 1990) and its resourcing (Church of England 2001c) while Gill and Burke (1996), Adair and Nelson (2004) and Grundy (2011) argue that a rediscovery of strategic and shared episcope combining trustworthy oversight and leadership builds effective clergy and parishes. Applying an anthropological lens to the 'clergy species', a key challenge to professional clergy identity is that some parish clergy feel that they have been edged to 'the hinterland' of public life (Percy 2006: 188) with a declining authority (Higgins 2001). They may be uncertain how their activities fit in with both other specialists and volunteers and feel a counter-cultural remnant within a postmodern environment. The clergy wellbeing report *Affirmation and Accountability* does not pull its punches about role confusion, ambiguity and overload. In relation particularly to clergy in crisis, it observes: 'we meet many clergy who fundamentally don't know what they are 'for'. Without this anchoring central knowledge they are prey to a host of inappropriate expectations, fed further by their own anxiety. At times of rapid and far-reaching change, within both church and society, this is an organizational problem, not just an individual one' (Lee and Horsman 2002: 7). By contrast, the women and men clergy in our research did bring a personal vocational professionalism to what they were trying to do and had a grounded view of their priestly duties and obligations. All understood who they were, what they were supposed to be doing and why, even if spiritual and pragmatic demands on their bodies and souls were not always easy to meet. However, within the context of professional identities our respondents reflected on a number of organizational and personal issues such as gender and impression management which made it hard to fit in with the expectations of the Church.

Gender and professional work

The entry of women's bodies into masculinized spaces marks an innovative 'professional project' (Witz 1992) for the Church of England. The progress and perils of careers in women's bodies pursued in traditionally masculinized medical spaces are highlighted by Martin (1987) and Pringle (1998), while *The Woman in the Surgeon's Body* contended that 'surgeons often define their masculinity through their work and view women as devaluing and threatening the worth of their achievements' (Cassell 1998: 600–1). There may be an unacknowledged clergy equivalent, 'I am a priest therefore I am a man' in some male clergy opposed to the ordination of women. To explain the persistence of discrimination in medicine Pringle and Cassell rely extensively on Bourdieu's theory of *habitus* (Bourdieu 1984). This perspective identifies and classifies the embodied aspect of social difference (Lash 1990) in which the female *habitus* hinders integration into masculine cultures. While a recent examination of emotion, performance and the body in women teaching male managers is optimistic (Swan 2005), Puwar's revealing research into gender and race in parliamentary politics is cautionary. Puwar (2004) found parliamentary institutions in denial about difference, despite the liberal rhetoric proclaiming neutral professionalism. Gendered and racially differentiated bodies were deemed 'space invaders', and out of place in relation to an invisible centre: 'There is a huge amount of resistance within the professions to making the gendered and racial nature of the environments visible. There is a reluctance to face up to how different staff members are afforded the advantage of 'ontological complicity' (Puwar 2004: 153–4).

In a Church where feminist theology is well established (Fulkerson 2003, Muers 2005) and where women are gradually progressing into senior leadership (though not yet as bishops in England) Jamieson (1997) explored power, authority and relationships from her perspective as an Anglican diocesan bishop in New Zealand. Through her experience as a woman with authority in a hierarchical institution where women have historically been second class citizens she tackles the fundamental problems facing outsiders who become insiders. Like Puwar, she notes the gap between the rhetoric and practice, and between the structural authority and the idealism of the Church. Paradoxically however, some outsiders are not welcomed. Research about male spouses of clergy indicates how the latter 'experience the non-identity' (Page 2010: 293) suffered by their female spouse predecessors. An interviewee referred to the occasional superior behaviour of some women priests towards lay women, perhaps because the latter now represent a nonidentity which female clergy believe they have left behind. Such behaviour could be constructed as unsupportive, and characteristic of a 'Queen Bee' syndrome in which high-ranking women are seen to be pulling up the sisterly drawbridge once they themselves achieve seniority, preferring to work with men and to preserve their own position as one of few women in powerful roles. Mavin (2006, 2008) has, however, deconstructed the concept of Queen Bee as oversimplifying the complexities faced by senior professional women. Mavin argues that, especially in male-dominated occupations, women are under more scrutiny than men in equivalent roles. They may be faced with unrealistic expectations regarding their ability to show sisterly solidarity through challenging gendered and embodied practices (in this case, the association between masculinity and the priesthood) which have been in place for centuries.

Impression management

Embodying one's professional occupation correctly is clearly important for both women and men. Singh, Kumra and Vinnicombe (2002) explore the tactics of women trying to fit into predominantly male environments. In the Church of England talk of clergy ambition and career paths is generally frowned upon. Even now the Church still uses a language of 'vocation and preferment' and promotion through informal processes which men have learned to negotiate using impression management strategies. The experience of over a decade of women priests and their progress into more senior posts as Area/Rural Deans, Archdeacons and Cathedral Deans confirms that the gender nuances of the 'promotion game' found in secular research are there also in the Church. Singh's research set us thinking about the behaviour of the people we work with in academia and the Church and who might perceive us as doorkeepers in relation to career opportunities. We recognize the behaviour in female and male colleagues in Singh's description of self-focussed impression management tactics: presenting a professional demeanour, diligent preparation and commitment in ministry beyond supervisory expectations, adding value and getting a reputation. Women clergy in particular have to negotiate remaining feminine while erasing gendered prejudices about ability in order to embody priesthood as generally understood in the Church. As in other walks of life so for clergy the 'workplace has become the point of convergence of a number of themes' (Morgan et al. 2005: 9) – gender and bodies, power and emotions, impressions and achievements.

Work and embodiment are thus linked to the extent to which the work is carried out under the gaze of others (Haynes 2011). Being called upon to present oneself in particular ways raises questions of gender and the relation between the performance and the audience (Collinson and Collinson 1997). As for the actor in the theatre of life (Goffman 1959: 244) so also for the priest and her/his congregation. Indeed style of dress may be important as part of the 'aesthetic labour' of celebrating or camouflaging difference (Morgan et al. 2005: 7, 11; Haynes 2011). This leads to some paradoxical results in the ecclesiastical setting. Although some women have adopted a traditional dark suited and clerical-collared approach, rather more have transformed the clerical shirt (blouse) into a rainbow of colours and styles. Further research is needed to discover whether those women who have reached the most senior positions tend towards a more collegial (traditional, male) dress and demeanour. The difficulty of achieving the invisible professional costume in Parliament without compromising race or gender (Puwar 2004: 78) is in the Church masked by androgynous liturgical robes and the clerical collar as professional signifiers, a dramaturgical 'disembodiment' (Morgan et al. 2005: 4) achieving visible invisibility – the woman in priest's robes, the priest in the woman's body.

According to Singh (2002) male strategies for promotion focus on gaining an early understanding of the prevalent success model in their organization and emulating it through hard work and fitting the mould. In our Church experience some women have tried even harder to outdo (and perhaps become victims to) previously male preoccupations with competitive church-growing, overt busyness and neglecting their families (Kuhrt and Bentley 2001, Thomas 2006) and there were some indications of this in the clergy interviews. Carole for example stressed how much she had energetically enlarged her congregation, 'we built up to between 40 and 50 on a Sunday which is very good particularly for a small village'. Linda seemed ambitious and admitted not giving her youngsters 'my personal attention all the time' and that with her ordained husband, 'we've allocated time tonight to sit down and talk through some issues . . . family communication isn't what it should be at the moment . . . we tend to take each other for granted'.

This suggests less gender differentiation in that both men and women were clear that 'reading the organization' in terms of identifying key practices and behaviour was necessary to progress. Some clergy don't quite realize the unspoken conventions required to 'fit in' and 'get on'. For example, turning up for a deanery service but declining to robe with clergy colleagues, preferring a seat in the congregation instead. In the Church, self-image and organizational image are not always consistent and learning to become more visible (without being marked out, Puwar 2004) does not come naturally to many clergy, male and female alike, who may regard self-promotion with suspicion. It seems unlikely however that impression management will disappear from organizations and their aspirant staff. Indeed it is arguable that the Church of England needs a great deal of it as it seeks to survive its 21st century identity crisis.

Cultivating virtue

The professional impression communicated by the clergy is indeed a topical concern for the Church. A key to the vocational identity of clergy is their understanding of disciplined professional behaviour. As we have already noted the Church of England is embracing a range of measures to tighten the framework for standards and self-regulation including Clergy Discipline and Terms of Service, appraisal and a rigorous approach to safeguarding children and vulnerable adults. For clergy these arrangements apply not only to working hours but all of life in a unique way. Clergy are not the only profession where errant behaviour outside the workplace can have consequences. For example a GP who received a police caution for assaulting staff in the dining car of a mainline express train was warned by a disciplinary panel of the General Medical Council about his future conduct and the risk of bringing 'the profession into disrepute' (Greenhill 2008). A clergyperson would attract similar attention. However the difference is that a married GP having an adulterous affair with another person (not a patient) is unlikely to be brought before a medical council, losing her/his job and home. Under the Clergy Discipline Measure a similarly errant vicar is most certainly at risk of lengthy prohibition.

Of particular interest here however are the *Guidelines for the Professional Conduct of the Clergy*, produced by the clergy themselves (Church of England 2003b). These are nonstatutory and a practical commentary for daily life based on the Ordination Services (Church of England 2007a). The Archbishops' foreword suggests to the clergy that the *Guidelines* 'should be re-read at regular intervals . . . at the renewal of ordination vows or on some . . . significant anniversary' (Church of England 2003b: vii). Importantly they contain a reflective section (Bridger 2003) which aims to provide a theology of professional responsibility based on three principles: covenant, agape and virtue. The first can be summarized as a promise 'to go the extra mile' – clergy behaviour is expected to exceed purely contractual minimums. *Agape* is the Greek New Testament word for loving care, gifted freely whatever the response from the other – clergy labour with people from all walks of life for love's sake. Both covenant and agape underpin the clergy's pastoral care role, emphasizing an unselfish ministry shaped by the needs of others and the need for the careful use of power in relationships with vulnerable people.

The third principle, virtue, has a particular elegance, promoting the idea that the character of the professional is as important as the code to which he or she adheres. This strikes at the heart of ordination, emphasizing personal integrity – what clergy do is governed by who they are. Disciplined bodies (Foucault 1977) are characterized by obedient souls (Rose 1999). However this cannot be left to chance and clergy 'must *deliberately* cultivate Christian character and virtues' in their work and 'habits of the heart' in a healthy spiritual life (Bridger 2003: 19–20, original italics). Within Christian morality virtue ethics has been a strong ideal: trustworthiness, prudence and holiness of life spring to mind and the early Christian values of love, joy, peace, patience, kindness, generosity, faithfulness, gentleness and self-control (Galatians 5: 22–3). In his reevaluation of contemporary moral philosophy, *After Virtue*, MacIntyre pointed to the 'construction of new forms of community within which the moral life could be sustained' beyond the philosophy of the civil state or the theology of the Church (1985: 263). Gill argues that virtue ethics is most persuasive when applied to 'empirical social communities' (Gill 2012: 222) and so it emerged that, in our research interviews, within clerical society the cultivation of virtue is a persuasive driver for clergy behaviour and the quest for priestly authenticity.

Ministerial review

The question of how virtue should be measured is a difficult one. A variety of Ministry Development Review schemes for the clergy have gradually been introduced in dioceses over the past decade to help the clergy reflect on how they use their time and set priorities. The concept of 'appraisal' does not sit easily in the lives of Church of England clergy who have traditionally been entrusted to work largely unsupervised, protected by freehold and the stipend from the parochial laity and the diocesan bishop. Few interviewees felt undermanaged though two indicated that they would appreciate a more regular personal meeting with their Bishop. Five participants believed accountability was to God and their own responsibility. Certainly clergy still have professional freedom to shape the hours and content of their working day on a spectrum 'from dedication to indolence' (Hinton 1994: 313) and John, an interviewee confirmed this:

> I have a lot of freedom to determine my own working pattern and there is very little sense of accountability so there is not that direct line management going on. I don't have targets, you know . . . bums on seats . . . all these things.

Unsurprisingly therefore clergy have expressed mixed views about greater professional surveillance: some resist what they see as interference in a self-regulating vocational life, others embrace the idea but paradoxically haven't found the appraiser or the outcomes sufficiently critical. Some clergy find 'the paradigm shift to collaborative ministry' stressful (Cranwell 2008). A priest from an industrial relations background writing in the church press argued that clergy appraisal is not yet focussed enough on a genuine 360-degree critical review of performance that can pick up difficulties and training needs before break-down occurs. The advent of national terms of service however now requires accountability and a compulsory approach to clergy Ministerial Development Review (Church of England 2008c, Rooms and Steen 2008) akin to the professional development reviews regarded as standard practice in most organizations. This has necessitated a more defined approach to work goals within ministry role descriptions and some assessment of the priest's achievements by lay leaders in the parish (Church of England 2005b: 62–6). In addition capability and grievance procedures are now in place for when there is a dispute about a priest's performance.

Already in dioceses a number of tools are usually suggested to assist clergy preparation for their annual ministry review interview, for example a ministry inventory, a life events and stress indicator exercise and keeping a 14-day diary. Diocesan reviewers have noticed some resistance to keeping and/or reporting details as part of the review scheme interview. However, following up Church contacts we were able to talk with five parochial clergy (three men, two women) beyond the Managing Clergy Lives research sample who provided information about their diaries and work–life balance. Two of the clergy were currently Area/Rural Deans while one had been in the past. Because clergy record their use of time in their own way it is difficult to make precise comparisons. However their comments provide a window into clergy daily life. One Area/Rural Dean kept a detailed 14-day diary. Married to a working spouse and with young children he recorded 21 per cent of waking hours as 'family time' with an additional 6 per cent and 8 per cent respectively for recreation and relaxing and 2 per cent at the gym. He managed two full weekdays off, a week apart, during the fortnight but we do not know how interrupted the remainder of his 37 per cent time off may have been, especially the time spent at home in the vicarage. He recorded an average 56-hour working week, categorized as follows:

Administration 8%
Worship and sermon preparation 19%
Occasional Offices (Baptisms, Weddings and funerals) 7%
Church meetings 13%
Community meetings 7%
Prayer 7%
Reading 2%
Support and planning 6%
Visiting/pastoral care 3%
Study and research 8%
Mentoring and leadership 5%
Area Dean's duties 10%
Training/teaching 5%

An incumbent of a rural benefice recorded a 46.8-hour average working week divided into five areas of activity:

Pastoral care 24.8%
Teaching 25.8%
Administration 21.2%
Prayer and worship 17.2%
Training 11%

Although he claimed that he only exceptionally missed his day off each week, his 14-day diary revealed otherwise! Another priest, leading an urban ministry team, managed two full days off – a Saturday in week one, and a Friday the following week (to accommodate weddings). However what was noticeable in her diary and the two previous examples was the length of clergy working days. Although she juggled with daily family interludes five of her workdays stretched across 14 hours and only two workdays were of less than double figures. In response to a question about appropriately adjusting one's work–life balance one female Area/Rural Dean reported,

'No, it is worse than it was, even though I protect my day off on the whole very successfully. Apart from my day off recreation is almost non-existent'. Another priest summed up the dilemmas of time succinctly: 'Work–life are not opposites for me. Work–home would be a better polarity' reflecting perhaps a common attitude among Church of England clergy. Since ministry is not confined to set hours and because clergy are based at home with computers and I-phones work and time off are at best blurred, and sometimes an air of desperation comes across. Peyton recently challenged a priest, 'did you really send this email to me at 2 am? Do take care of yourself!' evoking the response, 'Whoops, spotted!! Thanks Nigel'.

Complementing ministerial review the Church requires its clergy to participate initially in Curate Training and then Continuing Ministerial Education over the years. Among clergy there is perhaps a growing appreciation of and commitment to developing one's ministry and oneself. Some Dioceses direct their clergy to courses such as Arrow (CPAS 2012) and the Clergy Leadership Programme (Leadership Institute 2012) to enhance their ministerial aspirations and development and in particular developing spiritual maturity, reflexive practitioner and missional leadership abilities.

Clergy careers

While clergy were generally unanimous regarding their commitment to a life-long sacrificial embrace as regards God, they were less certain about earthly interpretations of how sacrifice should be understood. The organizational structure of the Church of England is a particularly flat one. The vast majority of clergy are working in parishes and the avenues for increased pay and promotion to senior status are very limited. Nevertheless these organizational and career realities do not prevent some clergy from harbouring ambition at some point during their ordained lives and the topic became apparent in eight interviews. Indeed the statistical indication that being an Area/Rural Dean increases a clergyperson's chances of preferment may in itself raise the hopes (and lead to disappointments) for some. Despite an overall reticence, within our research a number of women and men clergy clearly aspire to the 'ladder' and are anxiously hopeful or disappointed.

Ambition, preferment and disappointment

Richard, an experienced market town incumbent, for example has struggled to get a cathedral post and wonders whether women priests have the advantage of a 'hidden agenda'. Certainly the Church is now more proactive towards female preferment. However Puwar's observation that the relatively fewer women in an organization render them noticed more easily (Puwar

2004: 92) does not automatically translate into the unfair promotion of less able individuals. The Church's review of senior appointments in *Talent and Calling* conceded that a lack of detailed data about the relative age, experience and qualifications of women and men entering senior posts made it impossible to reach an objective conclusion about gender and fairness. The long-standing system of the Preferment List which contains the CVs of nearly 600 talented clergy recommended by their bishops for promotion to cathedral, archdeaconry or episcopal posts continues to operate uneasily beside a mixture of advertised and closed search and appointment methods (Church of England 2007d). The limited number of 366 senior appointments thwarts many personal ambitions and even knowing that one is on the List can have that corrosive effect on character described by Sennett (1999) on some clergy. Over the years the Church has counselled priests to develop a realistic view of their ambitions and disappointments (Hardaker 1998, Clergy Appointments Advisor 2011). In particular there is recognition (Lee 2006) that when preferment or moves do not happen the last years of full-time stipendiary ministry can be a time of frustration rather than fulfilment for many clergy. Some clergy find it difficult to face another decade of doing 'more of the same' (Lee and Horsman 2002: 13). A number of clergy in the sample like Richard were indeed frustrated, even bitter that they had been overlooked. Jean expressed the most frustration among the interviewees in being unable to secure the advancement she craved:

> I can't even get on the Archdeacon rung of the ladder after various attempts . . . I could not understand why I wasn't, with my wide range of gifts, why I wasn't getting interviews if five Bishops were telling me, 'I think this is the route you should be going' . . . there has been a high personal cost . . . I think what I have found enormously difficult in this process has been to trust the system.

Jean also held an advisory role to the Bishop so her last disappointment was particularly difficult:

> for me the hardest road was the final one I did apply for because . . . they did appoint a woman and she is good news I am sure, at least from what I gleaned from her, I was pleased that she had got the job but I was gutted that I didn't because I really wanted it.

The progress of the Church of England's clerical feminization since 1994 confirms the North American finding (Nesbitt 1997) that not all able women clergy will gain promotion. In the end Jean wonders why her honest ambition and seeking to be faithful to God, together with bishops encouraging her to apply for Archdeacon posts, have not got her anywhere. She says she will not try again.

Another participant, Julian admitted to wondering what he might do next and that he would quite like his interviewer's job, that is, being an Archdeacon:

> The thing that would be of interest to me . . . is actually doing your job. I think that the whole business of church management and strategy and making the Church as good as it possibly can be is something that pleases me. And I say that with some hesitation because it is all about servanthood and not that wanting to be an important person. But . . . the more I think about it and pray about it . . . that is the kind of skill set that I seem to have acquired by default. I mean, having said that, if that doesn't happen, it is not the end of the world.

Sometimes ambition is projected onto the clergy with unsettling consequences. John was unexpectedly approached by his Bishop on the margins of an unrelated Church meeting and prompted to apply for a Residentiary Canon post in his cathedral. The potentially harmful raising of false hopes in clergy in a throwaway remark by a Bishop is criticized in *Talent and Calling*. However, John realized that he might be seen as a 'plausible candidate' but 'emotionally I was all over the place' and the interviewer was left unsure whether John would apply or not. Just being told by one's Bishop that he is going to place you on the List can be an unnerving experience. Jacqui for example found that 'being on the Preferment List . . . was quite a shock actually.' She was recommended as a potential Archdeacon and was excited by the prospect yet realistic, 'because I am all too aware that nothing may happen you know'. It subsequently did when she was appointed an Archdeacon in her own diocese.

An Anglican theology professor and one-time General Synod member of the Crown Nominations Commission (the advisory body for diocesan episcopal appointments) has suggested that ministerial personalities are prone to having either too high, or too low, a view of ministers and ministry. In the 21st century we can either exaggerate the importance of clergy, or we can undervalue them and give them little respect (Thistleton 2006: 63–4). It is probable that both flattery and a lack of appreciation are equally damaging for clergy morale and in this respect clergy do report sometimes getting mixed messages both from their parishioners and the hierarchy. However not all ambition proves seductive. Mark chose to take up parish ministry instead of a cathedral post and he explained why:

> They were two completely different jobs. One was a parish job, the other was a Residentiary Canon's job with a social outreach kind of brief . . . and the interviews were in the same week. These were the first set and the others were going to happen later in the week and I came here and I didn't hear from here but I rang the other place and said that I wasn't going because having come to a parish situation I knew when I was here

that that is actually what I needed to do at that time and that I could pick up the other agenda at a later point if I wanted to.

It struck us as a courageous thing to do because in a flat organization the odds are against getting a second chance, but Mark replied, 'It didn't feel brave at the time, it felt a kind of "I can do no other" sort of experience'. Like Jacqui his honesty was also subsequently vindicated when he was appointed as a Residentiary Canon at another cathedral.

Towler and Coxon (1979) indicated that making a variety of moves between parochial and specialist ministry might indicate a preferment path in the Church of England. Recent longitudinal research into clergy patterns of service (Barley 2009) explores contemporary trends and in the light of our selected research sample it should be noted that the Archbishops' Appointments Adviser has indicated that success in the role of Area/Rural Dean can lead to inclusion in the 'talent pipeline' (Church of England 2007d: 30). For these clergy statistically there is a 112/700 (16%) one in six chance of such a promotion to Archdeacon, which is certainly better than the 112/8616 (1.2%) one in 77 chance at the point of Ordination. The fact that in many dioceses the role and responsibilities of Area/Rural Deans are being significantly enhanced will certainly further highlight the career channel to becoming an archdeacon.

Given that the vast majority of clergy will not however experience preferment to a senior role other moves or additional responsibilities take on an enhanced significance. Clergy make lateral moves to broaden their experience and to face fresh challenges. Family considerations for a spouse's career or children's education may also play a part in timely moves, or conversely in staying put, often leading to contented stability in a particular locality. Some clergy don't consciously cultivate career paths or find competitive recruitment congenial, Simon being one:

I don't like the idea of looking at the Church Times and applying to parishes. I would far prefer a phone call saying, 'I know you have been there for x number of years, would you be prepared to look at y?' and if that happened I would treat it very seriously.

Whether or not the Bishop telephones with such a suggestion, over the years, clergy transfer from one kind of parish to another. The new post typically might offer a different context, perhaps with a larger scope for leading a ministry team or training a curate. Other clergy transfer from the parish to sector and specialist ministries, as chaplains in secular institutions or as diocesan advisers, sometimes returning to a parish again later. These varied experiences were reflected in the research sample of Area/Rural Deans. It was striking how, many years on, sideways moves within the Church of England can still provide a sense of personal advancement. During his interview Ralph indicated how a recent invitation to move to a diocesan clergy training role was itself the fulfilment of a latent ambition closer to the academic career he 'gave up' many years ago in order to become a parish priest.

The advent of women clergy and 'two-clergy couples' in the Church of England has introduced a double dynamic of ambition and career development. Within marriages there can be competing expectations about whose career move takes the lead next time. Given the demands of residence for parochial posts and competition for specialist appointments achieving a satisfying or remunerated outcome for both individuals is challenging. Equal opportunities best practice breaks down within the particular requirements of the ordained ministry and as observed in other sectors (Gatrell and Swan 2008) institutional resistance remains. Nevertheless, for Linda the increasing openings for women to reach senior positions in the Church have awakened her sense of ambition and altered the previously gendered career assumptions of her two-clergy marriage:

> When I started that was a very distant future and therefore I didn't have anything to lose in that sense. It wasn't as if I was going to have to worry about my next job and partly because I'm married to a clergy person . . . both he and I are limited by the other as to what our next jobs can be anyway . . . so we're not on that ladder to somehow thinking . . . this is where we're going to go. We've always got to take into account the other and that will limit the choices we have.

Labour without reward

Clearly parish clergy are not 'in it for the money'. However our research reveals the subtle economic opportunity cost of being ordained. Whatever else they might be doing with their lives few clergy regret ordination but do absorb its consequences in their personal financial circumstances. For the less fortunate there is a significant level of anxiety which is affecting clergy morale in a largely private and hidden way. Warren found that 'many clergy highlighted the lack of money as a major cause of stress' (2002: 123) but did not explore the topic in detail. Lee and Horsman (2002) were concerned that the commitment of clergy and their families should not be exploited by unreasonable expectations yet they did not question either the concept or current value of the clergy stipend as contributory factors. Enquiring into clergy stress Thomas (2006) did not specifically explore financial worries though they were reported in the 'additional comments' section of questionnaires completed by just over a thousand clergy respondents.

The frequency of concerns expressed in our clergy interviews about personal finance, despite the fact that it was not a primary topic of our enquiry, was disturbing. We had not anticipated writing at length about clergy finance but the respondents' concerns became obvious after early conversations and continued throughout the interview sample. Eighteen respondents volunteered particular or extended comments relating to the economic downside of an ordained life in the Church of England and there were references to finance in virtually all the interviews. It was interesting to record how the subject arose spontaneously in the interview conversations. The questions probing clergy 'regrets' and 'future hopes' and discussion about spouses' occupations and vicarage family life regularly triggered comment about the cost of living on a stipend, anxieties about pensions and retirement housing and this data provided an opportunity to fill the gaps in the previous research.

Within this commonality the contrasting circumstances of clergy households generated differences in the outlook of each priest we interviewed. Clergy sensed that their stipend might seem poor if they ministered in an affluent parish, yet could be riches in an impoverished community. Meyrick (1998) reported a similar variety of often strongly held views among the clergy spouses she researched. Those clergy who offered the most accentuated comment in our research were generally those who felt financially poor, or badly treated by the Church, or especially anxious about managing in retirement. Those clergy with working spouses, and/or who had inherited family property or retained and often let their preordination home clearly expressed greater financial security. Either way clergy sit uneasily within socio-economic categories. Keith said that clergy 'are what my wife calls the posh poor' echoing Meyrick's view that 'the clergy . . . are middle-class men [sic] living in upper-class houses on a working class income. While this may no longer be completely accurate, there is still, for many, a perceived discrepancy between the demands of the job and the financial package that accompanies it' (Meyrick 1998: 104). As Mark and others commented in interviews, parish clergy do not receive bonuses for ministry excellence nor always feel sufficient 'affirmation, whether that be money or perks or status . . . that other people might get through bonuses . . . its very intangible . . . and sometimes I just think it needs to become physical'.

Pauline's account

Pauline is single and one of the younger women Area/Rural Deans interviewed. Employed in finance before ordination, her financial critique of working as a clergy person is particularly interesting. She makes a number of sharp points about how the Church of England values its clergy through financial compensation and housing arrangements. Firstly, Pauline doesn't agree with the way the Church of England in recent years has benchmarked clergy stipends with teachers' salaries:

> I do get really stroppy and this is probably the bad side of having been an accountant. I mean nobody goes into ministry for the money and it is fine not to earn, I mean be non-stipendiary . . . I don't have a problem with it

... what I have a problem with is when people make spurious claims ... I mean the whole thing about comparing to primary head school teachers and then, well [20% less] because clergy have a vocation and teachers don't. I mean that is basically insulting to the head teacher ... well, any I know.

As a result although she enjoys being a priest, Pauline echoes Burgess (2002) in distrusting her employer:

Yes I think you have to be absolutely certain that this is what you are called to do. Because if it is what you are called to do it is the best job in the world and I wouldn't really change it however much I moan. But if it is not then you are going to suffer and I would also say, as a general rule of thumb, don't trust the Church of England any further than you can throw it.

Pauline confirms the view that clergy do make a connection in their minds between the value of the Church of England remuneration package and feeling valued by the organization.

Secondly, Pauline felt cheated by the Church over her home ownership prior to ordination:

I was the kind of generation when I went to theological college, I was made to sell my house and now I am thinking ... my mortgage? Now I have not got a hope in hell of ever having anywhere to live of my own. That was a stupid mistake – thank you Church of England.

There is an almost biblical suggestion here of a demanding sacrificial commitment to sell-up and follow her vocation. Pauline is also unconvinced that the Church correctly calculates the added value of the provided house on top of the stipend: 'When we are talking about how much you earn there is included £15,000 for your house, but when they are actually calculating the pension that is not included in your remuneration'. This value is now calculated on a mortgage cost basis, £9740 in July 2010 (Church of England 2010b: 17). Parish clergy receive only a stipend and no extra housing allowance, for example to set up a mortgage for their retirement housing provision and the vicarage is discounted as a pensionable asset. She knows that while clergy may enjoy living in their vicarage the 'added value' of a 'tied asset' is something of a contradiction in terms: 'It is just like, how stupid do you think we are? So that is the kind of thing that gets me cross'.

Stipends and pension worries

Christian tradition has typically admired simplicity of life and been suspicious of clergy affluence. The remuneration package for today's Church of England clergy – stipend, housing and pension – described in *Generosity and Sacrifice* (Church of England 2001a) reiterates the financially sacrificial nature of the stipend when compared with secular professional salaries. Historically stipends related directly to wealthy patrons and glebe land revenues and there were wide disparities between a parish appointment to a 'good living' or a poor one. Indeed the egalitarian purpose of the Church Commissioners, founded in 1704, was to augment the stipends of poorer clergy. The comprehensive Paul Report (Church of England 1964) marks the 20th century watershed leading to the more realistic deployment and payment of the clergy. Hinton argues that in modern times a national Church of England stipend has spared clergy from 'most of the personal financial problems which beset their predecessors . . . they are neither indecently affluent nor excruciatingly poor' (1994: 90). While our clergy interviewees appreciate this many were circumspect about the daily economic experience of their ordained lives.

For example, setting a National Stipend in the Church of England while allowing regional variation remains open to criticism. James, a young priest married to a GP gets 'annoyed at Diocesan Synod when some lay people speak with some pride that we have the lowest stipends in the country. It makes me very cross that I think we have just gone over £20,000 and I know clergy in this deanery . . . one family relies on Family Tax Credits to survive'. Mark also commented on how the regional variations in stipend levels and the differential cost of living can work against clergy budgeting: 'In Birmingham you could buy a coffee in the high street easily for 50p. I came to London I took a pay cut of £1500 and the coffee was three times the price'. Perversely both these dioceses paid below the national stipend figure in 2011. The disparity of diocesan arrangements has grown in recent years and illustrated in Table 4.1.

Table 4.1 *Diocesan clergy stipend variations in the Church of England 2010–2011*

STIPEND VARIATIONS 2011

The National Stipend Benchmark 2011–2012 was £22,810 and set to be paid to all full-time stipendiary clergy of incumbent status. Although the majority of dioceses kept within ± £500 of the Benchmark 16 out of 43 dioceses paid below the NSB.

Guildford Diocese paid the highest stipend £25,056 (+2246)

13 Dioceses paid more than £23,310

4 Dioceses paid less than £22,310

Durham Diocese paid the lowest stipend £22,000 (–810)

Source: Church of England (2011b: 9)

The effect on clergy mobility of regional stipend variations is unknown. However for families a stipend is rarely enough and a spouse's additional income can make a big difference to household budgets and aspirations for vicarage children. Fiona, a young married vicar with a working husband and school-aged children, described some of the financial pressures:

> Our children cost us a lot of money with the activities that they are involved in and I laughed when you said 'go out for a meal' – what with? It is spent on singing lessons and all the other things that the children go to. We might afford the Two for One!

She enjoys her local gym for personal wellbeing and meeting parishioners there but the subscription eats into monthly pay. She realized that, 'if I was back out in the big wide world and I was the main bread winner I would be working and earning twice as much as what I am'. Fiona looks at clergy colleagues and is worried about further problems ahead with her growing family:

> There are some clergy within this deanery who are looking at resigning as a full time stipendiary incumbent, possibly transferring to non-stipendiary ministry and going back out into the work place because they cannot financially get children through university . . . with ageing parents to look after and no other source of income coming in, so there is no way they can earn extra money like you can in other businesses.

Another priest, Mark who is single recognizes among his deanery clergy colleagues the link between professional affirmation and financial insecurities:

> In other roles you would get more opportunities for affirmation, whether that be money or perks or status or all those sort of things that other people might get, or bonuses or whatever. Our role is not like that so the affirmation comes in very intangible ways . . . I know very few [clergy] who actually are in it for that, but that doesn't mean to say that those things suddenly disappear because they are all real human aspirations and our high ideals are not always matched by what is really going on . . . I don't know of many people who consciously moan endlessly about money . . . there are one or two who do.

The onset of financial turmoil in the markets, recession and price inflation since 2008 has increased clergy anxiety and makes efforts by the Church of England to enhance the value of the stipend even more difficult. Indeed many dioceses have frozen stipends or given minimal increases. The long term solution for clergy financial and domestic security would involve a fundamental shift away from the historic dependency culture that 'the

Church will provide'. A more fitting 21st century remuneration package might include a more substantial stipend, a partially contributory pension scheme and participation in savings and housing schemes from the earliest point of entry into the ordained life (Church of England 2001a: 78).

During the period of our research interviews the occupational pension environment and housing market were particularly volatile and economic difficulties in the United Kingdom continue. These realities, well documented in Church circles and the media, were doubtless preying on the minds of our clergy interviewees. Tony felt he had 'job security, as far as it goes . . . but pension? No!' In particular clergy knew that the Church of England, in common with many other organizations responding to their actuarial review, proposed to reduce the benefits of its Clergy Pension Scheme to offset the climbing cost of provision funded largely by the voluntary giving of church members. Some carefully crafted modifications were implemented following a fraught debate in the General Synod.

From a dispassionate perspective the Church of England Pensions Scheme remains by modern standards a sound one in that for clergy it is noncontributory and provides fixed benefits. In addition the Clergy Housing and Retirement Ministry scheme (CHARM) is a voluntarily established provision by the Church Commissioners offering limited equity-sharing and renting arrangements for the most needy clergy. Because pensions have historically been regarded as deferred stipend clergy have typically fought to keep these pension expectations even at the cost of suppressing stipend increases. The fact that over the past 20 years the profile of serving clergy has been steadily aging may well contribute to this mind-set. The average age for both women and men stipendiary priests is now 51 and for self-supporting clergy it is nearer 60; significantly 22 per cent of paid clergy are already over 60 (Church of England 2012).

The clergy in Carole's deanery are talking about 'clergy morale and I think that for all the same reasons . . . I think everybody is labouring really. I think one of the big things is pensions, housing and that sort of thing and if you feel that you are labouring away with perhaps few results with not much at the end of it, it can become quite sort of worrying'. Ordained 16 years, she is beginning to plan for retirement and said, 'I had something come through about my pension the other day which is not looking brilliant and it is certainly less than I was expecting it would be . . . the Church that I entered into . . . seemed to have prospects and seemed to have security . . . certainly had a pension and the prospect of a decent retirement and that is not I think the Church that we see today.'

Housing anxieties

A common theme among a significant number of interviewees of varied ages was the fear of having nowhere to live following retirement. Their anxiety partly reflected the emotional shift from provided accommodation to home ownership with its associated costs and responsibilities and partly the housing market conditions prevailing at the time of the research. It seemed then that house price rises were accelerating beyond the means of many clergy. However since the interviews house prices in the UK have plummeted by 30 per cent while equity markets and hence clergy savings have experienced considerable volatility. Clergy remain uncertain and some are remaining in paid ministry longer than planned, to accrue more pension or to continue earning until the economic outlook improves. They may have a long wait.

The Church of England acknowledged the need to assist poorer clergy at retirement in the early 1980s (2001a: 95) and since then that the requirement to live in a tied house in a particular community represents the key disadvantage of the parochial ministry. Geoffrey's perspective was typical:

> I don't own my own house so I am just now in the process of thinking we need to buy a place to retire to and all the sort of financial and upheaval things of that whole aspect, I think at present such money as we have is in the stock market and soon as we get that out and put it in a property it would be a good thing to do.

Interestingly two-clergy spouses' accounts of parish ministry (Nash 1990, Meyrick 1998) do not mention retirement housing as a concern. However it has become more urgent for many vicarage families, clearly exacerbated by house price inflation during the past decade as Geoffrey knows:

> I think part of me will breathe a sigh of relief when we have a house that we are letting out to somebody that is ours and that is becoming quite an urgent matter and one is anxious to get that right and also of course with hindsight would have put money in property a lot earlier than this but didn't know the way that property prices would go.

Alistair reflected similarly, 'If I had been much more calculating then I would have bought a house in my first curacy . . . I didn't realise it was going to be an issue'. Richard finds himself 'lying awake at night' worrying: 'We haven't got any money and we have to buy a house at 65. So I rather wish that we had – in some ways it would have been nice to have had that – done what many clergy now have done and have bought their house and at least have somewhere to go'. He says that he is the only clergyperson in his deanery without a property, 'I am the only one that doesn't. More and more . . . seem to have their own property' and now his wife is 'just beginning to feel it would be quite nice to have somewhere for ourselves but that is not a possibility at the moment'. The continuing care needs of an elderly parent however cannot be ignored: 'It is absolutely awful because it all depends on whether my mother needs to go to a nursing home or not. If she does then we are in big trouble. If she doesn't – actually saying that is horrendous – but that is the situation'.

The impact of clergy divorce is particularly disastrous financially, reducing the value or availability of already limited assets. For example Charles's circumstances make him anxious about the future:

> I have got no house . . . and I can see myself having to go on working until I am really quite elderly . . . I have a very small pension from the school but I was only there eight years and I have got no savings really. And obviously when I was married it was just understood that when anything happened to her parents then there was a house and home that we were due to inherit which has all gone by the wayside now.

Not all clergy vocalize worries and Robert for example tried to appear more relaxed:

> I'm not a worrier; I'll probably start worrying about where I'm going to live about two months before I retire; obviously I'd have to do it before then; but I don't really worry about these things. Where we go will depend somewhat on funding because obviously some parts of the country are better to buy property in than others if you've not got very much money. I don't think there's much chance we'll stay on . . . that's prices here.

Matthew and his wife, also ordained, illustrate how a few contemporary clergy families might circumvent traditional parochial ministry arrangements and get into the property market at the same time. Both are in the process of changing their ministries, Matthew to a training post and his wife to a non-stipendiary parochial role, which will release them from the requirement to live in the vicarage and their 'plan . . . would certainly be to buy a house locally and keep sending the boys to the same schools'.

Research by the Church of England suggests that an increasing number of clergy nowadays own a property. Enquiries among stipendiary clergy found that 38 per cent did so (2001a: 39). Subsequently the Housing for Clergy in Retirement Survey reported that 52 per cent of respondents owned a residential property but that nearly a third are looking to the Church to support them into housing at retirement. The survey was a limited sample and weighted towards older clergy, nevertheless it also ascertained that across all age groups, more clergy than not are very worried about how they will manage financially in retirement (Church of England 2007h). In our research however considerably fewer participants talked about residential property ownership. It may be that a few clergy in the sample with assets from previous careers owned property which they leased to tenants and therefore felt more financially secure. Six interviewees spoke of the benefits of already owning a property, mostly for personal recreational use rather than tenanting for income. Significantly, these clergy indicated that they knew they were not allowed to use their other property as a vicarage substitute, commuting into the parochial workplace as necessary. This confirmed their acceptance of disciplined bodies and governed souls since these Church of England clergy simply did not abuse the possibility, even though the houses described in the data were typically less than a couple of hours' journey away which encouraged regular use. For example his house on the south coast gives Mark, a young single priest in metropolitan London, a place away from its noisy demands and an important sense of longer term security. Sarah's cottage has helped her to organize proper time off:

> Has been my salvation really in some ways; because it's made me take time off . . . I couldn't work out what I wanted to do for a long time and part of that dilemma was I felt a moral thing about not having a second home, not having a property that's empty most of the time.

Roger and his wife have been renovating a cottage in a beautiful part of the country for over 20 years. Throughout his ministry it has been 'a constant other place' to be, both a 'bolt-hole' and a project. Janet was the only priest interviewed in a 'holiday house', a compact and newly built starter-home on a pleasant little estate in a country town. She said that she enjoyed using it regularly because the design of her vicarage lacked privacy and she cared for an elderly relative at home. Roy who was interviewed early in his retirement had owned the property for some years as a base for his wife's teaching career in an adjacent county and diocese.

John described how inheriting a house provided some additional income and security for his children and freedom of manoeuvre for him and his wife. Significantly he also saw it as a potential way out of being a parish priest in the vicarage forever:

> My wife's parents both died and left her a small house, nothing great, which means that in you have got to that point where you think, we have done this for twenty years and we had no alternative because we need to keep ahead because we need to provide for the children and a family. That situation has changed in that sense now and there was a sense of freedom. You can say, okay, you can carry on doing this and you carry on doing this because you want to do it, but economically it is feasible for you to do something else and that opened our thoughts up.

Resentment

The second criticism raised by Pauline earlier in this chapter was evidence of a disturbing research finding from five respondents concerning advice about house ownership given by the Church of England to them prior to ministry training or ordination. It appears that during the 1990s, before rapid UK house price inflation, those going into the ministry were sometimes advised by Directors of Ordinands and church leaders to sell their homes. This coincided with the steady increase of older ordinands leaving secular careers with houses and mortgages and very different financial circumstances to those candidates of the mid-1970s who were typically single or recently married and under 35-years old and invariably without property. Some reasons given to the would-be second career clergy emerged in the interviews: to rid yourself of the mortgage debt or the responsibility of being a landlord, to help support you financially through your training course, even 'clergy shouldn't own property' or, 'don't worry – the Church will look after you'. If 5 from our sample of 46 interviewees are anywhere near representative there may be a legacy of resentment corroding the morale of some clergy. The retirement housing needs survey tends to support this picture (Church of England 2007h). It found that nearly a quarter of respondents did own a property but sold it before being ordained (particularly those aged 46–55), and 16 per cent sold after their ordination. Among these once-owners the vast majority (82%) either sold the property to fund training or pay off debts, or felt they could no longer afford the costs given the modest stipend to which they were now entitled. With the benefit of hindsight and the financial services regulatory regime prevalent in the United Kingdom, senior figures guiding individuals towards ordination would nowadays be keen to stress the need to stay in the property market on the basis of professional and independent financial advice provided outside Church structures. The dilemma is that those allegedly once told to sell their houses now may have no retirement provision.

Fiona's story illustrates this well. Fiona and her husband owned a house but 'were encouraged not to have a mortgage which is a shame because it would have been OK. We had one when we were in the Forces . . . we got a mortgage straight away when we got married, and we rented the property out . . . so we had the income from that'. Fiona started training in 1996 and believes, 'apparently I was one of the last' to be so advised. She recalls the reasons given were that a prerequisite for selection for training was that ordinands should not be in debt nor perhaps have the burden of mortgage payments for a house they would never live in. 'That was the correct advice at the time . . . or deemed to be . . . and we are in different situations now and unfortunately life is like that sometimes'. With an air of fatalism she weighs up whether the sacrifice was worth it. 'Everybody gives up something or sacrifices something . . . we chose to do . . . what we were encouraged to do. We could have said no. Hindsight is a wonderful thing'. She knows of other clergy in her diocese in similar circumstances who feel like her: 'I am feeling quite angry that I gave up all of this and I am getting nothing back'.

Kenneth and Charles expressed similar regrets in their interviews. Charles and his wife had owned a house in the past when both had secular jobs but when he went to theological college, 'it was felt that we couldn't manage the mortgage and so we sold the house. Six months later the Church would have taken the mortgage on and put missionaries in it'. Likewise, Kenneth gave up his house on entry into ordination training. He had been a teacher and was close to paying off his mortgage. Ordination was the fulfilment of his life's vocation, 'but financially . . . it was the worst mistake I ever made . . . we were very comfortable, lived in a house that two or three years down the line we could have called our own'. Kenneth came into ministry 'with a view that, yes, it is not a well-paid job; you are not going to live in the lap of luxury; you are going to have twelve/sixteen hour days [we] accepted all of that but at the end [the Church] does care for you. And now maybe that caring is not there'. He worries about 'the possible change in pension settlement' and retirement housing in particular: 'The housing market has doubled on average in the last ten years . . . we sold our house at the time the market was going down so we sold our house two months before we could have got another £15,000 for it so that has gone. Investments have gone down so a "two up, two down" will probably be our final abode'. Kenneth's son is going to be ordained, 'and he has been told by his sponsoring diocese that at the end of his ministerial life when he gets to 70 they can't guarantee a house or a pension'. Kenneth worries about the economics of it all for the future of the Church of England.

Two things strike us as remarkable about these accounts: first, the degree of uncritical compliance with the Church's directions by some ordinands in past years and, secondly, the hiddenness of the issue in Church life. The first point confirms that a culture of obedience takes effect immediately an individual offers for ordination in the Church. A theological and ecclesial socialization based on biblical and monastic traditions, giving up worldly goods, takes place. 'To labour and not to ask for any reward' is a strong self-sacrificial guiding principle within Anglican ministerial culture. Second, the statement in *Generosity and Sacrifice* that 'ordinands have not been required to sell any house they owned to fund training since 1990' (Church of England 2001a: 78) may not be entirely correct. The experiences reported to us suggest that some encouragement to sell houses during candidature for ordination continued after 1990, while telephone interviews conducted for research about clergy retirement and housing (Church of England 2007h, 2008d) revealed similar stories. One of our interviewees, Angela, attended a Church of England preretirement course and reported that a Pensions Board manager had come across this issue. Angela sold her property in 1990 when she moved into the curate's house that came with her appointment. She recalls that the Archdeacon indicated the proceeds would help with training expenses and removal and set-up costs. More recently Angela saw her old house advertised at a 200 per cent premium. The legacy of these reported experiences is that because clergy felt unable to challenge the Church's expectations they remain unreconciled. None said it was a sacrificial embrace too far and all remained faithfully in post, but were clearly hurt and anxiety lingered.

A household contract?

Labouring without reward and embracing self-sacrifice through organizational culture, work and family life have been explored by previous researchers (Sennett and Cobb 1972, Collinson 1992, 2003, Collinson and Collinson 1989). Sennet and Cobb found that the working man's [*sic*] sense of 'sacrifice' held a moral claim over both employer and family and served as an incentive to children to better themselves through education and higher aspirations. The breadwinner's sacrifice however binds the family in a contract that also limits their choices: 'the sacrificer does not ask his family whether *they* want him to sacrifice . . . there is created in many families a kind of exchange relationship, a series of unspoken, individual expectations of obligation towards each other based on the respective sacrifices of each' (Sennet and Cobb 1972: 126–9). This analysis encapsulates the emotional and economic situation in many 20th century vicarages prior to the significant growth of two-income clergy households. In our research 28 spouses undertook paid employment (not necessarily full time) outside the home while a handful of others were home workers, valued carers of dependent relatives or unpaid parish secretaries (see Table 4.2).

Warren found that 'financial needs prompted the spouse to work outside the home' and led to a feeling of inadequacy among some male clergy that they could not provide for their families (Warren 2002: 123). It certainly can be the case that the major earner is the spouse who effectively

Table 4.2 *Paid employment of interviewees' spouses*

University counsellor (female)
Teacher (5f)
Doctors' receptionist (2f)
Clergy (3f, 3male)
Family support worker (2f)
College lecturer (f)
Nurse (f)
Actor/writer (f)
Legal secretary (f)
Volunteer co-ordinator (f)
Senior nurse (f)
Computer engineer (m)
Doctor GP (f)
Gardener (m)
Teaching assistant (f)
Counsellor (f)
Local government officer (f)
N = 28

subsidizes parochial ministry. However this was perhaps marginally so for only half a dozen clergy in our sample and no spouses were reported as commanding large salaries. Part-time, modestly remunerated roles were more common.

The growth of non-stipendiary ministries in the Church of England described in Chapter 1 certainly represents a significant form of sacrificial service in the Church. Although non-stipendiary clergy whose principal occupation is secular employment or home-work have occasionally been appointed as part-time Area/Rural Deans in recent years, there were no examples in the research sample. However for two-clergy couples, as Table 4.3 shows, three Area/Rural Deans (two women, one man) undertook the role on a less than full time, less than full stipend basis within two-clergy job share arrangements.

This finding reinforces the gendered part-timeness of women's sacrificial experiences in the ordained ministry noted by Nesbitt (1997), Bentley (2001) Kuhrt and Bentley (2001). In the sample six spouses of interviewees were themselves clergy though only two of these received a full stipend. From an economic perspective what appears to be significant in this research is the way that any additional income eases the sacrificial cost of ministry, particularly for families with school and college-age children, even though it may cause other household tensions. For example, the dilemmas of career and motherhood that may leave mothers in a 'no-win' situation (Gatrell 2005: 94) were noted by James who recognized that his wife wished to

Table 4.3 *Type of appointment and remuneration in two-clergy couples*

Area/Rural Dean Interviewee	Clergy partner post	Remuneration
Female Full time	Male Full time	2 × 1.0 stipends
Male Job share	Female Job share	2 × 0.5 Stipends
Male Full time	Female Part time	1 Stipend × 0.5 Salary
Female Part time	Male Part time	1.5 × Stipends
Male Full time	Female Full time	1 Stipend × 1.0 Salary
Female Job share	Male Job share	2 × 0.5 Stipends

combine her medical career with child care at home but ended up working full time for lifestyle reasons:

> In an ideal world [she] would like to have taken a gap from medicine or to go down to a very bare minimum to keep her hand in whilst the children were younger than they are now. We looked at it and yes, we could have made that choice, but when you think of how that would have changed our lives we felt that was not a positive thing. But she does speak about the fact that she does need to work and that can lead to some stresses.

Clergy respondents were also concerned that their sacrifices might disadvantage their children and they worried about behaviour and influences, schools and careers – stemming from their parental choice to live and work in disadvantaged areas. Linda's teenagers are fairly robust in their inner city environment 'but still need a little bit of TLC' and clergy in her position, like other middle class parents, occasionally choose to purchase independent education outside the parish at the cost of other possible expenditure. Alistair summed up the worries of a number of clergy:

> Quite a large amount of our income is going out to pay school fees which might have been used to pay a mortgage on a house to live and what we don't have at the moment is any spare money in which to use to pay for a mortgage, so there is this real fear about what is going to happen when we get to the point of retirement which is just over 8 years, so that is a cause of real concern.

Uneasy feelings of guilt were expressed in interviews that following a vocation in the Church sacrifices overall family opportunities. This is compounded by the fact that Church of England incumbents are usually educated to university degree level and might therefore have pursued other careers. The average age of ordinands has risen over the years – since 1994 the percentage of those aged over 40 entering training has risen to 60 per cent with the greatest number of overall recommended candidates now being from the 40–49 age band (Church of England 2012). The older age of entry may be correlated to financial resources accumulated prior to ordination that ease and enable the transition into second career ministry (Nesbitt 1997, Church of England 2001a: 38).

Many clergy have deliberately abandoned more lucrative careers to 'go into the Church' and required their families 'go along with this' despite the economic consequences or radical change of lifestyle – 'living in someone else's house' as Patricia put it, having moved her highly paid husband and five children. This was particularly borne out in the interviews when clergy spoke about house ownership, spouses' prospects and children. The modern concept of the Church of England stipend which has evolved between the Paul Report and *Generosity and Sacrifice* (Church of England 1964, 2001a) probably still assumes more government provision than is the case in changing socio-economic circumstances. Despite a small tax-free allowance against part of vicarage running expenses, the cost of fuel and household essentials is keenly felt where the stipend is the sole household income. The stipend has also not adjusted to new clergy anxieties, for example, about leisure expectations, dental costs, school and university fees and the mortgage prospects of their children competing with the continuing care of elderly relatives.

Accumulative opportunity cost

Although the clergy we interviewed expressed confidence in their vocational commitment, some participants sensed the passing years in ministry and what they 'might have been' in another life. For example as a businessman, civil servant or academic, a nursing director or a ship's captain, five of our sample would each have lived within a different remuneration framework than that provided by the Church of England. The range of previous occupations of the clergy interviewed was illustrated in Chapter 2 and across the research sample an accumulative economic opportunity cost emerged. Surrounded by an increasing proportion of second-career clergy, older long-serving clergy may resent that their priestly lives nowadays seem less acknowledged by the Church. However it also affects younger clergy like Pauline, whose concerns about the valuing of clergy were reported earlier, or Adam whose 'cash rich, time poor' commuter parishioners with exciting career paths are an enviable reminder of his previous brief life as a corporate lawyer in the City: 'I sometimes feel jealousy that they can change jobs'.

It is important of course to recognize that clergy are not the only people who experience low pay and financial worries, or who make sacrifices. Others also accept poor advice, making career and financial decisions that later turn out to be the wrong ones. In many ways clergy enjoy significant job security. Our research findings do however provide a first-hand account of the material circumstances of contemporary clergy lives in a way that recent research has given insufficient attention (Warren 2002, Lee and Horsman 2002, Thomas 2006). Two respondents expressed views on this. Penny came into ministry from a well-paid secular career and had to make adjustments: 'I don't have a thing about money really and I actually think we are quite protected as stipendiary clergy . . . but when we came here I had a huge drop and it took us about a year to adjust and this place, as lovely as it is, costs a fortune to heat'. John also articulated some thoughts about the opportunity cost of going into the ordained ministry, saying that clergy have exercised a personal choice: 'the financial side is not something that we struggle with . . . I didn't want to have a job . . . I wanted to have a way of life'. Years on, life might seem better in a well-paid job yet he believes 'it is sacrificial to work on the shelves in Tesco you know, so yes, there are sacrifices but I don't want to be a bleeding heart about it'.

There is therefore a powerful belief that professional ministry is about 'labour without any reward' outworked in the sacrificial agency of clergy vocational behaviour as compelling as the sacrifices identified by Sennett and Cobb (1972) and confirmed by Collinson (1992) in working-class settings. Unable to be totally independent, clergy recreate their freedoms and rewards through ingenious ways of managing: indeed their life-long vocational commitment is so powerful that the consequences for domestic economics may sometimes seem rather secondary. We propose the notion of an 'accumulative opportunity cost' as a useful way of encompassing the theological, economic and emotional complexity of clergy lives. Our research reveals the desire among clergy for a combination of material and emotional compensation for their vocational labour which is perhaps not well understood by the Church. At the same time, among the same clergy, embracing sacrifice appears to be the hallmark of a life-long vocation in which the secular milestones of career rewards – status, promotion or a bigger salary – are largely unavailable for most clergy.

Emotional labour

When Hochschild wrote about North American airline cabin staff in *The Managed Heart* (1983) she recognized that the crews' contribution of 'emotional labour' to please customers was crucial to the maintenance of competitive advantage by their organization. She described emotional labour as a self-estranging process, for example, the 'professional smile': 'the idea that emotion functions as a messenger from the self, an agent that gives us an instant report on the connection between what we are seeing and what we had expected to see, and tells us what we feel ready to do about it' (Hochschild 1983: x).

For the airline, customer satisfaction generating repeat business was the commercial Holy Grail. Hochschild's insights into emotional labour and management, elaborated by Bolton (2005) into a typology of workplace emotion, carry many parallels with the Church and other voluntary organizations where managing the quality of service is fundamental because individuals with choices can take their discretionary loyalty elsewhere. During the past decade many dioceses in the Church of England have quite self-consciously developed mission statements with memorable strap-lines as marketing tools aimed at cementing members and encouraging newcomers into the fold. For example, *'Joining Together in the Transforming Mission of God: Living Worship, Growing Disciples, Seeking Justice'* proclaims the vision of the Diocese of Southwell & Nottingham. It is not difficult therefore to imagine that for clergy there is a degree of plausibility about emotional labour. The critical literature about disciplined bodies and governed souls points towards the professional vocational life of clergy in the Church of England as under pressure to 'manage the heart', not only during working hours but in all ordained life, 24/7, life-long.

Hochschild's concept of the managed heart encompassed two dimensions: the private and the public sphere. This notion of private and public identities resonates with the performative and backstage identities described by Goffman (1959) and connected discourses concerned with the nature of labour (Braverman 1974) and the role of emotion in organizations (Fineman 1993). Hochschild believed that emotional labour was implicit within over a third of occupations, notably those which required personal contact with the public. The cross-section was gendered towards female roles (supervised by men) but also included clergy and religious workers. A generation later when many customer-facing occupations have been replaced by technology – for example ATMs at banks, and call-centres – it is interesting to relate emotional labour to the Church of England's clergy. Bolton's subsequent approach highlights the complexities of 21st-century emotion management in different workplaces, including vocational professions, and the importance of personal agency in shaping emotional behaviour. Unlike Hochschild's actors, Bolton suggests that 'the postmodern employee may not go through a lengthy period of "deep acting", but might quickly "internalize the new feeling rules" in unstable social environments, rapidly learning how to present to customers and employers the embodied attitudes expected while keeping private space for the personal; the self'. This enables individuals to retain a sense that it is they who control emotional labour and 'it is not always the organization which defines the emotional agenda' (Bolton 2005: 90–2). Selling ourselves is a self-estranging process: 'the management of feeling to create a publicly observable facial and bodily display; emotional labour is sold for a wage and therefore has *exchange value* . . . the synonymous terms *emotion work* or *emotion management* refer to these same acts done in a private context where they have *use value*' (Hochschild 1983: 7, original italics). Clergy strive to achieve these through an appropriate pastoral manner, adept liturgical performance and convincing preaching. Hochschild described the detachment of the body in physical labour paralleling the detachment of feelings in emotional labour. What occurs is the transmutation of private emotions into public relations and in consequence individuals negotiate an increasing number of social worlds in modern life, learning to manage emotions and spontaneity.

This characterizes the ordering of clergy lives as articulated by the research participants themselves. Following Hochschild we observe how contemporary clergy make up an idea of their real self, an 'inner jewel that remains their unique possession no matter whose billboard is on their back or whose smile is on their face' (1983: 34). Clergy are a distinctive example of emotional labour precisely because work and life are uniquely embraced by ordination. Unlike commercial airline workers, 21st-century clergy find it less easy to subtract who they really are from the ordained parts. According to Foucault (1980b) and the *Ordination Services* (Church of England 2007a) God recognizes the authentic within vocational performance and confessional truth. Hochschild also recognized how institutions manage feelings. Translating her commentary into the Church setting we can see how it arranges the front stage for clergy, providing them with scripts and authorizing stage directors to coach the cast in performance. The clergy in this research talk openly about these arrangements and how they adjust to the ordained role and manage their surface behaviour and deeper emotions.

The public consequences of emotional labour are sharply circumscribed for clergy. In Hochschild's airline example where emotional labour is expressed through obedient body language of smiles, elegance and deference, it is acceptable for workers to feign feeling while experiencing personal emotional dissonance. For the parish priest there are some parallels: s/he must promote the values of the company (Church) as family, the workplace (parish, vicarage) as home. Clergy must welcome the customer into the theatre of family and home (church building and services) and deal with sometimes unresponsive passengers (congregation) managing difficult customers (parishioners) as though they were children.

To some extent therefore, the dramaturgical and presentational aspects of life identified by Goffman resonate with the lives of the clergy interviewed. In interviews Robert described 'ministry as a pantomime' while Daniel memorably confessed, 'you get your show' even at the most holy moments of priestly activity at the altar. Clergy, as Hochschild (1983: 115) wonderfully pictured it, 'must deliver an emotional tone road show', while managing their own, sometimes conflicting emotions. Across the wider organization a common standard is required, but supervision and surveillance of workers (the clergy) occurs with a light touch (the gaze of the Bishop or parishioners) because clergy have internalized company policy (diocesan directives) and 'know' what they must do through the emotional governance of the soul, by personal conscience and ultimately by God. Hochschild (1983: 119) asks a pertinent question: 'the whole system of emotional exchange in private life has as its ostensible purpose the welfare and pleasure of the people involved. When the emotional exchange is thrust into a commercial setting, it is transmuted. A profit motive is slipped in under acts of emotional management, under the rules that govern them, under the gift exchange. Who benefits now, and who pays?' In times of organizational difficulty, Hochschild's airline workers were shown to resist the authorities by withdrawing, or at least muting their emotional labour.

For priests, however, withdrawing emotional labour is not an available choice. On a practical level, when clergy feel pressured at work – perhaps due to worries about recession and Church decline – they are expected to keep smiling through. 'Managing an estrangement between self and feeling and between self and display' (Hochschild 1983: 131) is not an option for priests because they remain God's servants. Faced with such challenges there are three Hochschild questions which workers (clergy) might ask themselves:

'How can I feel really identified with my work role (ministry) and with the company (Church) without being fused with them?'
'How can I use my capacities (ministry gifts and abilities) when I'm disconnected from those (congregation, hierarchy) I am acting for?'

'If I am doing deep acting for an audience (congregation, Bishop) from whom I am disconnected, how can I manage my self-esteem without becoming cynical?'

On a personal level, the differences between clergy and airline workers are even more disparate. While acting – deep or otherwise – might suffice for the performance of the priesthood with regard to earthly beings such as Bishops and parishioners, an apparently obedient body falls short of what ordained priests believe is required of them by God. Within our clergy research sample Laurence alone talked about not believing: 'I have a non-realistic view of God which . . . but that is not my public persona'. Yet he remains in stipendiary ministry 'beginning a count-down to retirement . . . I have twelve years and I shall keep plodding away'. In a sense he leads the type of double life identified by Goffman (1956). Laurence admits that his 'is not actually a very good attitude' and that privately he may be 'more fed up' than his public performance suggests. He appears vulnerable to the 'diminishing congruency' which Webster (2002) diagnosed as so corrosive to clergy wellbeing.

Our interviewees were asked to describe when they felt 'most priestly', a question which evoked some powerful and convincing responses. It became clear that clergy value sincerity over personal and corporate guile and value authenticity over the managed heart. This accords with Hochschild's hypothesis that, 'the more the heart is managed the more we value the unmanaged heart' (1983: 192). Clergy authenticity is based on a purer demonstration of faith, obedience and self-sacrifice which reflects the influence of ordinal promises on clergy lives as priests avow a belief in the Panopticon. As observed at the start of this chapter, priests believe that Godly surveillance extends beyond the public performance of faith. Divine judgement of priestly obedience goes beyond what is embodied and intrudes into the innermost reaches of the soul. If priestly performance is not authentic, God will know. The priest will have failed in their ordination promises to devote the self to the service of God, who is both entitled and able to make windows of priestly souls. Parishioners, bishops, archdeacons and family members might thus be convinced by the performance of a well-managed heart – but for God, only authenticity will suffice.

Claimed for Christ's service

Our key finding across the broad range of Church traditions – catholic, central or evangelical – is that the majority of priests embrace a sacrificial understanding and ascribe an ontological dimension to their priesthood. The impression was more pronounced than expected given the ascendancy of evangelical models of Church of England clergy in recent decades and a commensurate diminishing of sacramental ontology. Clergy in the sample expressed an ontological understanding of the 'indelible character change' (Ward 2011: 90) brought about sacramentally in ordination. As argued by Herbert, T. (2008: 76) it seems that for our more Protestant, evangelical participants, the ordained priesthood of the Church is now understood as an expression of the unique sacrificial self-emptying of Christ.

Only two clergy talked in functional terms like Laurence, who emphasized a more pragmatic view of ordination as conferring organizational leadership and authority:

> Yes I don't have a sort of 'ontological' view of ordination and I mean I would be quite happy to say that when I retire I stop being a priest. I am not one for saying that priesthood lasts . . . I have a more functional view of it I think. It is a setting apart or a particular ministry within the Church.

Predominately, transformative and indelible perspectives ('I am changed for ever . . . I will always be a priest') resonated with our interviewees' descriptions. Clergy confirmed a shared understanding of ordination as a life-changing and life-long 'claim for Christ's service' (Pannenberg 1998: 398) that has served as an inspiration to generations of Church of England clergy of all complexions and continues to sustain them through many vicissitudes in the early 21st century. These clergy may be an example of a 'cognitive minority' (Berger 1969) whose world view self-consciously differs from wider contemporary English society. As the House of Bishops has stated, 'the Church's ministry is set apart, holy' (Church of England 2007a: 5). In other words it is not only praiseworthy to live a counter-cultural lifestyle, but sacrificially expected.

Clergy resist diluting their vocation because it is so unlike any other occupation. This pushes against conventional literature about vocational working lives and has not previously been highlighted in this way. Priestly identity is characterized by obedient clergy bodies, not simply instrumental to the Church as an organization but theologically governed by clergy souls. Embracing personal sacrifice is the hallmark of vocational faithfulness and priests need to feel authentic in this regard if they believe they are answering God's calling. Clergy authenticity is based on both this enduring trajectory and the sense that outward performance, or 'managed hearts' will be detected by God. However there is an emotional cost in terms of relationships and intimacies.

5

Lost Intimacies

I miss friends, having friends most of all.

PHILIP

There is almost a sense that if I have an intimate friendship with people in the parish then I am depriving them of their parish priest.

PATRICIA

Personal relationships

Understanding the experiences and meanings clergy give to their vocational commitments within the organizational, community and family contexts in which they exist is important. This chapter opens a window into clergy households exploring how clergy manage intimacies within a range of personal and family contexts. The findings suggest that many clergy, married or single, struggle to enjoy private relationships uncontaminated by public ministry: they experience a loss of intimacy, coping with varying degrees of loneliness and frustration. Now is an interesting time to explore how clergy and spouses are getting on since the ordination of women to the priesthood. In addition the Church now has experience of two-clergy couples (where each is ordained) and the particular issues that can arise when accommodating two priestly vocations in one relationship (Bentley 2001).

This chapter explores some critical approaches to friendship and marriage, the family and relational matters developed within the social sciences. We also discuss the pressures, for priests, of trying to balance social and ecclesiastical expectations about how clerics should lead their personal lives, alongside what they believe is required of them by God. We show how priests are constrained in their personal relationships: friendships, intimate relationships and marriage and how English parish clergy are a particular example of acute work–home dilemmas (Hochschild 1989, 1997).

The Church of England exerts considerable pressure on the ordained to maintain Christian moral standards in their personal relationships and household life:

FROM *ORDINATION SERVICES* (CHURCH OF ENGLAND 2007A)

Will you strive to fashion your own life and that of your household according to the way of Christ, that you may be a pattern and example to Christ's people?

From *Guidelines for the Professional Conduct of the Clergy* (Church of England 2003b)

The clergy are called to a high standard of moral behaviour.

Those who are called to marriage should never forget that this is also a vocation. It should not be thought to be of secondary importance to their vocation to ministry.

Similarly, those who are not married, including those with a vocation to celibacy, should take the necessary steps to nurture their lives, their friendships and their family relationships.

All should guard themselves and their family against becoming victims of stress.

Embedded within the Ordination Service and professional guidance for clergy is the expectation that priesthood imprints itself upon personal relationships. This chapter explores the consequences of this, illustrating that the distinctive features of the relationships which clergy in the Church of England nurture and experience are restricted choice and public scrutiny, hence the meta-theme of lost intimacies. Giddens's assertions that late modern society offers individuals an 'open character of self-identity and the reflexive nature of the body' and that 'the self today is for everyone a reflexive project' (1992: 30) are shown to have limited application to the clergy in this research. The transformation of intimacy has not penetrated the Foucauldian captivity of obedient clergy bodies as described in Chapter 3. The full range of Giddens's 'pure relationships' (1992: 58) and postmodern lifestyle options open to other professionals and the Church's laity is simply not available within the disciplinary and self-sacrificial boundaries of a clergy life.

As attitudes towards marriage and family life have liberalized for many people in a separating and divorcing society, so some vicarage households also contain the greater diversity of kinship ties associated with 'recombinant' or reconstituted families (Giddens 1992: 96). To some extent, the contemporary Church has adapted to recognize changing personal relationships within vocational life. For example, while the Church upholds a traditional view of heterosexual marriage as 'normative' and adultery remains a serious offence under the Clergy Discipline Measure (Church of England 2003a), pragmatically, divorce and remarriage are no longer absolute barriers for entering or continuing in clerical life. However, while the existence of gay and lesbian clergy within the Church has become more widely recognized and accepted (Changing Attitude 2012), as the Jeffrey John story shows, issues of same-sex partnerships remain contested by some within the Church when it comes to episcopal appointments.

Amidst a background of changing family practices, the Church of England has commissioned remarkably little empirical research, quantitative or qualitative, into what we term 'clergy household studies'. This is a more inclusive term than the traditional or ideal-sounding 'vicarage family' and more responsive to the actual diversity found among 21st century clergy domestic arrangements. Household, as proposed by Morgan (1996: 23), is a useful theoretical and empirical research approach to clergy lives as yet not adequately explored.

Table 5.1 illustrates the vicarage household characteristics of the 46 Area/Rural Deans interviewed. Happily it proved possible to gather a variety of married and single households, with or without children and other residents within the research sample, successfully capturing a range of personal relationship issues. Although each clergyperson was interviewed alone, factual information about the shape of the vicarage household visited was recorded. Additional qualitative information captured in ethnographical field notes was impressionistic or mediated by the interviewee.

Table 5.1 *Household characteristics reported in the research sample*

Male clergy 32
Female clergy 14
Ethnic minority 1 (1 man)
Disability 0
Married currently 34 (6 women, 28 men)
Married with children at home 21 (3w, 18m)
Married 'empty nesters' 10 (1w, 9m)
Married with no children 3 (2w, 1m)
Clergy with other adult residents 4 (3w, 1m)
Two-clergy married couples 6 (3w, 3m)
Single currently 12 (8w, 4m)
Gay 2 (1w, 1m)
Civil Partnerships 0
Divorced 3 (2w, 1m)
Separated 0
Widowed 0
Remarried 0
Recently retired 1 (1m)

Our research data provides insights on the conduct of relationships in the pressured atmosphere of vicarages, displaying the 'working-out' (Finch 1989, Finch and Mason 1993) of many emotional (Hochschild 1983, 1989, 1997) and work–home issues. Because the Church's moral and lifestyle expectations apply not only to individual clergy but also to their household, it emerges that there are a lot of 'negotiated commitments' (Finch 1989, Finch and Mason 1993) to be undertaken by the clergy in their vicarage family and parish contexts with regard to how priests and those close to them manage their lives.

Friendship

Many clergy in this research, married and single, reported the professional sacrifice and social isolation of not being able to develop friendships freely. Most accepted this situation with difficulty, trying to keep up with family and maintaining (albeit intermittently) long-standing friendships, often clergy peers from theological college days now dispersed around the country. Philip, married, expressed isolation from intimacy and feeling depersonalized in the clergy role:

> The problem is, I quite like having friends but I've found this role, or this time the most difficult to make friends . . . Because the normal conversations that you would have with friends include talking about a lot of the things that you would normally talk about. You can't talk about church activities because it usually involves individuals and you can't be indiscreet about people as you would in normal conversation.

A key finding in this research is that marriage and ministry and friendship sit uneasily together. The vocational requirements and public nature of ministry appear to dissociate the clergy from their spouses and from the possibility of open friendships. Both spouses are 'married to the ministry' and are seen as such by parishioners, as Philip found: 'Too often I feel as though the Vicar is invited to a social occasion rather than Philip and Debbie. I go along and they'll say you're invited because of you, and then "could you do the Grace for us?" O.K. I don't mind but if I'm off duty, I'm off duty, and I'd like to just be somebody else who happened to be there'. In social situations it is the ordained officeholder who is viewed as present rather than two individuals or a married couple with separate professional careers and Philip finds it depressing, 'It's probably more to do with me than the job' but his sentiment was by no means exceptional in the sample. Patricia expressed the particular need for women clergy to find a way of developing friendships away from ministry and marriage:

Friendship I find is very difficult as well in ministry. I find it difficult to just talking to colleagues. Male colleagues seem to find no problem in making friendships and sorting out the role somehow and it does seem to be a gender issue. I don't know whether that is sweeping generalization . . . because of my feeling about priesthood about being set apart . . . I find it difficult at heart to think about making friends with people in the parish because I just think I would find it difficult to share intimate discussion with a member of the congregation.

Perhaps unsurprisingly, priests who felt the issue of friendship most keenly were the single clergy. Warren noted that for single, married and divorced clergy alike the local congregation has the potential to provide a type of 'family belonging' (Warren 2002: 47). However we have noted at a number of points the boundaries which clergy have to negotiate between public and private spaces. The finding here is that personal friendship and intimacy are rarely achieved when clergy are in role. Indeed a dysfunctional congregation can harm vicarage families as well as being a challenge for the vicar. Benjamin recalls how his wife and children felt bullied by church members and their expectations and 'stopped going to church in the end because, I think it was nearing Christmas Day, and she used to come home from church in absolute tears'. Under stress he thought of quitting his post and even contacted the diocesan psychiatric advisor, but then he and his wife 'had a conversation in bed one night and we came up with a plan . . . an idea of a strategy'. Benjamin decided to confront the trouble-makers, 'I basically got up the following morning and sorted them all out so that actually the parish was survivable and we had a way forward. And that little conversation one night, no one really knows about'.

Clergy understand that vicarage hospitality is an expectation that comes with being a parish priest whose home is in a tied house. Julian confirmed that 'there were one or two expectations about using the garden for stuff and we are very happy to accommodate that . . . I mean the garden is lovely and it is nice to share it'. Garden parties are a favoured way of entertaining large numbers and these occasions ('invasions?') can be fun (as well as a big task for the vicarage household) and are enjoyed by younger vicarage children who get lots of attention and by single clergy, especially men, who get lots of gendered help. Whether clergy describe the provision of hospitality in positive or negative terms, the research participants definitely regard such events as 'work' within the church community and not time off with chosen friends in an extended family. As part of their local leadership role Area/ Rural Deans also offer hospitality to clergy in the Deanery Chapter at their vicarages as a way of building up professional friendships and collaboration, and countering clergy isolation. Penny for example tries to create relaxing space at her vicarage for the local clergy so that they feel able to talk about what is really going on in their ministries and lives. Similarly Daniel and his wife particularly enjoyed the warm friendships forged through good food and time to talk:

> People get on well and we have time for one another. At our deanery meetings we have nice meals. We had one just two days ago and I said to a new priest, 'well, we have good food in our deanery meetings' . . . and I said 'when we have a little bit of time, then we do a little bit of business.' Personally I think building relationships does quite a lot of good to the morale of clergy. Clergy are already overburdened. They are already stretched and if only they could develop a way in which they could relate and share each other's difficulties and joys.

The findings confirm Lee and Horsman's assertion (2002: 150) that Area/Rural Deans are keys to promoting professional intimacy among the parish clergy of the Church of England as a way of countering stress and loneliness. However even Daniel and Penny's enthusiasm is borne out of their professional role with colleagues, not of their own choosing and deeper personal friendships were located elsewhere in their lives.

Home alone: single clergy

There were 12 currently single clergy in the sample of Area/Rural Deans, 8 women and 4 men, but their domestic circumstances varied greatly. Just 7 priests reported, strictly speaking, living alone at the vicarage. A common finding among single clergy is the way in which the congregation, parishioners and local clergy colleagues provide potential friendships, and a broader or even alternative sense of family belonging. Equally significant however is the finding that single clergy (as do married clergy), find it difficult to have friendships that are uncontaminated by their ordained role in the Church. Their difficulties are accentuated by the embodied realities, namely resident presence in the vicarage and the blurring of work/leisure and public/private distinctions. Mark summed it up: 'Is a dinner party work or not? I don't really think about having friends in the parish'. In order to appear equitable to all parishioners Mark distances himself from close friendships within the parish which might become too much hassle. He believes that true friends are the people a priest keeps up with after s/he moves on from the parish:

> There are clearly people who I would feel more affection towards than others and my experience from my previous jobs is that there are always a few people who remain on my Christmas card list after I have left . . . and a smaller group than that who I actually have some contact with as friends, but that seems to kind of filter down quite naturally.

Clergy simply do not take advantage of the reflexive interpersonal possibilities that exist for other professionals, and which Giddens (1992) characterized as the transformation of intimacy in a postmodern society. It seems they desist because it would undermine the whole point of their ordained life and their promised commitments to God and the Church that this entails. Clergy, single or married, are married to the ministry. They may possibly be the last remaining professional group who are so constrained, and expected to lead exemplary lives within certain boundaries defined by the Church and its teaching. The case of the drunken vicar enjoying 'swinging holidays' (partner-swapping) with her husband (Dixon 2008) was as much surprising as rare. Clergy appear to accept the Church's authority regarding acceptable priestly behaviour.

Ordination does seem to restrict friendships and consequently getting close enough to significant others to progress to intimate relationships/sexual partnerships and possibly marriage. Developing prospective partnerships through cohabitation is not an option for the ordained. Surveillance of the vicarage daily by parishioners, intermittently by archdeacons and ultimately by God and the conscience of the individual priest, significantly discourages the heterosexual and same-sex live-in arrangements that are routinely available to other public professionals. Causality remains an interesting question: is it the case that the Church inflicts its demanding moral standards on pliable ordinands, or conversely, does it attract those who cannot forge intimate or permanent relationships elsewhere in life? Kirk and Leary (1994: 94) and Warren (2002: 101) argue from a psychotherapeutic perspective that some clergy look upon the Church as a new family, an emotionally safe place that fulfils their longings for acceptance and affirmation. Interestingly the two male clergy interviewed who turned out to be 'children of the vicarage', having vicar-fathers, were both married with children and appeared professionally competent, personally self-confident and (compared with some participants) particularly contented with their lot.

The ageing profile of Church of England clergy as a second career may also influence this debate. When Peyton was ordained in 1976 as a bachelor aged 25, alongside other bachelors it was assumed (by him and parishioners) that he would at some point marry – or not, as the case might be. Fewer contemporary clergy colleagues were already married. There has not yet been a sufficient wave of unmarried, younger female ordinations to test whether women would have similarly open expectations. What would be interesting to know, is the statistical relationships between gender and singleness in contemporary stipendiary clergy. It appears from our research that those single clergy who do wish to develop more intimate relationships and enduring friendships experience significant disadvantages and find their situation disheartening. The four younger single clergy in the sample illustrated their frustrations and uncertainties. The two women priests made it clear during their interviews that they would prefer heterosexual relationships and marriage but feared they might always be alone. The sexuality of the two male clergy remained hidden behind general conversation about friendship and clergy isolation.

Sarah spoke of the difficulties she found in making friends in her parish where 'I was the youngest church member and I have found that very difficult and quite isolating and quite lonely . . . I've found we haven't really had shared interests'. Sarah found parishioners 'always willing to accept an invitation to the vicarage. There was a lot of curiosity about the house; I felt, I do still find that quite difficult, people are very curious and come to satisfy their curiosity, not because they want to engage with Bible study or whatever might be happening here'. Sarah happened to be interviewed the morning after a particularly unpleasant Parochial Church Council meeting where she had been on the receiving end of lot of male aggression. She felt 'terrible, not as bad as it has been . . . I mean I didn't come home and cry which is what I have done before, but I did come home and have a very big gin and tonic! And I stayed up very late watching a DVD'. Often, single priests have no-one at home to off-load onto or to provide comfort and reassurance. Sarah revealed something of her underlying feelings when she remarked 'that I got into a particular genre of novel that, where, single woman thinks she's happy, finds she's not, meets a man, gets married. And I just thought – I can't be having all this. There's more of that than you think there is!'

Mark spoke of his need to keep up with friends: 'I have a whole series of friends and I would say they are on the whole more important to me than my family because I see more of my friends . . . than I do my family and most of my friends also go back quite a long way . . . I find it quite difficult keeping in touch with people and I find that I am letting people down an awful lot friendship-wise'. He realized that he sometimes just doesn't get out of the parish, physically or emotionally and tries to 'catch up, but there is very little spontaneity and that is kind of sad I think'. Mark also found loneliness in the lack of close clergy colleagues:

> When I first got here it was hard because I had no other priest colleagues and I had come from a situation where I had four or five immediate colleagues and it was desperately lonely . . . the latter bit of my time in the previous job hadn't always been happy but when I got here the thing that I really felt very strongly was that even if you have colleagues you don't get on with they are better than no colleagues.

Nicholas, who once considered a vocation to the religious life as a monk, now works in an Anglo-Catholic urban parish where he keeps 'open house' at his vicarage and where some parishioners particularly like to befriend 'Father'. This cuts both ways: 'I dislike it if I think people are getting over familiar but on the other hand (and perhaps I am making a rod for my own back) because I like having the house . . . and having parishioners round and I quite like it if people want to come and be part of things and . . . it is a great place . . . and the parishioners are in and the fridge is better stocked afterwards!' Nicholas recognizes however that he cannot be a 'special friend' to lonely or demanding parishioners and he keeps a boundary of personal intimacy: 'The church can provide support and friendship and encouragement but . . . the priest . . . that "special person" – I don't think the priest can come up with those goods'.

For Pauline ordination somehow cut off the path to marriage and children. Some alternatives open to the laity such as sex and children outside marriage are largely denied the clergy by virtue of ecclesiastical discipline:

> Well that is probably my biggest regret actually. I was 30 when I got ordained and you know I had relationships then . . . nobody's asked me out since I got ordained . . . so I'm kind of thinking there might be a connection since I didn't have that much trouble before, and actually I just have been too busy being ordained. I mean it's something you worry about but, so when will I fit that in?

This has left her with heartfelt sadness:

> So now I have got to 44 and I've realized that you know it is too late for children and statistically speaking my chances of marriage aren't that high so that's pretty much it. Yes that is my biggest regret. I mean having said that, I wouldn't have done anything differently, but it's a high price for me.

When it was suggested that forgoing motherhood sounded like a great sacrifice Pauline responded firmly and with emotion: 'Yes it is . . . it is . . . I mind'.

Carole, divorced prior to ordination and with an adult daughter living with her in the vicarage, spoke of possibly remarrying at some point: 'I haven't ruled out the possibility that I might get married so I don't know what the future holds'. She mentioned it more than once and it was obviously on her mind. She entered the priesthood under the misconception that because she was divorced, 'I understood that if I were to be ordained I wouldn't be able to remarry . . . now that was not true but that was what I thought. It was a bit different in those days anyway and I certainly believed I couldn't have remarried and been ordained'. She later discovered this was not the case 'which just seemed so silly'.

> However, by that time it was too late: who wants to marry a vicar? One of the things that I think is very tricky if you are on your own, and it applies to men and women; it applies to single, divorced or whatever is: how do you have personal relationships in such a public life?

Carole underlined how difficult it can be for clergy in the Church of England to develop intimate relationships without surveillance or interference. Consequently, priests become extremely cautious about how they conduct their personal and intimate lives: 'I mean I am sure that people would be very supportive but it is the goldfish bowl existence isn't it and that applies to everything you do. It is not just about relationships it is everything that you do is known about and you don't have the same privacy that other people might enjoy'. Carole mentioned a current male friend but avoided any details.

Four long-serving women clergy seemed content in their single lifestyles. Beryl focused on her large family and circle of friends: 'a lot of who I am comes out of my family. And I've got very, very good friends, not particularly locally – I mean I've got friends locally – but the ones I would holiday with or would share what's really going on in my life. I'm fortunate and so they mean the world to me really and it's out of those relationships I think I tend to live out of that'. As a collaborative person she seeks out good working relationships with colleagues that bring friendships but, like Nicholas, she monitors the boundary between the clergy job and personal privacy:

> Probably a lot of that is about personality. I value my privacy, I value space and freedom; I'm an extrovert too so I will explore. If I get in and I'm exhausted I will and go out and see someone or I'll phone somebody up, you know. I'm not good at re-charging my batteries on my own. Having said that I'm quite happy to have periods on my own and I enjoy space and all that sort of stuff. If someone comes along who threatens that for me or starts to enter a space that, at that particular moment, feel I want to myself, I find that quite difficult. And there are people who latch onto you . . . and you sort of feel stalked almost.

Everyday friendships do provide social glue for some single clergy. Angela was in the process of moving vicarage within her deanery when interviewed. She clearly enjoyed working on her own from the vicarage and spoke warmly of her friendships with parishioners and local clergy colleagues. However she also regularly returned to another part of the country where she had grown up to visit her mother and also had plenty of contact with her adult children whose family photographs remained on display amidst the packing cases. In addition she was still in contact with her former husband whom she divorced prior to ordination. Jean also found that careful friendship in the parish could make an important contribution to her well-being: 'certainly when I think of my last parish experience a churchwarden and his wife were my sanity, my saving grace and I could go and tell them how it truly was from my perspective and they kept their counsel'. Nevertheless she found most personal support from 'my closest friends that I see every week, they live 45 minutes away'. Janet felt that in pursuing ordination she had sacrificed her career and marriage prospects and years on was, 'very comfortable in my own company and I think that is one of the inner strengths. For a single person you have got to be at ease and comfortable with yourself. I can be very happy here with my music, no television, nothing, just the quietness and I enjoy it'. We noted that their lives shared three common features: they lived alone, they were 'pioneer' women priests in the Church of England with many years ministry experience, and they each had enjoyed considerable professional careers in finance, health care and the civil service prior to ordination.

Clergy marriages:
the transformation of intimacy

Restrictions on intimacy are not limited to friendships but emerge within clergy marriages. Researching 'marriages in trouble', Brannen and Collard (1982) argued that marriage and family are problematic social constructions, linked to the traditional power elites of the churches, the politicians and the law. A generation later the underlying questions have not gone away. Families, parenting, household structures and finances, and children's well-being are central to social and political concern, while the debate on private lives and public interventions remains contested from all sides. What difference do marriages make amidst a range of relationship options? Interestingly, a report on families in Church and society, *Something to Celebrate* (Church of England 1995b) ran into difficulties with conservative Christians precisely because it described unjudgementally the variety of sexualities, cohabitation and family configurations available in contemporary society alongside more conventional Christian marriage, the decline of which remains a concern within conservative sectors of the Church.

Giddens questioned the dominant assumptions about the role of personal identity and sexuality in contemporary culture, emancipating traditional static views about personality and sexuality, and developing beyond Freud and Foucault a sociology of what he terms 'reflexivity' (1991: 53) and 'plastic sexuality' (1992: 27). Similarly, Bauman (1993, 2003, 2005) has coined the term 'liquid' for postmodern lifestyle arrangements. The transformation of intimacy, in which feminism (Butler 1990) has played a key role by claiming gender equality in intimate relations, is the democratization of the personal: 'sexuality functions as a malleable feature of self, a prime connecting point between body, self-identity and social norms' (Giddens 1992: 15). Although his argument that traditional heterosexual marriage is being eroded by a range of lifestyle options is compelling, his vision of individualistic adult relationships gives less attention to residual social variables such as employment and wealth, class, ethnicity, and religion which differentially affect relationships and families. For example, Giddens does not explore the nature of parental commitment once children are part of the family, and children's own agency as they grow up as observed by Smart and Neale (1999). Beck and Beck-Gernsheim (1995) explore further the contradictions of gender relations, marriage and family practices, especially the tension between tradition and modernity for women as mothers and men as fathers. Unlike Giddens's rather clinically negotiated 'pure relationship', for Beck and Beck-Gernsheim monogamy and children are 'inner anchors' that are powerfully attractive in character. In addition, extended lifestyle choices may lead to more complexity and relationship breakdown. Divorce and children rarely lead to a completely clean break as implied by Giddens, rather a legal battleground for gender rights and responsibilities and complex parent–child relationships. Although it is not always clear how much agency or intentionality the authors invest in adult behaviours in contrast to their subjection to wider social forces, Beck and Beck-Gernsheim recognize the demanding emotional work of intimacy and the 'hard labour' of parenting Gatrell (2005).

While Giddens, Baumann and Beck and Beck-Gernsheim address emerging personal, offspring and financial relationships in late modernity their fresh vision of plastic sexuality, liquid love, marriage and the family is nevertheless unavailable to clergy because they cannot move on relationally without negative professional repercussions. Serial monogamy is discouraged in the Church not least because of the implications for children to whom the Christian faith attaches great importance. The Church's view of family life continues to regard heterosexual marriage as a key building block in a sustainable society and something worth celebrating. As we discuss below, those outside this paradigm, including gay and divorced clergy, illustrate the current challenges facing priests to integrate both personal and communal ethical values within their ministerial lives.

Married to the ministry?

As indicated in Table 5.1 a clear majority within the clergy research sample, 34 (74%) of the Area/Rural Deans were currently married and 21 (62%) of these married interviewees were caring for children at home. A further 10 clergy and their spouses were 'empty nesters', their young adult offspring having moved away from vicarage accommodation. The 3 clergy interviewed who married later in life and were childless constituted a distinct minority (6.5%) household type in the research sample.

In *Married to the Job* Janet Finch (1983) showed how work-related structures limited the choice of spouses and created public figures by proxy. Prior to women's ordination Kirk and Leary (1994: 55) maintained that Anglican clergy marriages were based on companionship rather than sexual attraction. Their research on clergy and their spouses found that 'shared values and belief, similarity of background, personality, niceness, decency and stability' were of greater importance. Such a conclusion seems difficult to prove and our research did not interview spouses. Warren (2002: 102–3) found that clergy she interviewed emphasized how much they valued the 'affirmation and practical assistance' of their spouse, whether or not they pursued their own career. Fresh research is ongoing into the construction of masculinities and femininities in spouses of Church of England clergy (Page 2008) and quantitative research by the Church of England into clergy patterns of service (Barley 2009) may expand into qualitative explorations including enquiries about clergy households.

It would be interesting to know whether significant experiential differences exist between couples where marriage precedes ordination and where ordination precedes marriage. Either way it may be argued that spouses and family somehow honour and share God's call of the wife/husband to ordination, and that this ensures authenticity and stability (Reid and Reid 2009: 195–6). Despite the idealized aspirations of some newly ordained and their spouses our research suggests there are no ideal clergy marriages or vicarage families. Clergy households like all households are a problematic set of relationships, processes and constructions (Brannen and Collard 1982, Morgan 1996). One clergy research participant, Philip, believed that marriage and children changed him more than ordination, which came later in his life and which reconfigured family life. Our findings confirm that traditional expectations of clergy spouses following their husbands' vocations obediently as home-makers are now significantly eroded in the Church of England. The advent of working spouses, women priests and two-clergy couples, gay and lesbian clergy relationships and the application of modern employment practices to the clergy have led to a variety of family and household arrangements. During our fieldwork Civil Partnerships became available in the United Kingdom though no clergy in the sample had yet taken advantage. As illustrated in Table 5.2 31 spouses of clergy interviewed enjoyed their own careers and work and only three older women appeared to currently fulfil a traditional, stereotypical 'vicar's wife as unpaid curate' role (Meyrick 1998: 9). In the church literature tales of vicarage life are periodically told by spouses, traditionally wives (Nash 1990, Henshall 1991, Grayshon 1996, Meyrick 1998). With the advent of clergy husbands a new genre is possible and the website http://cucumbersandwiches.tumblr. com (Clergy Husbands 2008) provides a forum for their views. Of the six married women priests in the research sample three were married to clergy men and the three remaining husbands enjoyed various professional occupations, though one had recently retired. It was outside the scope of our research to interview clergy spouses and only 15 of them including two husbands were met very briefly on vicarage visits. However, Page's recent research demonstrated 'that clergy husbands are rejecting the clergy spouse identity, based on a model previously believed to have been forged by clergy wives, and are instead constructing the role they play on their own terms. It also appears relatively easy for them to reject this identity, for the parish does not have the same expectations of them as they perhaps would of a female spouse' (Page 2008: 40–1). Echoing the work of Gatrell (2005, 2008) on gender, parenting and work, Page argues that the tasks available

Table 5.2 *Occupations of interviewees' spouses in the research sample*

University counsellor (female)
Care of the elderly (f)
Teacher (5f)
Doctors' receptionist (2f)
Clergy (3f, 3 male)
Family support worker (2f)
Retired nurse / traditional spouse (f)
College lecturer (f)
Nurse (f)
Church administrator (f)
Actor / writer (f)
Legal secretary (f)
Volunteer co-ordinator (f)
Teacher / traditional spouse (f)
Senior nurse (f)
Traditional spouse (f)
Computer engineer (m)
Doctor GP (f)
Retired engineer (m)
Gardener (m)
Teaching assistant (f)
Counsellor (f)
Local government officer (f)
N = 34

are gendered so that traditional vicar's wife jobs are deemed feminine and frequently lie with the female vicar. It is these tasks that the men are rejecting, not an engagement with the local church *per se*.

Male clergy meanwhile are only expected to be the vicar and our own interviews showed this sharply for single clergy where the men are offered domestic support by parishioners which is withheld from single women priests. Warren, approaching clergy marriage from a psycho-dynamic point of view, concluded that 'it was in the home that their [the clergy] psychological make-up was seen at close quarters and worked out' (Warren 2002: 123). She argues that the priest's internal emotional strength to maintain ministry is key but that complementary emotional nourishment is necessary within the vicarage household if relationships are not to break down. She believes that many clergy are 'living with the cracks' in their relational lives at home (2002: 124).

The relationship between gender and spouses' occupations among married stipendiary clergy raises two interesting questions. Do married clergy tend to have spouses working in less or more demanding careers and is the answer gendered? Furthermore it would be helpful to know if the answer and its gendering have changed or become more accentuated since 1994 when women were ordained priests in the Church of England. Is it also the case that married women clergy are more likely to have husbands who are not immersed in demanding careers of their own? The research findings presented in Chapter 4 about the opportunity cost of ministry suggested that in very few cases were high-earning careerist spouses significantly subsidizing the ministry of their partner. It is believed that few clergy and their spouses with separate professional careers located at geographical distance have double domestic arrangements, using two residences and coming together at either as convenient. One would be a church property and the other a flat or house most likely owned as the couple's stake in the property market preretirement. At a parochial level the practice is rare and not encouraged as it is thought to endanger marriages and family life. Among bishops, deans and archdeacons there have been examples in recent years, including a two senior clergy couple making similar arrangements utilizing separate church properties. As far as we could ascertain there was a single example among the married couples in the Area/Rural Deans sample where separate careers were being pursued within marriage at geographical distance, using two domestic bases.

The majority of married clergy in our research sample appeared to be managing marriage and ministry in rather different ways. As Page (2008, 2010) shows, much depends on how involved the spouse actually is in parish life. A number of male clergy with working wives valued their partners as 'critical supporters' who perhaps picked up on things in church or at meetings, hidden from the vicar. Adam was confident that, 'well, my wife would be the first one in talking through issues and sharing and it is the case often that comments or criticism come back via her, which happens in every vicarage I should think'. However the go-between role could become a very negative experience, with a spouse divorcing themselves from church life in order to protect the marriage and I gained the impression that Alistair very much wished it was otherwise:

> If you ask my wife . . . one of the main reasons that she went back to work was to get out of the parish. She is not very keen on the people . . . her own social background is a bit different to this and she has always felt a bit intimidated by that. But she never felt welcomed and although I have said to her, 'you cannot make friends with parishioners you know that is a rule you need to live by' she wouldn't believe it and in the end she tried to make friends and then she found that she was being betrayed and she realised that the people who were trying to be friendly with her were trying to gain her confidence to get at the vicar, either for good or ill, it doesn't matter what it was, and when she found these things were happening she withdrew very much from a public face really.

Colin's wife was one of the very few 'unpaid curates' in the vicarage: 'She is a great supporter . . . I couldn't work if she didn't share the enthusiasm. It all worked out very well because she didn't want to be a clergy wife in a parish when I was first ordained. She said I could live with you being a clergyman but I can't live with being the vicar's wife at the moment and then the time came when she had made that adjustment and she was quite happy to go into a parish'. The division of ministry roles remained traditional and gendered: 'We work well as a team because I am the presenter but she has all the best ideas . . . with the children's work but she is not an up-front person'.

Quality time-off together remains a key issue for most married clergy, particularly those with children, the difference from other families being the external intrusions at home. Robert and his wife addressed this from the start:

> when we had the little kids with us, we always had some time to ourselves . . . we'd go away for a weekend, leave the kids with family or friends . . . so we always planned that in because I think the danger is if you don't do that and you don't have interests and time together and you've only got the children, when they fly, you haven't got anything, you suddenly realise there's this great void and you've not very much in common anymore other than your family.

Fiona and her husband guard their 'precious Friday night' when the teenagers are busy with activities. Although Jeremy and his wife have local friends, time at home can be preferable to yet another local social occasion where there are unspoken expectations from parishioners:

> It is hard though because particularly Saturday nights ever since we have been married we kind of try desperately Saturday night is kind of our time. The kids go out and do their stuff, the kids eat early and I love cooking so Saturday night is kind of my opportunity to do something different and I am not normally the one that cooks so we kind of make that our one night that we get . . . and part of me when something happens on Saturday night that is in the parish when there is an expectation that you are going to go I really kind of I don't want to go and especially when you are stuck in those situations when you have to do a pile of small talk and you are thinking, oh, go away, you know?

On the other hand Penny and her husband appeared to relish the formidable round of parties that formed the social life of the affluent village where she was vicar. Penny felt able to both be visible and in role at these occasions but also her married self with her husband who very much enjoyed village life. They have no children so parish friends provide a wider social network. Penny was alert though to a darker side of excessive social compensation for overwork:

> there's a 'trick or treat' thing about clergy and alcohol . . . we all drink too much . . . we get home and shut the door . . . one of the good things

about going on retreat for a week is not having to worry about watching how much you've had to drink.

Irene had some useful advice to give clergy and their spouses about the personal and professional distinctions that should be maintained between marriage and ministry:

> all clergy need . . . a good spiritual director . . . so that they are not off-loading onto their spouses all of the time . . . and also for the spouse to have somebody that she can off load or he can off load to outside . . . I have difficulty getting over to people who don't understand . . . the difference between confidentiality and secrecy. People say there should be no secrets between husband and wife but if you are told something in confidence it doesn't mean to say you have got to tell that to your spouse and a lot of people, clergy and laity, find that very difficult.

Marriages at risk

For a variety of reasons some clergy marriages run into difficulties. Although clergy marriage separations and divorce are below the national average they raise anxieties in national Church leadership (Warren 2002: 97). Archdeacons typically work with the pastoral consequences for clergy families and parishes: the few clergy who abandon the vicarage and their families usually do so because they are also abandoning ordained ministry. Despite the clear advice to clergy to nurture their marriages a common cause of discord appears to be a lack of investment in that relationship by the clergyperson compared with his/her investment in the priesthood (Greenwood 1994: 165–6) and their spouse's growing unhappiness with 'marriage to the ministry' – that is to say with vicarage life, their partner's working practices and the lack of privacy, a home life and possibly personal and sexual intimacy (Meyrick 1998, Warren 2002). Critical incidents occur when clergy spouses seek to divert attention away from ministry and the vicar responds claiming the moral high ground with some reason why a ministry task or somebody else's needs must come before marriage and family who, as one priest admitted, can come 'tenth on the list'. For spouses the desire to be free from a clerical lifestyle and 'normal' again intensifies and the relationship dries up. Because of the Church's powerful moral expectations a public presentation, 'keeping to the script' (Goffman 1959), may be maintained for a long time before a spouse finally leaves the vicarage, with or without the children, for a new partner or not.

As Keith remarked in the very first research interview, 'people can be very good at hiding things and even within a cell group; I really don't think we always bare everything'. The Irish survey of Anglican married clergy and their spouses (Church of Ireland 2008) highlighted the fear that any show of weakness or turbulence in either parish or family life might appear simply as failure to those in authority. Irish vicarage couples also worried where to turn to when difficulties affecting family life became overwhelming. Fear of ecclesiastical and public disapproval often delays separation for years, confirming the possibility that even among clergy, intimacy within a marriage may be lost, the couple's relationship taking on the character of a 'tenancy arrangement' (Beck and Beck-Gersheim 1995). Since 1983, the support group Broken Rites has assisted Church of England clergy marital casualties (Broken Rites 2012) campaigning for prevention and better after-care. Most dioceses provide a confidential counselling service for clergy and their families at one remove from the authority structures of the diocese.

In interview Charles spoke of his marriage breakdown, explaining why he thought his wife left him for another local man, also in public life:

> As time has gone on she has longed to be normal . . . to have her own house with a mortgage and everything else . . . we have a fairly large group of friends I suppose, a lot of them have no connection with the church at all and she very much wanted to be part of that and obviously there are certain things I wasn't part of because of living in a church house . . . and she found that quite difficult.

Charles admits that marriage to his ministry wasn't working for her:

> what I saw as being having got into a sort of comfortable routine she saw I think as being completely stifling and 'I'm 40 and I have got to do something' and that happened and to be fair it sort of almost wrecked her health for a time and I think she probably did the right thing by going.

Charles continued his ministry, now several years divorced, in the parish. His daughters remained with him at the vicarage before moving on to university and work. The divorce has caused painful issues for him: 'A sense of guilt I suppose that I am not . . . what I should be. It came as a complete bolt out of the blue when my wife decided . . . after twenty years . . . I suppose you want to feel that you are setting a good example to everyone else and this isn't the way to do it'. He expressed gratitude that his diocese 'is vaguely okay about me being divorced but I suspect remarriage would be another issue altogether'.

In another interview, Derek spoke frankly of the difficulties he and his wife had in reconciling his ministry to their marriage. He feels she may have underestimated what a vicar's life was like and that 'I will just resign myself to the fact that actually this is not working for the time being . . . and in order to sustain the marriage . . . I need to look elsewhere; I'll never be looking at my ministry as a mistake. But looking at it and accepting that actually in order to keep the marriage together I need to do something else'. Derek is also resentful that his wife is critical about his pattern of working and time off and wants his undivided attention. Negative family issues complicated matters further: 'difficulties we have with her parents who are very anti-me and very anti-church . . . so right from the beginning of the marriage they've been very anti the whole thing . . . and they've worked very hard against us . . . to split us up'. Derek seemed however unable to articulate a broader appreciation of family members' different needs or a joined-up solution and the interview ended with the impression of an unhappy vicarage couple at risk.

The domestic and lifestyle changes consequent to 'second career' ordinations usually challenge relationships and can sometimes undo marriages. A sharp example was revealed by Patricia whose blossoming ordained career as an older woman clearly caused problems for her recently retired husband. She reported his irritation that being a clergy husband living in a vicarage was not his idea of retirement:

> What has caused the most anxiety I suppose is my husband having to adjust to being the vicar's husband and whereas for most of our married life I have gone where his work was and we lived abroad twice . . . and suddenly the boot is on the other foot and suddenly I am the important person and he is not quite making tea and scones but it has been quite a challenge for him . . . I know that this is partly in reaction to seeing his job and status going down and he is seeing me changing from being in the home and looking after children and things.

She recognized that ordination training had '*changed me fundamentally*' and that challenged her husband even though he had originally supported her calling. Patricia was anxious about her ministry prospects because of her husband's reaction to further change: 'Just dealing with his unhappiness really . . . it is going to be difficult because while he is unhappy he would not want me not to take another post because of him, so it will be a time'. She has sought the help of a counsellor: 'I have actually been going to counselling . . . I now see it much more as his problem and his difficulty and so that has helped'.

Patricia was keen to be interviewed away from her vicarage and her experience shows that spouses can regret or even resent that the person they married has become a vicar with a lot of unwelcome implications for marriage and the family. In our research nine clergy households had experienced this transition, yet their marriages seemed to have survived intact for a significant number of years. In just two instances women became traditional 'vicar's wives' as a result. More usually the ability for the spouse's career to continue without too much disruption was a positive driver. For example, following his ordination, Roy and his wife bought a small house outside the parish to enable her to continue teaching during the week in a neighbouring county, and she returned to the vicarage only at weekends. Few clergy in our research had either the appetite or resources to take such a calculated approach. However the range of their spouses' occupations illustrated in Table 5.2 suggests that work outside the vicarage is a significant factor in maintaining clergy marriage and family life, not only economically as we noted previously when counting the cost of ministry, but also relationally by affirming the spouse's individual identity beyond the public gaze and expectations of marriage to the ministry. Therefore Philip's wife is professionally fulfilled heading a school department, Penny's husband keeps very busy running his gardening business and Keith's wife commutes to her counselling job each day while their priest spouses remain, embodied in the vicarage.

Occasionally clergy just quit the vicarage and their marriage, sometimes for a new partner but by no means always. Where sexual intimacy outside marriage and the vicarage is the main attraction, the media's interest in clergy adultery and scandal – 'Vicar runs off with . . .' (Gysin et al. 2008) and the weight of the Clergy Discipline Measure (Church of England 2003a) ensure that an individual's ministry implodes. Another thread seems to be a crisis of personal Christian faith and a loss of vocational energy for an ordained role in the Church. It is as though marriage to the ministry predisposes that a marriage is endangered when the ministry grinds to a halt, although causality is probably reciprocal and reinforcing. As we noted at the outset, such exits are probably rare, although the research evidence is limited. On the basis of the research sample we can only point to one interviewee, Laurence, whose ministry and marriage both appeared to be at risk. He talked about the erosion of his Christian belief and his tiredness in ministry, contrasting with his passion for cultural trips abroad (without his hospital chaplain wife and teenage children) and it seemed as though his heart lay elsewhere:

> I think I have three choices really. One is to stay here. The second is to look actively for another job in about a year or two years but I am not sure I could face another parish job like this, I am not sure I would have the energy to start again somewhere. And so we have toyed with the idea about whether I might look for a foreign chaplaincy or something like that. The other thing we half wonder about is whether I would take early retirement, [my wife] would carry on working which she enjoys very much, so yes, we are certainly beginning to look at all of those options.

Family practices

Within the social sciences both Giddens (2001) and Morgan (1996) would agree that the family has long been a discreet topic area and a dimension of all social enquiry. The main concepts under scrutiny are: kinship, cohabiting, marriage, divorce, remarriage, lone-parenting, gay and lesbian partnerships, ethnic family diversity, reconstituted families, absent fathers, childlessness, domestic abuse and child abuse. Many of these subjects have been politicized and moralized as British society adapts to changing attitudes, technologies and threats. The alleged breakdown of the family or 'family values' is frequently characterized in the media as symptomatic of social collapse (Cameron 2009) and attempts by successive UK governments to secure improvements through education, employment and social services have only been partially successful.

While accepting greater family diversity within secular life, the Church continues to stress the ideal of faithful relationships, life-long marriage and family life for its clergy. Priestly bodies are held in a theological and ecclesial version of the panoptical obedience described by Foucault (1977). Moreover the clergy accept such obedience as essential to fulfilling their vocational commitments in an exceptional example of the self-governed souls characterized by Rose (1999).

Families have always embodied complex relationships. Morgan finds 'family practices' (1996: 11) a helpful term to describe the complex embodiment of modern family configurations and the variable set of negotiated relationships and meanings they contain. Family practices constitute a process rather than particular activities according to neat socio-economic categories – gender, children, work or class. Morgan applies the term 'household strategies' (1996: 22) to describe how families and households function. His preference for 'household' rather than 'family' is argued because it does not imply a single unit that operates in a unified or uniform way. Marriage, family and household are therefore three different interlinked dimensions of family practices. Thus sociologically the family exists (or doesn't) less as an institution, more as a process or biographies. Family practices are constructed cognitively and emotionally, providing significance between the self and society, and are a way of understanding social life beyond the confines of 'the family' (Morgan 1996: 187, 199).

The 'traditional' picture of clergy households in the past is probably of a married man with a wife, children and servants living in a capacious vicarage anytime between the early 19th century and the Second World War. More recent vicarage literature (Nash 1990, Henshall 1991, Meyrick 1998, Burton and Burton 2009) still includes echoes of that picture now broken by the dimensions of late modernity, in particular the social marginalization of the Church in English society and the destabilization of the 'class embedded-ness' (Morgan 1996: 67) of the clergy. Paradigmatically the ordination of women has changed gender stratification in the Church for ever and has changed the shape and structure of contemporary and future clergy households.

Happy families?

As embodied sacrifice overtakes everything in the priest's life, one asks who else is making the sacrifice: the spouse, the children, and is family life a casualty? Trevor commented that 'some clergy are very boring and can only engage with work, and their families are forced to engage with them through work'. The findings of our research confirm that clergy families negotiate the complexities of life pragmatically, understanding that ordination and parish work have family implications. Families resist or tolerate the pressures of living in a vicarage, balancing these with the advantages and make their home there. There were both heroic and dysfunctional examples in the interviews and we would be cautious in suggesting that vicarage family life, *per se*, is any more demanding than family life elsewhere, for example than for families caught up in the expectations of the corporate business world or the armed forces, health care or farming. The vicarage 'tied house' is not the only kind of tie or intrusion that the working world imposes on workers and their families.

What can be said of Church of England clergy however is that their family life is under surveillance by the parish, the church authorities and God beyond an employers' basic requirement that post-holders do their jobs properly. The subtle ways in which this is experienced and dealt with by the clergy was described by participants in their interviews. They confirm what Burton and Burton (2009), reporting mid-1990s clergy family interviews, call a Double Bind: 'they wanted to put their family first, but they accommodated to the situation by putting the job first, with the family drawn into the heart of the task' (2009: 149). Some clergy in the research admitted to hardly seeing their spouses, especially working spouses. For Richard and his wife who works for social services Sunday afternoon is a tiny island amidst busyness: 'I had a number of colleagues working with me so we could arrange things in such a way that I didn't have to work Sunday afternoon and that made things bearable, because she works Monday to Friday it was difficult to do things otherwise'. Clergy like Neil and Julian who were married to teachers were frustrated to discover on their day off that 'even teachers have homework' or that their spouse could happily enjoy school holiday time at home in the vicarage just when the vicar was desperate to get away: 'it is one thing she really can't get her head around . . . she can't quite see it and even if I say to her, "imagine it was a load of parents from your school . . ." ah, but "that is different" and she can't quite see it as an issue'.

Colin admitted that his working practices as a priest might have endangered his family:

> I am not good at saying 'no' and in some ways it would have been better if I had said 'no' to a few more things but I am glad to say that it hasn't ruined our family. We are still a very happy close knit family. They all descend upon us for Christmas and we have a great crowd . . . I love it when they come and I love it when they all go home.

Jeremy found that meals were an important family time, 'in this house . . . we have got into the habit of . . . 6 o'clock until 7 the world has to stop for us because that is the only time we ever get . . . but mostly Monday to Friday that is the only time we eat together really'. James protected his family time by keeping the vicarage at arm's length from church business. The vicarage was located just a bit further away from the church building than most in the sample. James was not unsociable and some meetings and social events did take place in the vicarage. However as he explained, 'there is that wonderful sense of being able to go home at night and the way that we operate is that our home is first and foremost our home and then we invite people to join us at home for things'. James also made a significant point about the dangers of bringing family life into public worship: 'a decision I made about home privacy was that I wouldn't do sermons where the children were, you know, illustrations of vicarage life and I just don't do that, so I try and have that sense of privacy there'.

One or two clergy commented on the ways in which their vicarages were conducive or otherwise to family time together. The Church of England has a guide for vicarage size, design and construction (Church of England 1998) taking account of the property's semi-public purpose. The provision requires two reception rooms, a study and four bedrooms though the configuration, grounds and location and variable standards of repair in dioceses may not satisfy all clergy households. Church meetings at the vicarage compromise other family members, as John put it, 'if I have a meeting here there is a cost because we are a one TV, one car, four computer family . . . so in a sense it is saying to my son, "I am sorry, do you mind but I am having a meeting?" Now it doesn't happen often . . . but yes, we do have things from time to time here'. Neil had recently moved into a brand new, full specification vicarage and was delighted with it from a family point of view, saying, 'a properly designed vicarage makes all the difference'.

Because of their exposure to public life and parishioners, vicarage children are usually well socialized and not slow in coming forward to challenge their parents and the downside of being a vicarage family. James, married to a GP, admitted that their young son sharply reminded them of his existence by becoming naughtier the busier his parents were. Tony's children devised their own narrative to describe frequent parental absence, calling him 'meeting man' because he finds it difficult to say no to parochial involvements in and beyond the vicarage:

I can't remember saying 'no' to anything fairly recently. I try to say – well I have said no to some things recently – but by saying there is no way that I can take X on if you are thinking about trying to get me to take X on I can't do it because I just recognize that my children call me 'meeting man'. Sometimes I am going to so many meetings, that is all I have done you know, 'meeting man'. So, joking – but sometimes it is true you just rush from one meeting to another with a wad of papers in hand.

It is reported (Meyrick 1998, Burton and Burton 2009) that vicarage children can also feel more vulnerable to parishioners' criticisms than their peers and will fiercely defend themselves and parents when pushed. Occasionally the pressure becomes impossible and Thomas (2006: 20) suggests that 'clergy children are much more likely to need psychiatric help than children from other professions'.

The age and stage of vicarage children exercise considerable influence on if and when clergy move jobs. Simon was very settled, 17 years in the same parish largely, he said, because no job offers or opportunities arose when the 'education slots' were available: 'There was a slot when our three children were at primary school, before number one went to secondary school, there was a slot there where I looked at some parishes . . . and there is a slot now although nothing particular has appeared'. It should be remembered that we no more had access to interview vicarage children than we did the clergy spouses (in fact remarkably few youngsters were seen, most interviews being during the school day) therefore the data only provides one family member's view – the clergy one. Over the sample the extent to which clergy mentioned their children was uneven. Some were prominent in interviews, others absent.

Several clergy were caught up with the wider responsibilities of an extended family. Malcolm explained that he and his wife cannot agree about what is best for her ailing mother with Alzheimer's and it is a source of emotional and financial tension. Malcolm feels that his wife is focused primarily on her mother and on neither their marriage nor his ministry, confirming the findings of Finch (1989) and Finch and Mason (1993) about the obligations of kinship. Consequently home life is 'Well, it's a bit fragmented, very fragmented really . . . I think if I were really honest we are a bit dysfunctional family wise because of this. And part of the problem is I think I disagree with her philosophy about her mum really. She knows I do. I think we should at the moment be working hard to get her mum on to the list of several nursing care homes [my wife] is doing all of these hours, she's got mum on her brain all of the time, she's getting very tired'. For a number of other clergy the proximity of grandparents provided support for the vicarage household, particularly the grandchildren where both parents were working. Fiona warmly appreciated her close-knit family nearby: 'All of my family have settled here. My parents were quite happy to come over and stay. My Dad . . . loves coming here and chilling out. My sister lives down the road and is more than happy coming up with her family'.

The arrival of women clergy has opened up a critical awareness of a gendered division of labour within the ministries of ordained men and women. Because Area/Rural Deans have access to other clergy and their domestic situations they sometimes compared their own family practices with their knowledge of other clergy households in the deanery. For example Fiona noticed that some male clergy colleagues rationalized their selfishness: 'I have known male clergy who when the children are very small will arrange Evening Prayer each day at 6 o'clock so that the wife would have to organize bath time and bed time and it fitted in for them. It was a legitimate excuse not to be around at that moment . . . in fact one told me that he was deliberately doing it'. Fiona's comments echo Hochschild (1989) and Gatrell (2005, 2008) who observed that while many husbands of women combining career with childbearing were taking more time for their children they 'cherry picked' which tasks they undertook and there were still areas of traditional female domestic labour in family arrangements. Though some clergy in our sample certainly behaved otherwise, research by Page (2008) into clergy marriages suggests continued gendering within domestic life.

Fiona believes that men clergy are less comfortable than women clergy in multitasking, preferring to erect a barrier between being at work and being at home: 'For some they sacrifice their family ties and their own personal ties because the office is there and they can work in there and they can put themselves away and they don't have to face any of the other demands'. The concept of male clergy 'hiding in the study' cropped up periodically in interviews, for example Jonathan who 'can normally slip into the study to beaver away at something . . . for half an hour or an hour'. In a remarkable example of gendered multitasking Carole (divorced and with no partner) told me how her family expected her to lay on full Christmas festivities at the vicarage while meeting the seasonal expectations of her multiple village parishes:

> Family-wise I think I have made a lot of sacrifices. You are not around at the significant festivals that families get together – you are busy. Christmas has been a total nightmare here now I have . . . I forget how many services . . . I think it was eleven or twelve between Christmas Eve lunch time and Christmas Day lunch time to cover all of the different things that go on here . . . and I take all of those because there isn't anybody else to take them and . . . then come home at lunchtime on Christmas Day and cook for nine and then have my family time. Most of the time of which I am totally unconscious through wine and tiredness and that is just so ridiculous but I have grandchildren and I want to enjoy my other family life.

As might be expected among any 46 households, so-called 'recombinant families' (Giddens 1992: 96) were in evidence in some vicarages. Several clergy shared their lives with stepchildren and adoptive children and youngsters with a range of particular needs. Roy recalled the problems they experienced with an errant adoptive son, though did not believe his difficulties were exacerbated by vicarage life. More recently Neil had married a clergy widow with teenagers and was clearly adjusting to his lost bachelor status when interviewed. Their return from school triggered a fairly abrupt end to our conversation as he demonstrated keenness to reappear from the study for his new family. In the research sample three clergy (two women and one man) were divorcees and none had so far remarried, though one, possibly two, contemplated the possibility in interview. Within certain parameters divorce and remarriage nowadays are not impossible for clergy in the Church of England. The surveillance however is intrusive, the general rule being that the individual clergyperson and the new spouse should not have been the adulterous cause of a previous breakdown and the new relationship. This pastoral–legal approach is similar to that offered to laity marriage couples seeking remarriage in the Church. Remarkably, divorced candidates and those married to divorcees seeking ordination are interviewed by the Ministry Division along with their new spouse if they have one (Church of England 2011a). Divorced clergy can seek remarriage on similar grounds as the laity and sometimes do, usually very cautiously and only with their bishop's blessing.

Two-clergy couples

Two-clergy married couples face particular challenges in their working and domestic arrangements. Following Nesbitts's research in the United States (1997: 79–80) and early research by Walrond-Skinner (1998) in England, Bentley described how the Church of England struggled to accommodate two-clergy ministries let alone see the fresh possibilities for their deployment: 'there is little evidence of dioceses being proactive in the encouragement of couples into suitable posts' (Bentley 2001: 209). In the early days of women priests gendered differentiation in ministry was a concern for two-clergy couples. Dioceses were more likely to find stipendiary posts for male priests moving with an ordained spouse who was also changing post than vice versa. The NADAWM survey (2008) confirmed a continuing absence of 'facilitation of job-shares in the Church of England'.

The key issue, particularly parochially, is whether there is more than one paid post for two clergy in the deanery staff allocation and the diocesan budget. A variety of arrangements arises, the common feature of which is less overall stipend/salary and more part-timeness. The financial implications were noted in the previous chapter (see Table 4.3). There is a question whether two-clergy couples choose these arrangements for domestic work–home convenience, or are forced into accepting what the Church is prepared to offer. Two-clergy couples can find it difficult to find two full-time posts in the same or close by parishes. Table 5.3 illustrates the types of ministries undertaken by six clergy couples in the research sample.

As evidenced by our findings, three ordained spouses work in sector ministries beyond the parish, one job-share was coming to an end as one partner moved into a training role based elsewhere and another job-sharer was seeking to expand her time occupied in a currently unpaid assistant diocesan role. One parochial job-share was continuing successfully. A married clergy job-share in the same parish(es) may be great in theory for the parishioners and the diocese, providing two clergy for the price of one, however in practice this could put pressure on the marriage. An interviewee, Irene commented, 'I try and block out Friday so that we have both got the

Table 5.3 *Ministry combinations in two-clergy couples*

Area/Rural Dean Interviewee	Clergy partner post	Additional information
Female	Diocesan Director of Education (male)	Two posts and locations Two Stipends
Male	Parish priest (female) Same parish	Job-Share 2 × 0.5 Stipends
Male	Hospital Chaplain (female) Part time	Two posts and locations 1 Stipend + 0.5 Salary
Female	Parish priest (male) Same parish	2 × Part-time posts 1.5 x Stipends
Male	Hospital Chaplain (female) Full time	Two posts and locations 1 Stipend + 1.0 Salary
Female	Parish priest (male) Same parish	Job-Share 2 x 0.5 Stipends

same day off. There are people that moan that we have the same day off but I do point out to them that they expect a day off with their spouse. The same as our last parish in London . . . I couldn't have the same holiday and I wrote and complained to the Bishop that we took the same holiday'.

The limited data gathered in the research tends to agree with Bentley (2001) and NADAWM (2008) that the opportunity and appetite for clergy job-share is limited and that the potential working intimacy of parish job-share appears to work only for a few self-selecting clergy. Two respondents working alongside clergy spouses in shared parish posts offered contrasting perspectives. Matthew found it uncomfortable in practice and was moving to a post in theological education, leaving his clergy wife to run the rural benefice. He was also moving his desk from the present two-desk study to the sanctuary of an upstairs bedroom: 'Yes, we get in each other's way a lot . . . I think that this new scenario will, we hope, give her actually the space to further fly. I mean we have got different styles and she is exceptionally good at all age stuff and that is not particularly my strength'. Matthew discovered that job-sharing placed pressures on his marriage and bringing up their children: 'it does spill over into the way in which we might handle each other and our children because some of those become flash points'.

On the other hand Liz and her clergy husband addressed the problem by sharing the strategic ministry tasks across the parish according to their gifts and interests. Liz finds the traditional 'structures within the Church, doing the same job' frustrating. Fortunately her husband has the patience, 'and our ministries have separated and that is partly because actually our skills are very different and my ministry has become much more child/family/school focused and he is different and it is just has gone that way'. In addition Liz and her husband thought through the family practicalities carefully:

> We took a job and a half because, for us as a family and us as a couple, we felt if we did that we could more or less manage between ourselves to care for our children without involving others. We haven't got family structures locally or anywhere (and we never have had to support us). And when we moved here they were both at school and we felt yes, we can and we did use to find during the summer holiday it got pretty stretched after six weeks, but most of the time a job and a half, one of us could be in the house with the children and that sort of thing. It is inevitably changed because their pattern changed. We started the job here when they were five and six and you have your meetings early in the evening when they are tucked up in bed. Now we are at the stage where . . . we can leave them a bit in the evenings and so we are in a stage where I think it is easier than it has been but it is finding quality time to spend with them maybe.

Liz finds that the demands of their jobs are on both her and her husband and time off 'bleeds quite a lot . . . we both take Thursdays together'. Quality time as a family is also hard won, sometimes because the children demand it. She recalled a conversation. Mum: 'So what do you want to do for half term?' Children: 'Please can we go away together for some time so that we are all together?' Mum: 'We do go away at holidays because if we stay here the phone just rings the whole time and we have a secretary who works in the house so there is no sort of quality time' and presumably no place to hide.

   Two-clergy couples with divergent foci of ministry for example, parochial/ diocesan specialist reported a number of issues that appeared to erode relationships and intimacies within the family. At a basic level getting two clergy together at home can prove difficult, as recounted by Linda from her inner city vicarage: 'It's easier in some ways in that we both know what that's like for the other and the fact that he's no longer in a parish but has a diocesan responsibility has meant that he's much more available in the evenings than he ever was. But then that tends to mean that he'll say, "well, why are you always out?" And he's got a point!' Gatrell and Cooper (2007a, 2007b) argue that the pressure to maintain a bodily presence at work over long periods is gendered, and embodied. Both clergy in this household appear to be placing their jobs before their marriage: 'So I think that sometimes he assumes that it's always me that does the over-work. In fact it's not always that and the difficulty we have at the moment is finding a day off together; because obviously his days off tend to be at the weekend and mine are often not at the weekend'. As discussed earlier excessive working hours, a lack of quality time off and privacy at home are key features of obedient clergy bodies which spell a particular danger for two clergy bodies living together in one vicarage. Linda echoed Fiona's gendered observation already quoted in this chapter that male clergy spouses, ordained or not, find multitasking at the vicarage difficult and resist its demands: 'A lot of my working life has been working around somebody else's agenda . . . the first one into ministry and a lot of time was focused about how we're going to fit it around his parish ministry . . . then my agenda then came in . . . that was a big shock for him . . . he had to learn to do that as well'. Confirming the gendered domestic tasking noted by Page (2008), 'he does multi-task very well now . . . but at first he was very good at compartmentalizing his work time . . . he didn't think about anything else'.

Two of our male clergy respondents were married to hospital chaplains. Healthcare chaplaincy can offer flexible part-time posts working set hours away from the home, which particularly for women, but for their husbands also can combine more easily with children and family concerns. In terms of the research sample Jonathan was an exceptionally relaxed interviewee, clearly at home in his vicarage, commenting that he didn't 'feel beleaguered . . . chased or hemmed in' by parish ministry and could take time off at home. He certainly benefited from a very settled household after many years in the same parish, significantly supported by grandparent backup and a very stable routine. We wonder whether his clergy wife felt quite the same because Jonathan admitted that 'in terms of relationships . . . I am probably much more kind of reactive . . . no, we don't have enough time to ourselves but then I suppose I objectively accept that reality . . . I think my wife finds that more of a tension you know . . . she always feels that she is tenth on the list'.

Laurence said in his interview that he and his wife who worked full time as a hospital chaplain found organizing quality time off together and holidays with four teenage children quite 'complex and erratic'. The need for an extra teenager's bedroom in the vicarage meant that Laurence had no study in which to separate work from home. He recognized that

> there can be stress when I am attempting to balance family and work when [my wife] is working and . . . generally that is fine, that is okay, but sometimes, yes, that can be a stress point. I mean I think it's generally a good thing that we have our own spheres of ministry though I think we can have a tendency to unload on each other.

Laurence referred several times to his need to escape from the parish and explained that 'I go away for a couple of weeks a year by myself' a unilateral action presumably enabling him to escape from his wife and children also.

Despite her relational approach Warren (2002) does not report on two-clergy couples. The limited findings from our research and NADAWM (2008) suggest that the ministries of two-clergy couples merit further research, exploring gendered and professional aspects of the ordained careers of two-clergy couples in the Church of England, updating Walrond-Skinner (1998) and Bentley (2001). Our findings suggest there is some evidence that ministries as well as marriages and the upbringing of children among two-clergy couples are vulnerable, also that the two-clergy version of separate careers in Church work appears to undermine domestic intimacy. There are indicators that behaviours in these clergy remain strongly gendered with patriarchy in the ascendancy. Two-clergy couples represent a two-way amplification of the experiences and issues found in this research to affect all those who are 'married to the ministry'. Following a conference for two-clergy couples which had revealed a lot of relationship tensions, Irene found herself thinking about the ordination vows quoted at the start of this chapter: 'What has God called you to be? Surely he hasn't called you to be at each other's throats. You are supposed to be selling marriage as well as the Church you know'. Interestingly this accords with research into dual role ministry (Peyton 1998, 2001) where individual clergy undertake two part-time posts with disparate foci, typically a parish and a diocesan role or chaplaincy in a secular institution. Although where such ministry is consciously a first choice it can be highly stimulating for clergy and their families for a particular period in their lives.

Clergy households and work–home balance

In *The Time Bind* Hochschild (1997) examined the relationship between working practices and family life in small town America. She found that despite the availability of some flexible working arrangements within companies, families experienced time compression in which 'work becomes home and home becomes work'. Hochschild describes this conflation as 'a new model of family and work life . . . a tired parent flees a world of unresolved quarrels and unwashed laundry for the reliable orderliness, harmony and managed cheer of work. The emotional magnets beneath home and workplace are in the process of being reversed' (1997: 44). Working parents struggle to compensate for the 'just-in-time' pressure placed on their child-rearing and marital relationships with 'quality time'. However achieving this often involves transferring the cult of efficiency from office to home and 'our family bonds are being recalibrated to achieve greater productivity in less time' (1997: 50). Hochschild argues that the growth in the employment of women offers an opportunity to reverse the time bind: 'at all levels of the workforce there are women and men whose potential selves are clamouring for more time at home' (1997: 258).

However in her earlier study, *The Second Shift* (1989) which examined two-career parents typical of mainstream America, Hochschild found strongly gendered second shift arrangements in which working women took the lead in housework and child care. Collusion by both partners in gendered behaviour led to jealousies and resentments affecting the health and well-being of both partners. Two careers are appealing but difficult in practice because the surface ideology didn't always match deeper feelings.

Women accommodate men to save the marriage: 'What often tipped the balance between a wife's gender strategy and her husband's was the debits and credits on their marital economy of gratitude . . . beneath the cultural cover-up . . . there is a quiet struggle going on in many two-job marriages . . . many women kept cautiously to those strategies which avoid too much change in men' (Hochschild 1989: 203).

Hochschild possibly romanticizes previous generations of work–home arrangements but it appears that Church of England clergy are an interesting case study for Hochschild's theory of permeable family–work borders. Parish clergy live with their work as well as their families within vicarages in ways that can be quite confusing and stressful. The comings and goings, the escapism to the 'other' work or life is space-time compressed into the vicarage. Among clergy in Liverpool Diocese 71 per cent agreed that they 'spend far too much (or a bit too much) of my time working and not enough at home or leisure' (Liverpool 2011). Previously Collinson and Collinson (1997) examined managerial responses to this challenge and concluded that individuals internalize surveillance and collapse the distinction between home and work. Many clergy are now women, in two-career marriages or two-clergy couples, thus gendered work–home lifestyles are open to inspection, much as Gatrell (2005, 2008) has critiqued maternity, parenthood and work.

Morgan notes how distinctions between the rational and the emotional shape ways in which family life is understood and family relationships constructed as sites where a lot of 'emotional labour' is performed or expected to be performed (Morgan 1996: 81). Church of England parochial clergy are a particular example. Clergy are invited pastorally into the intimacies and lifestyles of others while having to create their own, often with difficulty as some research into clergy lives has suggested (Lee and Horsman 2002, Warren 2002). Although the bishops disavow interrogating individuals on personal intimacies there remains an overwhelming expectation that clergy should 'set an example' (Church of England 1991: 44). In order to underline the importance of retaining a traditional view of vocational household in changing times the *Guidelines for the Professional Conduct of the Clergy* states that,

> The clergy are called to a high standard of moral behaviour . . . those who are called to marriage should never forget that this is also a vocation . . . it should not be thought to be of secondary importance to their vocation to ministry . . . similarly, those who are not married, including those with a vocation to celibacy, should take the necessary steps to nurture their lives, their friendships and their family relationships . . . all should guard themselves and their family against becoming victims of stress. (Church of England 2003b: 9)

As was discussed in Chapter 3 the mandatory residence in the parish in a particular vicarage, and presence and availability to parishioners is a key factor for clergy: the priest and her/his household are embedded in the parish. From the outset clergy realize that the Ordination service explicitly requires them to 'strive to fashion your own life and that of your household according to the way of Christ' (Church of England 2007a: 38) and this is often experienced as a pressure on vicarage households. The bodies of clergy spouses and children are therefore also under surveillance: family practices in the home are under scrutiny and clergy, their spouses and children frequently have to deal with impertinent intrusions into their behaviour and feelings (Meyrick 1998: 48–81).

Sanctuary from surveillance

Finding family sanctuary in a vicarage is not always easy as visitors and ministerial work seep between the study and reception rooms disturbing spouses and children alike. Clergy sometimes adopt deceptive strategies to avoid surveillance – drawing curtains, switching off lights, doorbells and answering machines. For a handful of interviewees (including two single clergy and a clergy woman without children at home) an upstairs room provided a refuge beyond the public gaze, as Alistair explained:

> The tiny bedroom on the south side of the house we call the studio and . . . that is a room we sit in and in fact it became particularly important when I did a Master's degree . . . that was the place I would go and sit to study and read. It can't be seen by anybody in the parish so we are completely isolated when we are there. The sun shines into it so it is pleasant from that point of view, not terribly big but the four of us can just about fit in and if it happens to be a day off or a Saturday or Sunday and we are here we will usually have tea there away from everywhere so there is a sort of intimacy in that space and that has actually been tremendously important.

Clergy work a six-day week and need holidays but are not always good about taking up their 36 days entitlement envisaged in Clergy Terms of Service. Some clergy disregard their family's needs, choosing to cling to work while others are disorganized, for example a vicar who came back in the middle of his holiday fortnight in order to take a wedding! Others with children and nonworking spouses may well have anxieties about cost. Some clergy combine holidays with doing 'Sunday duty' in a church somewhere nice at home or abroad, or even swap vicarages. Fiona knows of some clergy,

> who go and do holiday duty for a month in the summer. I have got a colleague who does that . . . in Jersey . . . and he loves every minute of it. He literally does the Sunday service and gets somewhere to stay for his holiday for a month. It will help them because his wife doesn't work

and they have got four teenagers so it helped them because they weren't having to pay an absolute fortune for somewhere to stay and they could get a decent holiday out of it.

This does not appeal to Fiona who cannot bear the thought of mixing a family holiday with work.

I don't understand folks who go for their main holiday to Christian festivals . . . and that is their family holiday. I don't mind going if I am taking a church group and we are doing it as part of our retreat thing from the church but 'no, thank you very much' it would be like a busman's holiday.

Fiona is clear about what refreshes her and provides quality family time together:

We do go abroad for our holidays every summer most years and we go and find remote little places. We went to Catalonia one year . . . we don't want big and lively we just want somewhere we can just . . . [the kids] well they just go in the water. They both love swimming and snorkelling and . . . we all like looking round. We are very much social people so we like looking at things and the history of things and doing lots of walks together . . . we are not really beach bums . . . we go and explore.

On the evidence of our vicarage interviews caravan holidays are particularly favoured among some clergy and their families, possibly for cost reasons, also the ease of taking the family camping to annual Christian festivals such as Spring Harvest, New Wine and Greenbelt. Philip recalled how 'when we first came into the Church it was the only way we could afford to get away . . . the children enjoyed it . . . and it meant that the five of us were able to get away for a week or two weeks at a time, afford it, and be away from the business. And we just carried on with that'. There is significance in the caravan as a vehicle of privacy and freedom, a 'towed house' rather than a tied vicarage. Clergy said how much they appreciated the ability to go at short notice, leaving ministry behind. For Kevin the caravan provided 'an opportunity to go away more economically more often and that does actually give us space which is time off for holidays which are genuinely off'. Jeremy admitted that the previous year for once he had taken a full family holiday and while recognizing the benefits also found it slightly unnerving when he got back: 'Well . . . spending three weeks intensely on holiday with the kids, no pressure at all and it was a really good time for us, we had a good time and I think day one back in here was "what am I doing?" In hindsight I think that was just part of me really trying to . . . revisiting what the vocation was about . . . it was just that kind of challenge of God saying are you really up for this?' Maybe this was the vocational panopticon reasserting itself?

Family relationships and work are therefore embodied in particular ways for clergy and their lives offer an insight into the rapid and continuing social changes under way in relationships, families and working arrangements at the start of the 21st century in which there is a fresh concern for the boundaries between work and home or other aspects of our lives. Houston (2005) and Stewart (2005) report the findings of a major research exercise examining work–life issues in UK families and communities. Houston finds a persistent work–life imbalance. Despite the advantages flexible working offers to both women and men and their work–life balance it is difficult to escape the conclusion that part-time (or other versions of gendered 'nonstandard' employment) can harm longer term career prospects. This is true for men and women; men are anxious about job security, pay and promotion, while women are often frustrated at not being able to find rewarding part-time work that reflects their experience and aspirations (Houston 2005: 1–10).

Lewis and Cooper (2005) report case studies about change in a variety of organizations exploring ways in which the dual agenda of workplace effectiveness and personal quality of life can be achieved. They found that long-term employer and employee commitment and awareness of wider societal changes was crucial to achieving greater work–life integration. Paradoxically, 'there is a danger that high levels of autonomy can create blurred boundaries between work and home, in which case people often "choose" to work longer and harder to fulfil all their demands . . . this tends to be exacerbated if jobs are seen as insecure' (Lewis and Cooper 2005: 122). Work–life issues are high on the agenda of Church of England clergy, married and single, female and male, as they attempt to manage the entirety of their lives. Research into clergy stress (Lee and Horsman 2002, Thomas 2006) highlighted the domestic/professional causes and symptoms of breakdown. Living in a tied house 'over the shop' within the parish, with all the problems of having a public office and meeting space within the private vicarage, gives rise to clerical perception that a work–*home* emphasis is more meaningful. Clergy behaviour is physically and emotionally restricted by the rules of their calling. Clergy seem to be simultaneously an exceptional example of 'blended' work–life integration and work–home identification or confusion.

'Issues' and secrets: same-sex relationships and the priesthood

An issue which further highlights the relational constraints under which clergy live is that of their sexual orientation. Burrell (1984) proposed that as a social construct sexuality represents a major frontier of control and resistance in organizations. In the context of the Church of England gay and lesbian relationships among priests and their partners are a source of heated debate. The official position of the Church of England on same-sex relationships remains opaque, as articulated in *Issues in Human Sexuality* a Statement by the House of Bishops (Church of England 1991) and reiterated in ensuing debates (Church of England 2003c). Unsurprisingly the Church of England policy has been challenged: Jeffrey John's *Permanent, Faithful, Stable* (1993), Michael Vasey's *Strangers and Friends* (1995) and *Voices on Homosexuality* (Bradshaw 1997) were particularly personal appeals that same-sex relationships could be faithful to scripture and morality and achievable in the life of the Church.

The consecration of a gay bishop in The Episcopal Church in the United States in 2003 triggered a global Anglican debate between conservative and liberal constituencies which the Windsor Report of the Lambeth Commission on Communion and subsequent 'Anglican Covenant' proposals (Anglican Communion 2004, 2011, Williams 2008) have not yet resolved. In the United Kingdom, news about Dr Jeffrey John (at the time of writing Dean of St Albans), has regularly filled the front pages of national newspapers since nine Church of England diocesan bishops wrote an open letter to the *Church Times* complaining about John's nomination as a suffragan bishop. Their concerns were that Dr John had been openly in a same-sex relationship for 20 years and held views departing from a heterosexual understanding of Christian marriage. Under pressure Canon Jeffrey John withdrew from this nomination. Conservative Anglicans were appeased, members of the gay Christian community angered, liberals disappointed and the general public bemused. At the General Synod meeting at York in July 2003 members of the Lesbian and Gay Christian Movement invaded the platform and disrupted business. They accused Church leaders of homophobia, 'not listening' and avoiding dialogue (Paflin 2003: 16).

As Hearn (1989) suggests, organizational attempts to regulate sexuality often serve only to complicate further the complex relationships between employees and their organizations. The lack of consensus within the Church of England about whether it does or doesn't condone same-sex relationships among clergy, whether or not gay male priests should be appointed as bishops and whether gay marriage can be celebrated are continuing sources of tension and media interest (Gledhill 2008). In 2012 Dr John was reported as threatening the Church with legal action on grounds of discrimination having been now rejected for the role of Bishop of Southwark. His situation has been mirrored in the television series 'Rev' where, during an interview for a bishopric, the Archdeacon (Robert) was pressed to disclose his life partnership with another man and was rejected on the grounds of his gay relationship.

Today, amidst a growing social and legal acceptance of gay relationships in Britain including marriage, many gay and lesbian Anglican priests are still struggling to become part of a more inclusive Church. The most obvious dilemma concerns the costly choice between the public call to be a priest and the expectation in some ministry contexts that gay and lesbian priests should hide their identity: 'keeping their sexuality concealed' (Furlong 2000:

363). Gay and lesbian priesthood certainly evoke different and sometimes vehemently held views which the Church of England finds difficult to handle. As Janet, one our research participants observed: 'The Church is still struggling with a huge issue about sexuality and gender . . . it is still completely obsessed with it'.

Gay clergy

We conclude this chapter with the stories of Jacqui and Ralph, the two priests within our sample who described themselves as gay. Neither lived alone. Ralph avowed a celibate priestly life and shared his vicarage accommodation with two lodgers. Jacqui was in a permanent relationship with another woman who lived with her at the vicarage. When planning the research we hoped to include both gay and lesbian clergy within the sample interviewed and in the event we were successful. However we neither knowingly recruited such participants, nor were intrusive lifestyle enquiries made when interviewing the nine single clergy in the sample. Without being asked directly however, two clergy – one male, one female – volunteered some interesting reflections about their sexuality. Jacqui's story and Ralph's experiences share some things in common, but with contrasting outcomes.

Jacqui spoke about her situation in some detail: 'I have got a partner and that is obviously the cornerstone of my support . . . and that is the relationship really that forms the basis of my emotional and spiritual support'. She was asked how well known her relationship was:

> I think it depends what you mean by 'known' really. The parish knows that we live together. We do everything together, we are on holiday together. When I am invited out to somebody's house for a meal my partner is invited as well. We are treated as a couple but how many people have actually drawn that particular conclusion I really wouldn't know. Some of the younger ones have I think but the older ones? There are a couple in the congregation who are very highly significant friends – they don't live together but they do everything together – they are not partners so I suspect a lot of people see it in a similar kind of mutually supportive very close friendship way. My Archdeacon knows and is very supportive [but] I don't know who else knows.

However Jacqui believes that her diocesan bishop doesn't have full information about her personal situation and that this may create 'issues about where I go next' possibly affecting her chances of preferment to a senior role or another appointment. Jacqui fears that 'people inevitably ask questions' and she wants to be honest rather than secretive: 'there are issues for me about how much I say, how I present it, how I respond if questions are asked'. She decided to talk to another bishop about a post that she was considering: 'I don't know whether he knew but I knew that he would be sympathetic and I talked to him and he said, "well, you have just got to tell the bishop you can't take on a job like that with the bishop not knowing." And there is a huge vulnerability about that and I suppose in a way it is always there and I suppose as I have taken on more responsibility and paths are opening up and those kinds of questions are probably more likely and it is quite hard to know how to handle that'. Meantime Jacqui feels 'very supported and very safe here and I think even if it came out, the parish, because they know me so well, would be very supportive but of course that is not the case, you have not got those brownie points stacked up, have you, when you go to a new parish? I don't know . . . we will have to see'. Jacqui's partner participates in church life 'fully and whichever church I am at she comes with me so there is no kind of deception or hiding anything'. Jacqui is anxious for her future: 'absolutely yes, I mean it may well skew things. It could blow the whole thing up you know'. However she is not involved in support networks of gay or gay Christian people, preferring to keep her personal relationship a private matter rather than a cause.

During the course of this research Civil Partnerships became available to same-sex couples in the United Kingdom and some Church of England clergy have entered into such arrangements. The issue for the Church and its clergy is squaring sexuality with a secular marriage alternative and the concept of celibacy. The Dean of St Alban's, Jeffrey John has articulated the arguments for permanent, faithful and stable Christian same-sex partnerships (John 1993) and subsequently entered into a Civil Partnership himself. In this research, neither of the clergy who told us that they were gay spoke of taking up Civil Partnerships now or in the near future. Gatrell and Swan (2008: 80–1) reiterate that coming out in the public or employment context is not a single event but a process of personal decision making and negotiation within relational networks and organizations. Jacqui's situation illustrates how entering a Civil Partnership would compound the issue of her sexuality for her employer, the bishop, hence her caution in order to preserve her relationships with both the bishop and her partner. Because of the continuing opacity and uncertainty from diocese to diocese for priests like Jacqui the dilemma is balancing intimate security with a successful career in a Church that does not yet openly accept gay clergy.

Ralph came to the view early in ministry that he would be sacrificing his sexuality for his vocation to the priesthood. The topic of Ralph's sexuality arose in discussion about his early vocational crossroads when he left academia behind and chose priesthood in the Church of England: 'Oh yes I think yes I have sacrificed but . . . it is a very willing sacrifice I think . . . well I am a gay and I suspect I would have had a partner if I hadn't been ordained because it is very difficult in the Church of England currently'. Ralph is sad and resigned to the political situation he finds himself in within the life of the diocese: 'it is not easy in this diocese you know and I am very fond of the bishop but he has got very clear views on the subject and I think that does make it more difficult you know'.

Ralph admits that looking back he might have welcomed a stable same-sex relationship: 'I suspect, but I don't know, I may not have done, one just doesn't know in life. You don't know . . . if I had been in a different sort of environment'. He believes however that his priesthood takes precedence over a potential gay relationship: 'you can't do what we do and form relationships with people who don't at least have sympathy with what you do . . . I mean it in a sense it the vocation that is the priority'. Ralph admitted that his was a hard personal sacrifice but that he had come to appreciate what he had rather than what he didn't get: 'I learnt to value friends and until recently I had two friends who have lived with me since their early 20s. They sort of came separately to me at times of difficulty and needing a roof and basically stayed . . . it is like having a family really, just a different sort of family'. Ralph admitted that at a personal, emotional level he occasionally wished that he could leave the ordained ministry and go off and be an academic and do what he liked with his personal life, laying the priesthood to one side. However, 'I think the problem I have is that I am here because I think this is where God wants me to be . . . and to me that is what any vocation is about really'. Ralph drew a distinction between the public/private lives of others where being gay 'is actually about who you are and there is a sense in which . . . it is part of who you are but you can have a private life' totally divorced from a professional career and the situation of the clergy where 'you can't if you are a priest because it is actually about a calling to a way of life'. Ralph appears to believe that for him a transparent celibate priesthood is preferable to a secret gay relationship and is more enduring and authentic for who he is and who God wishes him to be.

The accounts by Jacqui and Ralph resonate with the finding of Fletcher (1990) that despite good levels of job satisfaction, gay and lesbian clergy may experience greater anxiety, depression and physical manifestations of stress than their heterosexual colleagues. Whether or not gay and lesbian clergy were sexually active or lived with a same-sex partner, 'the work demands placed on the clergy due to their sexuality were perceived as very significant' (Fletcher 1990: 87). Contributing factors included anxieties about the Church's teaching on sexuality and secrecy from the bishop, media exposure and parish hostility, and the emotional energy required to maintain public and private personae. As Lee and Horsman concluded, 'the stress of secrecy can take a serious toll' (2002: 101).

The erosion of intimacy

The Welsh Anglican priest-poet R S Thomas whose poem 'The Priest' opened our book experienced the erosion of intimacy inherent in the ordained life. In another poem, 'The Word' he gave the topic a broader theological rationale. The Christian quest for intimacy with God serves to highlight the loneliness of the human condition. For parish clergy, ordination brings with it a paradox: access to a wealth of other people's life stories combined with a personal loneliness caused by the professional contamination of the private sphere.

The personal relationships experienced and related by the Church of England clergy indicate that combining ministry with a personal life and relationships leave clergy between a rock and a hard place. Priesthood imprints on all personal relationships a vocational commitment to the ordained life which can limit intimacies. The transformation of intimacy in late modernity continues to challenge the Church and its clergy. Just as the vicarage 'tied' house limits the bodies of clergy, 'marriage to the ministry' (signifying the private sphere being tied closely to the working world) shapes the character of their marriages, intimate relationships and family lives. The panoptical surveillance of clergy bodies by parishioners, the Church and God extends into the bedroom and intimate lives. There is nowhere to hide.

THE WORD

A pen appeared, and the god said:
'write what it is to be
man.' And my hand hovered
long over the page,

until there, like footprints
of the lost traveller, letters
took shape on the page's
blankness, and I spelled out

the word 'lonely'. And my hand moved
to erase it; but the voices
of all those waiting at life's
window cried out loud: 'It is true.'

R S Thomas *Laboratories of the Spirit* (1975)

6

Clergy Authenticity

*I sometimes feel like my outside and my insides
don't match very well.*

PAULINE

For clergy, aspiring to honesty about who they are, what they believe and how they are working is a daily challenge: it is difficult to sustain being a faithful priest for long by pretence. Our research shows how congruency between inner belief and the outer person; private thoughts and public behaviour, is both embodied and eroded in clergy lives. Paradoxically it presents in its absence when clergy, for example Pauline, report a lack of congruent meaning between her inner life and outward appearance. In interview Pauline talked of feeling intellectually understretched in her daily ministry, out of sorts with the leadership of the Church of England and personally very lonely. Pauline seemed not at peace with her personal and professional selves. Like Pauline, Bishop Penny Jamieson in New Zealand experienced the tension between her interior life and the demands of the job: 'for without that fundamental harmony my spirit would have died and I would have very little to offer; I simply could not believe that it was the will of God who had called me' (Jamieson 1997: 2). As Webster (2002) and Paveley (2008) have observed, when things go awry in ministry it is frequently because the different elements within clergy lives have ceased to be congruent.

We suggest that authenticity is a convergent explanation for enduring clergy vocational commitment. Examining the character of personal authenticity among the clergy research participants as evidenced in the data we discern the ways in which Church of England clergy are encouraged to cultivate professional integrity and virtuous behaviour. In a passage redolent of the Church's *Ordination Services*, Rose proposed that an 'ethic of authenticity' is required in the formation of a secure personal identity and a well governed soul in the face of potential hypocrisy (Rose 1999: 267). Priestly authenticity is perhaps what characterizes the sacrificially embodied clergy of the Church of England, underpinned by the historic theology and tradition of the Church. Parish clergy are strengthened by the principle that embodied presence and constant sacrifice is desirable, even essential for ministry.

An authentic identity

Our concluding chapter summarizes the emerging themes from a particularly productive interview question: 'when do you feel most priestly?' It also examines whether Area/Rural Deans are a sample where exemplary clerical performance is more likely than in the general clergy population. Warren (2002: 95) states that 'the question of what it means to be a priest is pivotal' for clergy wellbeing. The findings of this research confirm that it is the clergy's self-understanding of their priesthood which defines their role, gives them their identity and affects their relationships within the home, congregation and wider community. Bernauer and Mahon (2003: 169) argue that clergy authenticity is grounded in a 'salvation ontology' and from the clergy data described in the preceding chapters their view of who they are within the panopticon of God's estimation and in the eyes of their people influences their sense of purposefulness. In the previous chapter Ralph for example expressed his view that a transparent celibate priesthood is preferable to a secret gay relationship and is more enduring and authentic for who he is and who God wishes him to be.

One of the overarching findings in this research is the way in which the clergy emerge from their ordained captivity and its consequent disciplined bodies and governed souls with a personal identity and a sense of vocational integrity. Rose (1999) argues that such authenticity is possible when the mismatch between public conduct and private secrets is overcome in an exercise of self-evaluation. The vocational choice of the priesthood is a particular example of the 'personal assembly of religious allegiances' described by Rose (1999: 272). The ordained life may be a mixed blessing but in order to demonstrate personal integrity and social plausibility it has to be 'first choice' for each individual Church of England clergy person. However, personal authenticity – public and private – can be a struggle. It is what Jung called a 'healthy desire for selfhood ... the possibility of an integration ... [a] reward in an undivided self' (Jung 1974: 197). Personal congruence may be the inner ideal but there is an earthly wrestling in most clergy in this research. Clergy may conceal their anxieties through performance or feigning obedience but they believe that the God of the panoptic Ordinal searches into their hearts.

The Church is aware of clergy struggles to be authentic. As we noted in Chapter 4, clergy professionalism is based not only on a code of practice but also on the shared ethics of corporate character and integrity. We suggest that the clergy of the Established Church in the 21st century remain a particular kind of 'moral community' as proposed by Gill (1992, 1997), attempting to lead 'exemplary' professional lives (Greenwood 2009: 50) within an increasingly marginalized institution. Church of England clergy are encouraged by their leaders to deliberately cultivate Christian character and virtues, not leaving them to chance and to develop those 'habits of the heart' derived from the Ordination Service (Bridger 2003). Ordination to the priesthood is not only a single ceremony (deeply significant as we have demonstrated) but also the start of a life-long process, that of 'becoming priest' and an authentic integrated person. What the clergy say about embodying priesthood illustrates the quest for authenticity as a convergent explanation for clergy vocational commitment. During the interviews each participant was invited to describe 'when they felt most authentic, most priestly' and the responses provided some rich data about what clergy believe and experience as lying at the heart of the matter of their ordination and their clergy lives.

If, as observed in an industrial setting by Watson (2001: 66), individuals have a tendency to 'maintain a certain level of self-esteem' and internal integrity by emphasizing positive aspects of their otherwise unhappy situations and by projecting the blame on others for the negative experiences, care is needed in evaluating what clergy say about personal authenticity. We invited respondents to say when they felt happiest and most congruent as priests, hoping that clergy, steeped in a culture of confessional honesty would seek to be truthful. Indeed we wanted to uncover their ideal signifiers precisely because these anchor priests in an enduring vocational commitment, and conversely their absence is corrosive of clergy authenticity.

Most priestly? The heart of the matter

Virtually all the clergy interviewed seemed to grasp the question quickly and to have things to say about when they felt most priestly, most happy, most themselves. For many it was as though we had posed a question they had always wanted to answer but had never been asked. For others it set off an unfolding, thoughtful line of conversation. The findings reflected several dimensions of the embodied priest as a holy, representative person and as a multifunctional religious professional. In addition some interviewees offered reflections on the nature of their vocational endurance over the years.

Minister of Word and Sacrament

Unsurprisingly most respondents talked about presiding over public worship. Reviewing English parish clergy over the centuries Hinton argues that 'whatever else a parson does or refrains from doing, it is unthinkable that he [*sic*] should not lead public worship. It is his [*sic*] most characteristic activity'. (Hinton 1994: 223) Jonathan confirmed this:

> There is a sense of totality that you have to be authentic in all expressions of your priestly calling and that is being with folk and also, you know, presiding or leading worship. I think you have got to lead worship in an authentic way that people can be at peace with, at home with, you know, comfortable with as well as it being challenging too.

Adam enjoyed shaping and sharing in teaching and the Eucharist and 'walking home from a service that has gone really well'. Alistair was typical of a number of clergy in saying that he was most himself presiding at the Eucharist. The Eucharist, recalling the incarnational ministry of Christ and the Last Supper is a central Christian sacrament where the transcendent and the communal dimensions of priestly embodiment intersect, providing affirmation and authentic meaning. Other sacramental rites of passage such as Baptism and the care of the dying provide a similar focus. Imagining herself as most priestly Jacqui pictured herself

> at the altar presiding but also ... when I have been called to be with people who are dying. I pray with them and anoint them but it is the sacramental stuff I think really. Those kinds of moments when I suppose heaven and earth meet in a very profound and present way.

Penny spoke of the godly simplicity of 'taking Holy Communion to people' to the sick and housebound in the parish.

For some clergy the teaching ministry was more to the fore. Mark felt most priestly

> 'When I am preaching ... trying to share a conversation which is about this world and God.' Benjamin spoke of 'Small group work and training sessions and nurture courses ... the magic that happens because you are not expecting it but it comes out of the dynamic and conversations with the people.'

Roger took encouragement from 'seeing God working' through worship and teaching. Kevin took a holistic approach to the opportunities of the daily round of a pastoral parish ministry:

> Well, I think I feel if I have communicated something of the gospel to someone of whatever age, particularly the ministry that makes me feel like I am doing what I am supposed to be doing, called to do. Things for example like work with children, taking school assembly or perhaps ministering to a bereaved family or preaching in a way that you feel you are actually communicating and that people are understanding what you

are saying. These kind of daily things I think really if you like are what gives me the buzz and that make me sense that I am being the priest, the vicar in the most effective way really.

The power of forgiveness was a different perspective brought up by Linda for whom ordination represented an empowering and self-authenticating journey from a Christian background in which women were subordinate:

> Being a priest was an important part for me of completion, of bringing somebody to a point where I could offer them forgiveness ... as a spokesperson on behalf of God, not saying that I was God in any way ... I'm not trying to get into the female gender thing either here ... but actually recognizing that there was certain authority bestowed in what I was doing and an opportunity to bring somebody to forgiveness, to fruition and to understand fulfilment and that was important to me.

Unsurprisingly, given the force of located and regulated clergy bodies described in Chapter 3, clergy recognize the significance of their presence and visibility. Despite the negative constraints on their lives there are positives which help clergy feel at home in their parishes. There is a self-assurance revealed in some comments about priestly belonging to people and places. Sarah spoke positively 'about being a visible presence; sounds a bit Catholic for me but you know what I mean?' In conducting rites of passage Fiona recognized that clergy have 'privileged priestly access to family life over the years' giving rise to an intimacy with local people. Colin recalled how customer feedback can be particularly affirming, 'somebody said to me, "I have been to six funerals you have taken and you have not done a duff one yet"'. Derek succinctly defined his sense of public belonging in the local community: 'the pub landlord knows "your usual"'. Like other regulars this vicar has gained an acceptance in the pub as a local for local people. However none of this happens without some intentionality on the part of the priest. Jonathan related the question of authenticity to his belief in a ministry work ethic. His was probably less frenetic than the unhealthy long-hours culture typical of many clergy, but equally not a slap-dash approach: 'I mean I could do 24/7 and some clerics would do ten minutes ... there isn't necessarily a correlation between the amount of time you put in and the results you get but I think it is being authentic to me'.

Holy representative

A large number of responses focused on the public representative nature of priestly ministry in the Church of England, serving the parish community. Malcolm believes that a priest is 'a particular channel for God'. Keith, echoing the words of Archbishop Michael Ramsay (Ramsay 1972: 14), sees his priestly self 'as a man who stands before God with the people on his heart; I can't do better than that frankly'. Keith also spoke of the priest as an intercessor and bridge-builder, 'that's really where I am as a priest. For me the recitation of the Daily Office is a public duty … on behalf of the parish. It's not a private act of devotion; it's something I do for the people'. Tony and Patricia concurred: 'The work of the priest is the prayer … the work of prayer that you do with the people … saying words for the people'. Some clergy focused on their function amidst competing community needs. Liz, Julian and Beryl each spoke of 'building community and making a difference' … 'bridge-building, caring for people in the margins' … 'that sense of being a gatherer, builder of community'. Beryl, who worked in health care prior to ordination, developed the theme further, picturing herself as a midwife of community:

> So they tend to think you can fix anything. I think I would see myself too as … a sort of midwife, which is fully related to the fixer – enabling things to happen, to sort things out right. But it feels sometimes a bit like helping things into to birth but you can't do it yourself and you have to be alongside … just being with somebody … where something has to happen, or a group, or a deanery, or being a mum … but often not the one who can actually do the work.

Geoffrey, who pursued an interest in native North American culture and spirituality, made a remarkable connection between the Anglican parish priest and the shaman of traditional religions:

> I would say that I continue to be involved as the priest of the community because the Church of England is one of the few organizations in England that actually provides that genuine opportunity to be, if you like, the shaman of the community. To be the person who goes on the spiritual journeys and comes back with the spiritual wisdom that will be for the guidance and strengthening of the community. It is the only job that is available and although it has defects and limitations, although there are people within the communities who don't want to move, where the whole movement and change of community is so immensely slow – nevertheless it is the only job on the go that works and I think that does work for me and that is at the core of my motivation is to be the priest of the community.

Geoffrey felt most authentic and priestly as the shaman and to illustrate the point he described the recent funeral of a suicide, a large and difficult event in his parish in which he believed his role was to articulate community feelings and meanings in a pastoral theological way that resonated with people. He understood the importance of 'authentic spiritual leadership' (Dorr 2006: 7).

Clergy in this research clearly believe that they offer something beyond the generalist clerical professionalism noted by Russell (1980). Malcolm said: 'I'm not a social worker, I'm not this, and I'm not that and I'm not the other. I'm a priest ... parish priest or whatever. I have a particular role, in a particular ministry, which I don't have to re-define in terms of these other professional roles'. Matthew agreed that 'we bring something else' other than the technologies of the care professions. Neil wondered whether 'the freelance possibilities in a Church culture that has collapsed may be very fruitful and we will discover what priests are actually for'. John simply described the location of his authentic priestly self as, 'where I am working for the kingdom'.

Priest and person: the congruent me?

There are very few callings in the modern world which 'require the same degree of identification of the person with the job' (Church of Ireland Marriage Council 2008). However the clergy experience that all of life is affected by ordination does not automatically determine how priest and person are fused in a congruent whole. We discern a present-active concept of 'becoming priest', an ordained counterpoint to the 'emergent manager' of Watson and Harris (1999: 237) and recognize the continuous struggle for integrity in ministerial role and out of it. So for example Beryl believed that authentic priesthood cannot as it were be switched on and off: 'it's also about who you are and not what you do, and we all know that. What does that make of you as a priest when you're off duty?'

Robert provided a full and interesting explanation of how he managed his sense of self and priestly role as a single identity: 'I grew up in a time when clergy were clergy and were different to everybody else and from the very outset I decided that I was me first and a priest second. And I've always operated on that basis. Priest happens to be what I am and do ... I'm not going to be a different me as a priest to the me that I am normally, as far as I am able to do that'. However Robert realized that the wider public project ideals and identities onto clergy: 'Because obviously you have roles and people do have expectations and you do have certain public persona that you have to fulfil'. Robert believes that when he robes for church services he remains the same person: 'I wouldn't take a service dressed in my jeans and a jumper. I'll wear the gear that says I'm the priest up there. But I'm not going to be a different person as a priest'. However he admits that it is not always natural or straightforward: 'It's a difficult one to manage but I reckon basically you can do it. I don't find that split personality too much'. Robert also alluded to the vulnerability of the priest-person and trying to present a congruent identity for parishioners:

> you've got to be in some sense vulnerable because it's the you that people see, and it might not be sometimes what you want them to see, or it may

not be what they want to see; but you have to work away at that ...
the way in which you conduct meetings, the way in which you conduct
services ... and be as natural and normal as you can. I think in the end
people come to see that and respond to it.

Likewise Nicholas realized that accessibility for his parishioners also extended
to friends who appreciated him both as a priest and friend: 'From time to
time one's friends suddenly do come and talk because you are a priest as well
and I like that sort of thing because that is how it should be ... I think you
are a priest when you are seen ... and love and care for your parishioners as
well as doing the more obvious priestly things'.

However other research participants admitted the uncomfortable struggle
to achieve a congruent self, typically describing how their dramaturgical
presentation (Goffman 1959) in public ministry was complemented by a
private, backstage person. Matthew described how outwardly, 'What you see
is what you get. There is a kind of ease by which you put on a professional
persona'. However he added, 'I think mine, I suspect publicly that people
don't see anything like the level of impatience and frustration that I have'
and it was crucial not to give the game away: 'I think there are ... dangers if
you have too much of a split personality'.

Several clergy reflected theologically that congruence was particularly
characterized as God took control of who they were. Daniel celebrating the
sacraments in his multicultural city church described his deep feelings of
self-abandonment to greater forces, akin to Foucault's characterization of
the elegant docile body (Foucault 1977: 136–7). Following Goffman (1959)
Daniel delivers a public dramaturgical performance although inwardly he
feels rather overwhelmed:

> I am not explaining this very well ... when I am at the high altar even,
> I feel sometimes alienated you know I feel I am in a position where I
> cannot wholly say I am in control and yet the conditions want to be in
> control so that ... you get your show. But each time I say to a new priest
> I really struggle to be who I am because I am representing something
> bigger than I am.

Somewhat fatalistically Kenneth seemed prepared to sacrifice himself for
the sake of the greater demands of ordination: 'Does it matter who the real
me is ... as long as I am trying to fulfil the sacrifice?' Linda found the sense
of vocational separation unnerving, as though God had captured her in
ordination, enclosing her in a permanent new way of life: 'My priesthood it
isn't a job, it's just that, it's something to do with who I am now. And that's
quite daunting ... it does feel as if it's blocked me from other things ... it just
feels as if it is somehow an enclosure – in a positive sense I think'. Linda's
reference to 'enclosure' made connections with the Foucauldian and self-
sacrificial aspects of the ordained life explored in previous chapters.

Still called after all these years

Given that few clergy permanently quit ministry it was interesting to hear the research participants' accounts of how and why they endured in their vocational commitment over the years. Jonathan declared, 'No I am not a quitter' and felt a conviction about his original vocation which countered any notions of giving up the priesthood:

> I think it is being authentic to what you believe God has called you … I suppose it is about conviction … yes, you could give up but I would be unhappy giving up. I mean before I became ordained I was always thinking, 'what should I do?' I taught – drifted into this and that – feeling, you know, moderately fulfilled … what I actually wanted was to be ordained … I have always felt wonderful about it.

Beryl like a number of interviewees said that she never questioned her calling and Mark agreed, speaking almost of an original innocence, still intact: 'Who the real me is comes back to ordination, the call I think … there is kind of something about that kind of foundational naivety which is that stuff that keeps me going really'. Roger claimed that he 'Got ordained because it was the only way that I could get God off my back' while Nicholas reflected, 'just after I had finished university I thought … maybe that is what I would do but I don't regret … I can't imagine not being a priest now and that is because I feel … on the whole I am happy with the way things have turned out'.

Various positive things keep clergy enthusiastic amidst the challenges of ordained ministry. For Jonathan it was, 'The variety, the thought that you might be making a difference … the belief that I am actually engaging with crucial issues and have the freedom to do that. I can engage with folk in different walks of life about key issues'. Sarah, struggling to find personal happiness and ministry fulfilment in an unresponsive community, knows deep down why she perseveres even on her bad days: 'It has made me think well, why am I still here? And I think on my bad days it's because I don't think I can do anything else now. On my good days I still feel a sense of call and vision … and I see how far I've grown and I think well, actually I do have skills, I do have something to offer … actually we do have a sense of where we're going and it's hard to articulate but it is that sense of call'. Despite disappointments and tiredness, the majority of clergy in this research like Penny and Irene talk of 'keeping going in a life of service' – driven like Jonathan to overcome the frustrations:

> I think the challenge is finding the right voice or the right words to express that now and that to my mind is a wonderful challenge and that is something that drives me on so I don't feel I have ever felt like quitting. I mean, I have felt frustrated and occasionally beleaguered and over-burdened and frustrated and sometimes angry, you know, that things

don't work however much you try … it doesn't amount to a great deal or nothing appears to be happening because of the endless effort you might put in.

Carole finds it helpful to regularly recall where it all began: 'I always make a point of going to the Chrism Mass held on Maundy Thursday in the Cathedral at which we renew our Ordination vows. Now that to me is the most important service in the whole year'. Unlike some clergy who remain in parishes with diminishing enthusiasm, marking time to their retirement, Robert moved parish to face one final ministry challenge as a full-time stipendiary priest for a few years prior to his retirement and found the move energizing:

> I mean I still do it because I still feel called to do it. And that's always been there in me, that sense of call. But I do it first and foremost because I still feel called to do it. And I do it because I get tremendous fulfilment, satisfaction, enjoyment out of it. Not every day of course, it has its problems. Sometimes you wish you were anywhere but there. But by and large I wouldn't change it. I will stop doing it when I get to retirement age, there are a lot of reasons I'll stop doing it, but at the moment I still feel called to do it. I feel fulfilled, I feel challenge. That's the other big thing for me … if there's a challenge there and that was part of the point of moving and I feel challenged … and challenge reinvigorates me.

Behind these contributions lies a sense of ordination itself and daily ministry fuelling the courage to continue. An Anglican clergyman suggests that 'the only certain way a priest can deal with affliction is to remain convinced of the significance of his [sic] work' (Hinton 1994: 343). The progressive Roman Catholic theologian Hans Kung argued in *Why Priests?* that ordination gives the assurance that the priest 'is truly called and designated as the leader of the community … it can give him [sic] the confidence to match his vocation, the courage constantly to tackle the task anew, the trust that, despite all difficulties, doubts and temptations, enables him [sic] to persevere to the end' (Kung 1972: 70).

On the wall of Ralph's study hung a theological college graduation photograph of 30 or so male ordinands and staff typical of the period, the 1970s. In an ethnographical moment, pointing to the photo, the question arose, how many of Ralph's contemporaries had actually 'gone off the rails' or left the Church over the years? Ralph pondered carefully each figure in the portrait:

> One committed suicide. One had a spell outside ordained ministry but now functions as a non-stipendiary, he ended up in teaching. One had a spell of ill health but how far that was physical and how far it was psychosomatic I don't know, he ended up in the Roman Catholic Church.

Let's just look ... one took early retirement on health grounds ... apart from that ... he died tragically young. Apart from that we are all in stipendiary ministry.

Given the research indications that on average maybe 6 per cent of annual cohorts of Church of England clergy left ministry in the years 1970–2000 (Barley 2009), his dozen or so contemporaries were an enduring vintage.

Where are they now?

Indeed as far as we can tell from a limited telephone follow-up call 2 years on the vast majority of our 46 research participants appear settled. Some 80 per cent remain in the same diocese, frequently with expanding deanery, training or specialist roles. Four clergy (including one woman) gained senior promotion as archdeacons (three in their present diocese), one became a Residential Cathedral Canon, while half a dozen (mostly women) were made Honorary Canons. Two priests retired early on health grounds.

Some original interviews had indicated household tensions and we employed critical listening to discover whether these had deteriorated or had been resolved. However, no separations, divorces or major family disasters were disclosed, although spouses' employment, children's schooling and finance remained concerns for some clergy. Four interviewees within the six two-clergy couples in the sample were making changes to their ministry combinations and hours, juggling parish and specialist posts. The two who were most stable were married to female hospital chaplains, one vicar saying that his wife's full-time hospital role would determine his next ministry move.

The four clergy who moved diocese indicated that they did so in order to improve their careers and lifestyles. Two male clergy were looking for a final post that would stretch them in fresh ways and each had landed happily – one nearer a good location for his favourite outdoor leisure activities. Another expressed hopes that the move would help his wife develop her own career. The woman, single, who moved did so in pursuit of an infrequently available full-time diocesan specialist role. A degree of professional and personal loneliness had pervaded her interview and the new post conveniently brought her nearer family and friends.

As in the original interviews, additional telephone comments expressed anger and thankfulness in equal measure about 'the state of the Church of England' and their bishop's leadership and management style in the diocese. One interviewee was delighted to be asked by his bishop to consider a new post, while another was quite bitter and disparaging about the regime he had gladly left behind. Several clergy whose original interviews revealed ambition for preferment remained unrewarded and were continuing hopefully in the same post. Two traditionalist catholic clergy expressed distress about the General Synod debates on women bishops and were wondering about their future in the Church of England.

Dramatically one of the Area/Rural Deans in our sample subsequently abandoned his parish and wife for an adulterous affair with his female and married Associate Priest colleague (Gysin et al. 2008). The errant priest was prohibited under the Clergy Discipline Measure from functioning for life as a Church of England priest (his colleague was banned for 12 years). The diocese spoke of its high expectation of the clergy and the tribunal judge commented that 'the public must understand that the Church takes matters such as this extremely seriously ... those in public positions must consider those positions when making decisions in their private lives' (Ashworth 2009).

Taken as a whole these additional findings tend to confirm our analysis about the pastoral rootedness of clergy in dioceses and their attitude to ambition and career. The low diocesan turnover also confirms that clergy (particularly women) make a limited number of major career moves, more often developing their ministries where they are located. On the contested question of clergy leavers our window of research only records one participant doing so against a national average of 6 per cent suggested by Barley (2009).

Setting an example

At the outset we proposed that our clergy sample of Area/Rural Deans were key informants with a balanced perspective about priesthood. Certainly there was evidence that their additional local responsibilities heightened their aspirations to be a faithful and diligent priestly example of enduring vocational commitment to their fellow clergy. The role of Area/Rural Dean is a changing one, from purely a local spokesperson for the deanery and its clergy to a midway leader sharing in the bishop's vision and delivery of diocesan policy. In a strikingly rare reference in this research to social class Fred

> felt very often a square peg in a round hole ... the bishop said to me, 'you are the shop steward' and I said 'you call me a shop steward because I come from a working class background ... if I was more middle class you would say I had good management skills ... he just smiled.

Others also expressed mixed feelings, so for Jonathan, 'we have had some increasingly better Chapters but still modest in terms of numbers you know because I think that clergy are a cussed race who – I mean I can't be, I am Rural Dean, I am poacher turned game-keeper because I mean there were times when I didn't go to Chapter because I had too much to do and Chapter never seemed the place that was worth going to'. He tries a friendly hospitable approach though, 'what I do is, let's meet for a meal, we will all eat together, we will share issues and maybe talk a bit of theology and something like that'. However as Kenneth pointed out the number of clergy is reducing so deaneries are 'an uncomfortable place' to be modelling for the local clergy what Caroline called 'leadership with vision'. On the other hand virtually all participants valued their close working relationship with their archdeacon and the team of Area/Rural Deans in the diocese, Beryl's comment being typical: 'we've got a very good Archdeacon ... he's very accessible; I mean yesterday I needed to go and see him about a Faculty matter and phoned up ... and he said "oh that's fine come on over" and ... that makes a huge difference'. Interestingly the two key reasons why in their report on clergy stress Lee and Horsman (2002: 105) recommended that 'the role of Area/ Rural Deans should be enhanced' were precisely to provide sympathetic modelling of sustainable 21st-century priesthood and a meaningful link with the bishop's leadership.

Our participants appeared to be a stable presence in the local Church, knowledgeable, pragmatic and very hard working and confirm the loyal, 'conformist strand' first noted in a study of archdeacons (Peyton 2003: 42). The twin mandate from the bishop and their clergy peers perhaps motivates them to try and be well-organized, caring and hospitable individuals who empathize and watch over their clergy colleagues' triumphs and struggles. This may explain their keenness to talk about clergy finance more than we had expected and also their sensitivity to the very disparate personal and domestic circumstances of local clergy.

The interviewees clearly grasped the sacrificial nature of their vocation and its daily implications. In particular the major research finding that these clergy recognized a strong ontological (as opposed to functionalist) dimension in their ordination, whatever their church tradition, suggests a heightened awareness of an exemplary identity. For Irene this was a matter of personal and spiritual integrity: 'we have got to account for ourselves at the end of the day ... to make sure that we are self-disciplined ... as regards time off, prayer, balance between family and ministry – over the whole spectrum ... and to encourage self-awareness'. Area/Rural Deans gain respect for who they are as well as for what they do and thus need a relational, 'cheer-leading', consensual leadership style in order to succeed. Again, because their role could be a stepping-stone to preferment the motive for exemplary performance among the Area/Rural Deans is ever-present. Capable priests, younger or newer, and especially women clergy in the research sample knew of the career possibilities and some were quite ambitious.

Whether Area/Rural Dean households are more exemplary or atypical of the general clergy population is unclear. Our observation would be that the role heightens public/private tensions and amplifies those issues characterized as 'married to the ministry' in the previous chapter on 'Lost Intimacies'. The role and personal ambition may encourage some participants to have exemplary personal and domestic relationships but ambition fuelled by overwork and a fear of disappointment could equally undermine performance. Where Area/

Rural Deans are routinely expected to be exemplary is in their hospitality ministry, whether in meetings, meals, social events or personal accessibility. Thus they can be keen agents in modelling and promoting local trust and professional intimacy among clergy colleagues.

Belonging, believing and becoming

The theoretical debate about late 20th-century British religion has been characterized as a contest between a secularization model and a believing without belonging approach. The decline in English churchgoing predated any widespread decline in conventional Christian belief and we confirm how Church of England clergy have soldiered on, keeping the parochial system alive despite their possible professional marginalization as the generalists of last resort. Empirical research by Warren (2002), Greenwood (2009) and in our project confirms both the continuing residual Christian expectations of otherwise secularized or religiously plural communities and the key importance of the personal faith and integrity of priests themselves as the difference between enduring or quitting (Louden and Francis 2003, Greely 2004). Paradoxically while many of the laity have 'gone for good' (Francis and Richter 2007) we argue strongly here the reasons why the majority of clergy 'stay for good', affirming a priestly vocation to location and community. We conclude from our research that sacrificial marginality lies at the heart of clergy self-perceptions as they occupy 'that strange hinterland between the secular and the sacred ... acting as interpreters and mediators' (Percy 2006: 188). The Church of England could look to traditional ordination values afresh, harnessing them to contemporary clergy deployment patterns, pioneer and chaplaincy ministries.

In short, clergy as examples of 'religious bodies' (Shilling 2008: 166) endure when their 'being' that is the whole of their lives experience a convergent authenticity of Christian belief, professional belonging and personal development – *becoming* – across the years. Perhaps 'priest' is better understood as a verb rather than as a noun. Priestly embodiment is a work in progress, a process of embodying change. Watson and Harris (1999) developed the concept of the 'emergent manager' as a similar becoming over time while the Bishop of Oxford describes this congruent self in theological terms: 'When ministry is hard and people seem unresponsive ... it's a time to return to the confidence that God has called us to be here, now, and nowhere else ... and, many years on, by far the majority of clergy would still say that the best decision they could ever have made was to accept God's call to the life and work of a priest' (Pritchard 2007: 159–60). R. S. Thomas was right: 'priests have a long way to go, picking their way through the parish'. Our clergy research participants were certainly sensitive to their own vocational journey and the journeys of others and appreciated the insight that priests are not only ordained in a life-changing moment but are 'becoming priests' across a lifetime.

REFERENCES

Adair, J. and Nelson, J. (eds) (2004) *Creative Church Leadership*. Norwich, Canterbury Press.

Alvesson, M. and Deetz, S. (2000) *Doing Critical Management Research*. London, Sage.

Alvesson, M. and Willmott, H. (eds) (1992) *Critical Management Studies*. London, Sage.

Anglican Communion (1999) *The Official Report of the Lambeth Conference 1998*. Harrisburg, PA: Morehouse Publishing.

—(2004) *The Windsor Report*. The Lambeth Commission on Communion, London, The Anglican Communion Office.

—(2011) 'The Anglican Covenant: a *Church Times* Guide', 18 March.

Ashworth, P. (1999) 'O happy servants they!', *Church Times*, 3 September. www. anglicansonline.org/news/archives/churchtimes accessed 5 February 2009.

—(2009) 'Clerics removed from office', *Church Times*, 2 January, 6.

Avis, P. (2007) *The Identity of Anglicanism: Essentials of Anglican Ecclesiology*. London, T&T Clark.

Bagilhole, B. (2006) 'Not a glass ceiling more a lead roof: experiences of pioneer women priests in the Church of England', *Equal Opportunities International*, 25 (2) 109–25.

Ballard, P. (2000) 'The emergence of pastoral and practical theology in Britain', pp. 59–70 in Woodward, J. and Pattison, S. (eds), *The Blackwell Reader in Pastoral and Practical Theology* Oxford, Blackwell.

Barley, L. (2006) *Christian Roots, Contemporary Spirituality*. London, Church House Publishing.

—(2009) *Understanding Clergy Patterns of Service*. A Research Report by the Research & Statistics Department and the Ministry Division of the Church of England.

Barnes, E. (2001) 'The Episcopal Ministry Act of Synod', pp. 240–2 in Kuhrt, G. (ed.), *Ministry Issues for the Church of England*. London, Church House Publishing.

Bauman, Z. (1993) *Postmodern Ethics*. Oxford, Blackwell.

—(2003) *Liquid Love*. Cambridge, Polity.

—(2005) *Liquid Life*. Cambridge, Polity.

BBC TV (1994) *The Vicar of Dibley*, BBC 1 Series 1994–2007.

—(2010) *Rev*, BBC 2 Series One.

—(2011) *Rev*, BBC 2 Series Two.

Beavan, E. (2008) 'Curate gets death threat after hate campaign resumes', *Church Times*, 10 October, 6.

—(2011) 'Women Bishops approved', *Church Times*, 18 November, 4.

Beck, U. and Beck-Gernsheim, E. (1995) *The Normal Chaos of Love*. Cambridge, Polity.

Benedict (2003) 'St Benedict's Rule', pp. 7–100 in Ampleforth Abbey Trustees (ed.), *The Benedictine Handbook*. Norwich, Canterbury Press.

Bentley, L. (2001) 'Two-clergy couples', pp. 208–10 in Kuhrt, G. (ed.) *Ministry Issues for the Church of England*. London, Church House Publishing.

Berger, P. L. (1967) *The Sacred Canopy: Elements of a Sociological Theory of Religion* (1990 edition). New York, Anchor Books.

—(1969) *A Rumour of Angels: Modern Society and the Rediscovery of the Supernatural* (1990 edition). New York, Anchor Books.

Berger, P. and Luckmann, T. (1967) *The Social Construction of Reality: A Treatise on the Sociology of Knowledge*. New York, Anchor.

Bernauer, J. and Carrette, J. (eds) (2004) *Michel Foucault and Theology: The Politics of Religious Experience*. Aldershot, Ashgate.

Bernauer, J. and Mahon, M. (2003) 'Michel Foucault's ethical imagination', pp. 149–75 in Gutting, G. (ed.), *The Cambridge Companion to Foucault* (2nd edition). Cambridge, Cambridge University Press.

Betjeman, J. (1982) *Church Poems*. London, Pan Books.

Bolton, S. (2005) *Emotion Management in the Workplace*. Basingstoke, Palgrave Macmillan.

Bourdieu, P. (1984) *Distinction*. London, Routledge.

Bradshaw, T. (ed.) (1997) *The Way Forward? Christian Voices on Homosexuality and the Church*. London, Hodder & Stoughton.

Brannen, J. and Collard, J. (1982) *Marriages in Trouble: The Process of Seeking Help*. London, Tavistock.

Braverman, H. (1974) *Labour and Monopoly Capital: The Degradation of Work in the Twentieth Century*. New York, Monthly Review Press.

Bridger, F. (2003) 'A Theological Reflection', pp. 13–20 in *Guidelines for the Professional Conduct of the Clergy*. London, Church House Publishing.

Brierley, P. (2000) *The Tide is Running Out: What the English Church Attendance Survey Reveals*. London, Christian Research.

Broken Rites (2012) www.brokenrites.org.

Brown, C. (2001) *The Death of Christian Britain: Understanding Secularisation 1800–2000*. London, Routledge.

Bryman, A. (2004) *Social Research Methods* (2nd edition). Oxford University Press, Oxford.

Bunting, I. (1993) *Models of Ministry: Managing the Church Today*. Cambridge, Grove Books.

Burgess, N. (1995) 'Clergy Careers in the Church of England this Century', *Crucible: The Quarterly Journal of the Church of England Board for Social Responsibility*, July, 127–36.

—(1998) *Into Deep Water: The Experience of Curates in the Church of England*. Bury St. Edmunds, Kevin Mayhew.

—(2002) 'The Church of England as an employer', *Crucible, the Quarterly Journal of the Church of England Board of Social Responsibility*, January, 9–20.

—(2005) 'The strange case of the disappearing clergy: dropping out of full-time paid ministry in the Church of England', *Crucible: The Quarterly Journal of the Church of England Board of Social Responsibility*, January, 21–30.

Burrell, G. (1984) 'Sex and organizational analysis', *Organization Studies*, 5: 2.

—(1988) 'Modernism, post modernism and organizational analysis 2: the contribution of Michel Foucault', *Organizational Studies*, 9 (2) 221–35.

Burton, J. and Burton, S. (2009) *Public People, Private Lives: Tackling Stress in Clergy Families*. London, Continuum.

Butler, J. (1990) *Gender Trouble: Feminism and the Subversion of Identity*. London, Routledge.

Cameron, D. (2009) 'Family values the key to responsible society', www.telegraph.co.uk/news./politics accessed 10 March 2012.

Campbell, A. V. (1981) *Rediscovering Pastoral Care*. London, Darton, Longman and Todd.

CARIS (1996) *Knocking at Heaven's Door: Challenges and Opportunities Presented by the Casual Caller in the Parish*. London, Church Action & Response in Society.

Carrette, J. (ed.) (1999) *Religion and Culture by Michel Foucault*. Manchester, University Press.

—(2000) *Foucault and Religion: Spiritual Corporality and Political Spirituality*. London, Routledge.

—(2004) 'Beyond theology and sexuality: Foucault, the self and the que(e)rying of monotheistic truth', pp. 217–32 in Bernauer, J. and Carrette, J. (eds), *Michel Foucault and Theology: The Politics of Religious Experience*. Aldershot, Ashgate.

Cassell, J. (1998) *The Woman in the Surgeon's Body*. Cambridge, Massachusetts, Harvard University Press.

Caulkin, S. (2005) 'When the devil is in the details', *Observer*, 20 February, 11.

Changing Attitude (2012) www.changingattitude.org.

Channel Four TV (2005) 'Priest idol', 28 November.

—(2006) 'Gay vicars', 30 January.

Chapman, M. (ed.) (2010) *The Hope of Things to Come: Anglicanism and the Future*. London, Mowbray.

Chesshyre, R. (2005) 'Faith under fire', *Daily Telegraph Magazine*, 24 December.

Christou, S. (2003) *The Priest & The People of God*. Cambridge, Phoenix Books.

Church of England (1964) *The Deployment and Payment of the Clergy*. A Report by Leslie Paul for the Central Advisory Council for the Ministry, London, Church Information Office.

—(1983) *A Strategy for the Church's Ministry*. A Report by John Tiller for the Advisory Council for the Church's Ministry, London, Church Information Office.

—(1985) *All Are Called: Towards a Theology of the Laity*. London, Church Information Office.

—(1990) *Episcopal Ministry*. Report of the Archbishops' Group on the Episcopate, London, Church House Publishing.

—(1991) *Issues in Human Sexuality*. A statement by the House of Bishops of the General Synod of the Church of England, London, Church House Publishing.

—(1993) *Episcopal Ministry Act of Synod 1993*. London, Church House Publishing.

—(1995a) *Partners in Marriage and Ministry*. Advisory Board of Ministry Paper 11, London.

—(1995b) *Something to Celebrate: Valuing Families in Church and Society*. Report of a Working Party of the Board of Social Responsibility, London, Church House Publishing.

—(1998) *Parsonages: A Design Guide* (6th edition). London, Church Commissioners.

—(2000a) *Called to Lead: A Challenge to Include Minority Ethnic People*. London, Church House Publishing.

—(2000b) *The Canons of the Church of England* (6th edition). London, Church House Publishing.

—(2001a) *Generosity and Sacrifice*. The Report of the Clergy Stipends Review Group, London, Church House Publishing.

—(2001b) *For Such a Time as This: A Renewed Diaconate in the Church of England*. A Report of a Working Party of the House of Bishops, London, Church House Publishing.

—(2001c) *Resourcing Bishops*. The First Report of the Archbishops' Review Group on Bishops' Needs and Resources, London, Church House Publishing.

—(2003a) *Clergy Discipline Measure 2003*. London, Church House Publishing.

—(2003b) *Guidelines for the Professional Conduct of the Clergy*. London, Church House Publishing.

—(2003c) *Some Issues in Human Sexuality: A Guide to the Debate*. A discussion document from the House of Bishops Group on *Issues in Human Sexuality*. London, Church House Publishing.

—(2004a) *Review of Clergy Terms of Service*. London, Church House Publishing.

—(2004b) *Mission Shaped Church*. London, Church House Publishing.

—(2004c) *Protecting all God's Children*. The Child Protection Policy for the Church of England (3rd edition). London, Church House Publishing.

—(2005a) *Clergy Ill Health*. Deployment, Remuneration and Conditions of Service Committee of the Ministry Division of the Church of England.

—(2005b) *Review of Clergy Terms of Service Part 2*. London, Church House Publishing.

—(2006a) *Clergy Pensions – The Challenge Facing the Future*. London, Church House Publishing.

—(2006b) *Clergy Discipline Measure 2003: Code of Practice*. London, Church House Publishing.

—(2006c) *Church of England Clergy Diversity Audit 2005*. London, Church House Publishing.

—(2007a) *Common Worship: Ordination Services*. London, Church House Publishing.

—(2007b) *Quantity and Quality in Ministry*. Internal Survey for the House of Bishops, December.

—(2007c) *The Church of England Yearbook 2008*. London, Church House Publishing.

—(2007d) *Talent and Calling: A Review of the Law and Practice Regarding Appointments to the Offices of Suffragan Bishop, Dean, Archdeacon and Residentiary Canon*. London, Church House Publishing.

—(2007e) *Present and Participating: A Place at the Table*. A Report from the Committee for Minority Ethnic Anglican Concerns, London, Church House Publishing.

—(2007f) 'Present and Participating' *Report of Proceedings 2007: General Synod July Group of Sessions*, 38 (2) 228–49, London, Church House Publishing.

—(2007g) *Disabled Clergy in the Church of England*. A Report from the Committee for Deaf and Disabled People, London, Church House Publishing.

—(2007h) *Summary Report on the Housing for Clergy in Retirement Survey for the Archbishops' Council.* Ministry Division.

—(2008a) *Stipends, Process and Policy.* Deployment, Remuneration and Conditions of Service Committee of the Ministry Division of the Church of England.

—(2008b) *The 35th Report of the Central Stipends Authority 2007.* London, Church House Publishing.

—(2008c) *Ministerial Development Review: Interim Guidance.* London, Church House Publishing.

—(2008d) *Retirement Housing Review for the Archbishops' Council.* Ministry Division.

—(2010a) *Report of the Pension Ill-health Benefits Review.* Deployment, Remuneration and Conditions of Service Committee of the Ministry Division of the Church of England.

—(2010b) *The 37th Report of the Central Stipends Authority 2009.* London, Church House Publishing.

—(2011a) *Ministry in the Church of England* www.churchofengland.org/clergy-office-holders/vocation.

—(2011b) *The 39th Report of the Central Stipends Authority 2011.* London, Church House Publishing.

—(2012) *Church Statistics,* www.churchofengland.org/about us/ facts-stats/research-statistics.

Church of Ireland (2008) *A Digest of the Results of the Clergy and Clergy Spouse Questionnaire of April 2007.* Dublin, Church of Ireland Marriage Council.

Church Times (2008) 'Criticising the clergy? It's not all bad', *Editorial*, 6 June, 12.

Churches' Commission for Racial Justice (2003) *Redeeming the Time: All God's People must Challenge Racism.* London, Churches Together in Britain and Ireland.

Clergy Appointments Advisor (2012) www.churchofengland.org/clergy-office-holders/clergy-appointments-adviser.

Clergy Husbands (2008) www.cucumbersandwiches.org.

Cocksworth, C. and Brown, R. (2006) *Being A Priest Today: Exploring Priestly Identity* (2nd edition). Norwich, Canterbury Press.

Coffey, A. (1999) *The Ethnographic Self: Fieldwork and the Representation of Identity.* London, Sage.

Collinson, D. (1992) *Managing the Shop Floor: Subjectivity, Masculinity and Workplace Culture.* Berlin, Walter de Gruyter.

—(2003) 'Identities and insecurities: selves at work', *Organization*, 10 (3) 527–47.

Collinson, D. and Collinson, M. (1989) 'Sexuality in the Workplace: The Domination of Men's Sexuality', in Hearn, J. et al. (eds), *The Sexuality of Organization.* London Sage.

—(1997) 'Delayering Managers: Time-Space Surveillance and its Gendered Effects', *Organization*, 4 (3) 375–407.

Colquhoun, F. (ed.) (1967) *Parish Prayers.* London, Hodder and Stoughton.

CPAS (2012) *Arrow: Growing Leaders.* Church Pastoral Aid Society, Coventry.

Cranwell, B. (2008) 'Head off stress by getting feedback', *Church Times*, 13 June, 11.

Crockford (2007) *Crockford's Clerical Directory 2008/2009.* London, Church House Publishing.

Croft, S. (1999) *Ministry in Three Dimensions*. London, Darton, Longman and Todd.

—(2005) 'A Theology of Church Leadership', pp. 11–41 in *Focus on Leadership*. York, Foundation for Church Leadership.

—(2006) (ed.) *The Future of the Parish System: Shaping the Church of England for the 21st Century*. London, Church House Publishing.

Cross, F. and Livingstone, E. (eds) (1997) *The Oxford Dictionary of the Christian Church* (3rd edition). Oxford, Oxford University Press.

Davie, G. (1994) *Religion in Britain since 1945: Believing without Belonging*. Oxford, Blackwell.

Davison, A. (2010) 'Theology and the Renewal of the Church', Chapter 4 in Chapman, M. (ed.), *The Hope of Things to Come: Anglicanism and the Future*. London, Mowbray.

Davison, A. and Milbank, A. (2010) *For the Parish: A Critique of Fresh Expressions*. London, SCM Press.

Denzin, N. and Lincoln, Y. (eds) (2000) *Handbook of Qualitative Research* (2nd edition). Thousand Oaks, California, Sage.

Department of Health (2008) 'What is the European working times directive?', www.dh.gov.uk/en/Managingyourorganisation/Humanresourcesandtraining.

Dewar, F. (2000) *Called or Collared? An Alternative Approach to Vocation* (2nd edition). London, SPCK.

Dixon, L. (2008) 'Swinging vicar who turned up drunk at services is banned', *Times*, 12 November, 9.

Dorr, D. (2006) *Spirituality of Leadership: Inspiration, Empowerment, Intuition, Discernment*. Dublin, The Columba Press.

Dorrien, G. (2001) 'Berger: theology and sociology', pp. 26–39 in Woodhead, L. (ed.), *Peter Berger and the Study of Religion*. London, Routledge.

Drane, J. (2000) *The McDonaldization of the Church: Spirituality, Creativity and the Future of the Church*. London, Darton, Longman and Todd.

Elliott, J. (2005) *Using Narrative in Social Research: Qualitative and Quantitative Approaches*. London, Sage.

Evans, M. and Lee, E. (eds) (2002) *Real Bodies: A Sociological Introduction*. Basingstoke, Palgrave Macmillan.

Finch, J. (1983) *Married to the Job: Wives' Incorporation in Men's Work*. London, Allen and Unwin.

—(1989) *Family Obligations and Social Change*. Cambridge, Polity.

Finch, J. and Mason, J. (1993) *Negotiating Family Responsibilities*. London, Routledge.

Fineman, S. (ed.) (1993) *Emotion in Organizations*. London, Sage.

Fisher, M. (1999) *Religion in the Twenty-first Century*. London, Routledge.

Fleetwood, S. (2007) 'Work–life balance' *International Journal of Human Resource Management*, 18 (3) March.

Fletcher, B. (1990) *Clergy Under Stress: A Study of Homosexual and Heterosexual Clergy in the Church of England*. London, Mowbray.

Forward in Faith (2011) www.forwardinfaith.com.

Foucault, M. (1977) *Discipline and Punish*. Harmondsworth, Penguin.

—(1978) 'Sexualite et pouvoir', A Lecture at the University of Tokyo, quoted by Jordan, M, pp. 238–9 in Bernauer, J. and Carrette, J. (eds) (2004), *Michel Foucault and Theology: The Politics of Religious Experience*. Aldershot, Ashgate.

—(1979) 'On Governmentality', *Identity and Consciousness*, 6: 5–21.

—(1980a) *Power/Knowledge: Selective Interviews and Other Writings 1972–77*. Brighton, Harvester Press.

—(1980b) 'About the beginning of the Hermeneutics of the self', p. 179 in Carrette, J. (ed.) (1999), *Religion and Culture by Michel Foucault*. Manchester, Manchester University Press.

—(1988) *Politics, Philosophy, Culture: Interviews and Other Writings 1977–1984*, edited by Kritzman, L. D. London, Routledge.

Francis, J. M. M and Francis, L. J. (1998) *Tentmaking: Perspectives in Self-supporting Ministry*. Leominster, Gracewing.

Francis, L. and Richter, P. (2007) *Gone for Good? Church-leaving and Returning in the 21st Century*. Peterborough, Epworth.

Freidson, E. (1994) *Professionalism Reborn: Theory, Prophecy and Policy*. Cambridge, Polity.

Fulkerson, M. (2003. *Feminist Theology*, pp. 109–25 in Vanhoozer, K. J. (ed.), *The Cambridge Companion to Postmodern Theology*. Cambridge, Cambridge University Press.

Furlong, M. (1984) *Feminine in the Church*. London, SPCK.

—(ed.) (1998) *Act of Synod – Act of Folly?* London, SCM Press.

✓ —(2000) *C of E: The State It's In*. London, Hodder and Stoughton.

Gatrell, C. (2005) *Hard Labour: The Sociology of Parenthood*. Maidenhead, Open University Press.

—(2007a) 'A fractional commitment?', *International Journal of Human Resource Management*, 18 (3) 462–75.

—(2007b) 'Secrets and lies: breastfeeding and professional paid work', *Social Science and Medicine* 65: 393–404.

—(2008) *Embodying Women's Work*. London, Sage.

Gatrell, C. and Cooper, C. (2007a) '(no) Cracks in the glass ceiling: women managers, stress and the barriers to success', pp. 55–77 in Bilimoria, D. and Piderit, S., *The Handbook of Women in Business and Management*. London, Edward Elgar.

—(2007b) 'Work–life balance: working for whom? Parenting, paid work and the gendered body', *European Journal of International Management* (forthcoming).

Gatrell, C. and Swan E (2008) *Gender and Diversity in Management, A Concise Introduction*. London, Sage.

Giddens, A. (1979) *Central Problems in Social Theory: Action, Structure and Contradiction in Social Analysis*. London, Macmillan.

—(1991) *Modernity and Self-Identity: Self and Society in the Late Modern Age*. Cambridge, Polity.

—(1992) *The Transformation of Intimacy: Sexuality, Love and Eroticism in Modern Societies*. Cambridge, Polity Press.

Gill, R. (1977) *Theology and Social Structure*. Oxford, Mowbray.

—(1992) *Moral Communities: The Prideaux Lectures 1992*. Exeter, Exeter University Press.

✓ —(1993) *The Myth of the Empty Church*. London, SPCK.

—(1997) *Moral Leadership in a Postmodern Age*. Edinburgh, T & T Clark.

—(2012) *Theology in a Social Context: Sociological Theology Volume 1*. Farnham, Ashgate.

Gill, R. and Burke, D. (1996) *Strategic Church Leadership*. London, SPCK.

Gledhill, R. (2007) 'Hate campaign drives out woman priest', *The Times*, 8 December, 25.

—(2008) 'Archbishop believes gay sex is as good as marriage', *The Times*, 7 August, 1–2.

Goffman, E. (1959) *The Presentation of Self in Everyday Life* (1990 edition). London, Penguin.

Goode, W. (1969) 'The theoretical limits of professionalism', pp. 266–313 in Etzioni, A. (1969), *The Semi-Professions and Their Organization: Teachers, Nurses and Social Workers*. New York, Free Press.

Graham, E. (1996) *Transforming Practice: Pastoral Theology in an Age of Uncertainty*. London, Mowbray.

Graham, E., Walton H. and Ward, F. (2005) *Theological Reflection: Methods*. London, SCM Press.

Grayshon, J. (1996) *The Confessions of a Vicar's Wife* (new edition). Crowborough, Monarch Publications.

Greeley, A. M. (2004) *Priests: A Calling in Crisis*. Chicago, University of Chicago Press.

Green, A. (2009) *A Theology of Women's Priesthood*. London, SPCK.

—(2011) *A Priesthood of Both Sexes: Paying Attention to Difference*. London, SPCK.

Greenhill, S. (2008) 'A first-class fracas', *Daily Mail*, 19 March, 9.

Greenwood, R. (1994) *Transforming Priesthood: A New Theology of Mission and Ministry*. London, SPCK.

—(2002) *Transforming Church: Liberating Structures for Ministry*. London, SPCK.

—(2009) *Parish Priests: For the Sake of the Kingdom*. London, SPCK.

Griffin, D. (1998) *Spirituality and Society*. Albany, NY, State University of New York.

Grundy, M. (2011) *Leadership and Oversight: New Models for Episcopal Ministry*. London, Mowbray.

Guiver, G. (2001) *Priests in a People's Church*. London, SPCK.

Gutting, G. (ed.) (2003) *The Cambridge Companion to Foucault* (2nd edition). Cambridge, Cambridge University Press.

Gysin, C., McDermott, N. and Rees, G. (2008) 'Dear parishioners, the vicar has run off with his deputy', *Daily Mail*, 13 February, 39.

Hampson, M. (2006) *Last Rites: The End of the Church of England*. London, Granta.

Hardaker, I. (1998) *Occasional Papers of the Church of England Clergy Appointments Adviser*.

Hargrave, A. (2008) 'Written answer to a question at General Synod', 9 February.

Harris, H. and Shaw, J. (eds) (2002) *Women and Episcopacy*. London, WATCH (Women and the Church).

Haynes, K. (2011) 'Body beautiful? Gender, identity and the body in professional service firms', *Gender, Work and Organization*, doi:10.1111/j.1468-0432.2011.00583.x.

Hearn, J. et al. (1989) (eds) *The Sexuality of Organization*. London, Sage.

Henshall, A. (1991) *Not Always Murder at the Vicarage: A View of Clergy Marriage Today*. London SPCK.

Herbert, S. (2008) 'Priest's conduct was unbecoming, rules York Chancery Court', *Church Times*, 9 May, 29.

Herbert, T. (2008) *Kenosis and Priesthood: Towards a Protestant Re-evaluation of Ordained Ministry*. London, Paternoster.

Heywood, D. (2011) *Reimagining Ministry*. London, SCM Press.

Higgins, J. (2001) 'The declining authority of the clergy', *Crucible: The Quarterly Journal of the Church of England Board for Social Responsibility*, July, 167–70.

Hill, M. (2007) *Ecclesiastical Law* (3rd edition). Oxford, Oxford University Press.

Hinton, M. (1994) *The Anglican Parochial Clergy: A Celebration*. London, SCM Press.

Hochschild, A. (1983) *The Managed Heart: Commercialization and Human Feeling* (2003 edition). Berkley, California, University of California Press.

—(1989) *The Second Shift*. New York, Avon Books.

—(1997) *The Time Bind: When Work Becomes Home and Home Becomes Work*. New York, Owl Books.

Holloway, I. and Wheeler, S. (1996) *Qualitative Research for Nurses*. Oxford, Blackwell Science.

Holloway, R. (2012) *Leaving Alexandria: A Memoir of Faith and Doubt*. Edinburgh, Canongate.

House of Lords (2006) 'Work–Life Balance: Debate', 22 June, reported in *Hansard*, Vol. 683, No. 167.

Houston, D. (2005) *Work–Life Balance in the 21st Century*. Basingstoke, Macmillan.

Howson, A. (2005) *Embodying Gender*. London, Sage.

InterHealth (2008) *Caring for Those in Christian Ministry*. London, InterHealth.

Jackson, B. (2002) *Hope for the Church: Contemporary Strategies for Growth*. London, Church House Publishing.

—(2005) *The Road to Growth: Towards a Thriving Church*. London, Church House Publishing.

James, W. (1902) *The Varieties of Religious Experience: A Study in Human Nature*. London, Longmans.

Jamieson, P. (1997) *Living at the Edge: Sacrament and Solidarity in Leadership*. London, Mowbray.

John, J. (1993) *Permanent, Faithful, Stable: Christian Same-Sex Partnerships*. London, Darton, Longman and Todd.

Jones, S. H., Francis, L. J. and Jackson, C. (2004) 'The relationship between religion and anxiety: a study among Anglican clergymen and clergywomen', *Journal of Psychology and Theology*, 32: 137–42.

Jud, J, Mills, E. and Burch, G. (1970) *Ex-Pastors: Why Men Leave the Parish Ministry*. Philadelphia, Pennsylvania, Pilgrim Press.

Jung, C. (1974) *The Development of Personality [Collected Works Volume 17]*. New York, Bollingen Foundation and Princeton University Press.

Kirk, M. and Leary, T. (1994) *Holy Matrimony? An Exploration of Marriage and Ministry*. Oxford, Lynx.

Kuhrt, G. and Bentley, L. (2001) 'Women and ordained ministry', pp. 234–39 in Kuhrt, G. (2001), *Ministry Issues for the Church of England*. London, Church House Publishing.

Kung, H. (1972) *Why Priests?* London, Collins.

Lamb, C. (2012) 'The revolving door – woman who join, leave and return to the Catholic Church', *The Tablet*, 7 January, 4–5.

Lamont, R. (2011) *Leaping the Vicarage Wall: Leaving Parish Ministry*. London, Continuum.

Lash, S. (1990) *Sociology of Postmodernism*. London, Routledge.

Lawrence, C. (2001) 'Minority ethnic concerns', pp. 96–100 in Kuhrt, G. (2001), *Ministry Issues for the Church of England*. London, Church House Publishing

Leadership Institute (2012) *Clergy Leadership Programme*. Downham Market, The Leadership Institute.

Lee, C. and Horsman, S. (2002) *Affirmation and Accountability*. Dunsford, The Society of Mary and Martha.

Lee, J. (2006) *From Frustration to Fulfilment: The Final Ten Years of Licensed Ministry*. An Appendix to the Clergy Appointment Adviser's Annual Report to the House of Bishops.

Lewis-Anthony, J. (2009) *If You Meet George Herbert on the Road, Kill Him: Radically Re-thinking Priestly Ministry*. London, Continuum.

Lewis, S. and Cooper, C. (2005) *Work–Life Integration: Case Studies of Organisational Change*. Chichester, John Wiley & Sons.

Liverpool (2011) *Clergy Questionnaire*. Liverpool, Diocese of Liverpool.

Louden, S. and Francis, L. (2003) *The Naked Parish Priest: What Priests Really Think They're Doing*. London, Continuum.

MacCulloch, D. (2003) *Reformation: Europe's House Divided*. London, Allen Lane.

Macdonald, K. (1995) *The Sociology of the Professions*. London, Sage.

MacIntyre, A. (1985) *After Virtue* (2nd edition). London, Duckworth.

Martin, D. (1978) *A General Theory of Secularization*. London, Blackwell.

—(2011) *The Future of Christianity: Reflections on Violence and Democracy, Religion and Democratization*. Fareham, Ashgate.

Martin, E. (1987) *The Woman in the Body: A Cultural Analysis of Reproduction*. Boston, Beacon Press.

Mason, J. (2002) *Qualitative Researching* (2nd edition). London, Sage.

Mavin, S. (2006) 'Venus envy: problematizing solidarity behaviour and queen bees', *Women in Management Review*, 21 (4) 264–76.

—(2008) 'Queen bees, wannabees and afraid to bees: no more "best enemies" for women in management?', *British Journal of Management*, 19: S75–S84.

McGillion, C. and O'Carroll, J. (2011) *Our Fathers: What Australian Catholic Priests Really Think about Their Lives and Their Church*. John Garratt Publishing, Mulgrave.

McNair, S. (2008a) Centre for Research into the Older Workforce, www.niace.org.uk/crow.

—(2008b) *The Ageing Workforce and the Church*. Presentation, Deployment, Remuneration and Conditions of Service Committee of the Ministry Division of the Church of England, 5 March.

Meyrick, S. (1998) *Married to the Ministry*. London, SPCK.

—(2008) 'Campaign to up the aisle', *Church Times*, 26 September, 19, 22.

Milbank, J. (1990) *Theology and Social Theory: Beyond Secular Reason*. Oxford, Blackwell.

Moody, C. (1992) *Eccentric Ministry*, London, Darton, Longman and Todd.

Morgan, D. (1996) *Family Connections*. Cambridge, Polity.

Morgan, D, Brandth, B. and Kvande, E. (2005) *Gender, Bodies and Work*. Aldershot, Ashgate.

Morgan, G. (1997) *Images of Organization* (2nd edition). Thousand Oaks, CA, Sage.

Moynagh, M. and Worsley, R. (2005) *Working in the Twenty-First Century*. Leeds, Economic and Social Research Council and The Tomorrow Project.

Muers, R. (2005) 'Feminism, gender and theology', pp. 431–50 in Ford, D. and Muers, R. (eds), *The Modern Theologians* (3rd edition). Oxford, Blackwell Publishing.

NADAWM (2008) 'New Dawn II – 2008 … Women in ministry', A Report for the National Association of Diocesan Advisors in Women's Ministry, Liverpool, Diocese of Liverpool.

Nash, W. (1990) *Living with God at the Vicarage*. Nottingham, Grove Books.

Nelson, J. (ed.) (1996) *Management and Ministry – Appreciating Contemporary Issues*. Norwich, Canterbury Press.

Nesbitt, P. (1997) *Feminization of the Clergy in America: Occupational and Organizational Perspectives*. New York, Oxford University Press.

Nettleton, S. (2006) *The Sociology of Health and Illness* (2nd edition). Cambridge, Polity Press.

Norman, E. (2004) *Anglican Difficulties: A New Syllabus of Errors*. London, Morehouse.

O'Collins, G. (2011) 'What priests are for', *The Tablet*, 19 February, 16.

Office for National Statistics (2003) *April 2001 UK Census*, www.statistics.gov.uk.

Oliver, G. (2012) *Ministry without Madness* London, SPCK.

Paflin, G. (2003) 'Report of General Synod in York 11–15 July 2003', *Church Times*, 18 July.

Page, S. (2008) 'The construction of masculinities and femininities in the Church of England: the case of the male clergy spouse', *Feminist Theology*, 17 (1) 31–42.

—(2010) 'Femininities and masculinities in the Church of England: a study of priests as mothers and male clergy spouses', University of Nottingham PhD Thesis.

Pannenberg, W. (1998) *Systematic Theology Volume 3*. Edinburgh, T and T Clark.

Parish and People (2008) www.parishandpeople.org.uk.

Paveley, R. (2008) 'When it gets too much', *Church Times*, 25 April, 19.

Percy, M. (2006) *Clergy: The Origin of Species*. London, Continuum.

Peyton, N. (1998) *Dual Role Ministry: First Choice or Mixed Blessing?* Cambridge, Grove Books.

—(2001) 'Dual role ministry', pp. 206–7 in Kuhrt, G (2001), *Ministry Issues for the Church of England*. London, Church House Publishing.

—(2003) 'Being our selves: managerial roles and identities in Archdeacons', Unpublished Paper for Critical Management Course, Lancaster University,

—(2006) 'Women in the Episcopate', *Report of Proceedings 2006: General Synod July Group of Sessions*, 37 (2) 302–3, London, Church House Publishing.

—(2009) *Managing Lives: The Embodiment of Priesthood in Church of England Clergy*. Lancaster University PhD Thesis.

Pigott, R. (2007) 'Religion in British society', pp. 43–5 in *Britain in 2008*, Economic and Social Research Council, London.

Platt, J. (1981) 'On interviewing one's peers', *British Journal of Sociology*, 32 (1) 75–91.

Podmore, C. (2005) *Aspects of Anglican Identity*. London, Church House Publishing.

—(2009) *The Governance of the Church of England and the Anglican Communion*. London, Church House Publishing.

Pringle, R. (1998) *Sex and Medicine*. Cambridge, Cambridge University Press.

Pritchard, J. (2007) *The Life and Work of a Priest*. London, SPCK.

Puwar, N. (2004) *Space Invaders: Race, Gender and Bodies out of Place*. Oxford, Berg.

Ramsay, M. (1972) *The Christian Priest Today* (revised edition 1987). London, SPCK.

Ranson, S., Bryman, A. and Hinings, B. (1977) *Clergy, Ministers and Priests*. London, Routledge and Kegan Paul.

Reform (2011) www.reform.org.uk.

Reid, K. and Reid E. (2009) 'Honouring family and friends', pp. 181–96 in Frame, T. (ed.), *Called to Minister: Vocational Discernment in the Contemporary Church*. Canberra, Barton Books.

Roberts, R. (2002) *Religion, Theology and the Human Sciences*. Cambridge, Cambridge University Press.

—(2005) 'Theology and the social sciences', pp. 370–88 in Ford, D. with Muers, R. (eds), *The Modern Theologians* (3rd edition). Oxford, Blackwell Publishing.

Robson, C. (2002) *Real World Research* (2nd edition). Oxford, Blackwell.

Rooms, N. (2011) *The Faith of the English: Integrating Christ and Culture*. London, SPCK.

—(2012) 'Deep listening: a call for a missionary anthropology', *Theology*, 115 (2) 99–108.

Rooms, N. and Steen, J. (2008) *Employed by God? Theological and Practical Implications of the new Church of England Clergy Terms of Service Legislation*. Cambridge, Grove Books.

Rose, M. (1999) 'Explaining and forecasting job satisfaction: the contribution of occupational profiling', ESRC Working Paper 3, Future of Work Programme.

Rose, N. (1996) *Inventing Our Selves: Psychology, Power and Personhood*. Cambridge, Cambridge University Press.

—(1999) *Governing the Soul: The Shaping of the Private Self* (2nd edition). London, Free Association Books.

Russell, A. (1980) *The Clerical Profession*. London, SPCK.

— (2010) 'Cathedral Canon dumps his wife to move in with a married mother', *Daily Express*, 25 August.

Saint George's House (1998) *Marital Bliss and Ministerial Enigma*. Report of a Consultation, Windsor, Saint George's House.

St Luke's Healthcare (2011) *Continuing to Make a Difference*, www. stlukeshealthcare.org.uk.

Sandford, J. (1984) *Ministry Burnout*. London, Arthur James.

Savage, S. (2006) 'On the analyst's couch: psychological perspectives on congregations and clergy', pp. 16–32 in Croft, S. (ed.), *The Future of the Parish System: Shaping the Church of England for the 21st Century*. London, Church House Publishing.

Schon, D. (1987) *Educating the Reflective Practitioner: Toward a New Design in Teaching and Learning in the Professions*. San Francisco, Jossey-Bass.

Sennet, R. (1999) *The Corrosion of Character*. New York, W.W. Norton.

Sennett, R. and Cobb, J. (1972) *The Hidden Injuries of Class*. New York, Random House.

Shakespeare, S. (2000) 'The new Romantics: a critique of radical Orthodoxy', *Theology*, CIII, 813: 163–77.

Shilling, C. (1993) *The Body and Social Theory*. London, Sage.

—(2005) *The Body in Culture, Technology and Society*. London, Sage.

—(2008) *Changing Bodies: Habit, Crisis and Creativity*. London, Sage.

Silverman, D. (1993) *Interpreting Qualitative Data: Methods for Analysing Talk, Text and Interaction*. London, Sage.

—(2005) *Doing Qualitative Research* (2nd edition). London, Sage.

Singh, V, Kumra, S. and Vinnicombe, S. (2002) 'Gender and impression management: playing the promotion game', *Journal of Business Ethics*, 37: 1.

Smart, C. and Neale, B. (1999) *Family Fragments?* Cambridge, Polity.

Smith, D. (1974) *Clergy in the Cross Fire: Coping with Role Conflicts in the Ministry*. Philadelphia, Pennsylvania, The Westminster Press.

Smithers, A. and Robinson P. (2004) *Teacher Turnover, Wastage and Destination*. Centre for Education and Employment Research, University of Liverpool www.dscf.gov.uk/research/data/uploadfiles/RR553.

Sowerby, M. (2001) 'Vocation', pp. 88–95 in Kuhrt, G. (ed.), *Ministry Issues for the Church of England*. London, Church House Publishing.

Staples, W. (1997) *The Culture of Surveillance: Discipline and Social Control in the United States*. New York, St Martin's Press.

Stewart, P. (ed.) (2005) *Employment, Trade Union Renewal and the Future of Work: The Experience of Work and Organizational Change*. Basingstoke, Palgrave Macmillan.

Stoddart, E. (2011) *Theological Perspectives on a Surveillance Society: Watching and Being Watched*. Farnham, Ashgate.

Strauss, A. and Corbin, J. (1990) *Basics of Qualitative Research*. Thousand Oaks, California, Sage.

Swan, E. (2005) 'On bodies, rhinestones, and pleasures: women teaching managers', *Management Learning*, 36 (3) 317–33.

Swinton, J. and Mowat, H. (2006) *Practical Theology and Qualitative Research*. London, SCM Press.

The Tablet (2010) 'Airwaves to heaven', *Notebook*, 4 September, 21.

Thistleton, A. (2006) *1 Corinthians: A Shorter Exegetical Pastoral Commentary*. Grand Rapids, Michigan, Eerdmans.

Thomas, C. (2002) 'The disabled body', in Evans, M. and Lee, E. (eds), *Real Bodies: A Sociological Introduction*. Basingstoke, Palgrave Macmillan.

Thomas, P. (2006) *Bruised Reeds? A Report on Stress experienced by the Clergy*. London, St Luke's Hospital for the Clergy.

Thomas R. S. (1952) *An Acre of Land*. Montgomeryshire Printing Co.

—(1968) *Not That He Brought Flowers*. Hart-Davis.

—(1975) *Laboratories of the Spirit*. London, Macmillan.

Thorne, H. (1999) *Journey to Priesthood*. Centre for Comparative Studies in Religion and Gender, Monograph Series 3, Department of Theology and Religious Studies, University of Bristol.

Towler, R. and Coxon, A. (1979) *The Fate of the Anglican Clergy*. London, Macmillan.

Turner, B. (1984) *The Body and Society.* Oxford, Blackwell.

Turton, D. W. (2010) *Clergy Burnout and Emotional Exhaustion: A Socio-Psychological Study of Job Stress and Job Satisfaction.* Lampeter, The Edwin Mellen Press.

UK Government (2008) Population statistics for England, www.statistics.gov.uk.

Vanhoozer, K. (ed.) (2003) *The Cambridge Companion to Postmodern Theology.* Cambridge, Cambridge University Press.

Vasey, M. (1995) *Strangers and Friends: A New Exploration of Homosexuality and the Bible.* London, Hodder and Staunton.

Voas, D. and Bruce, S. (2004) 'Research note on the 2001 Census and Christian identification in Britain', *Journal of Contemporary Religion*, 19 (1) 23–8.

Walrond-Skinner, S. (1998) *Double Blessing.* London, Mowbray.

Ward, R. (2011) *On Christian Priesthood.* London, Continuum.

Warren, Y. (2002) *The Cracked Pot: The State of Today's Anglican Parish Clergy.* Stowmarket, Kevin Mayhew.

WATCH (2012) www.womenandthechurch.org.

Watson, T. (1995) 'Shaping the story: rhetoric, persuasion and creative writing in organizational ethnography', *Studies in Cultures, Organisations and Society*, 1 (2) 301–11.

—(2000) 'Ethnographic fiction science: making sense of managerial work and organisational research processes with Caroline and Terry', *Organisation*, 7 (3) 513–34.

—(2001) *In Search of Management* (revised edition). London, Thompson Learning.

—(2002) *Organising and Managing Work.* Harlow, Financial Times/Prentice Hall.

Watson, T. and Harris, P. (1999) *The Emergent Manager.* London, Sage.

Webster, A. (2002) *Wellbeing: Society and Church.* London, SCM.

Williams, R. (2004) *Anglican Identities.* London, Darton, Longman and Todd.

—(2008) 'Covenanted restraint', Concluding Presidential Address by the Archbishop of Canterbury at the 2008 Lambeth Conference, *Church Times*, 8 August, 2.

Winkett, L. (2010) *Our Sound is Our Wound: Contemplative Listening in a Noisy World.* London, Continuum.

Witz, A. (1992) *Professions and Patriarchy.* London, Routledge.

Wolkowitz, C. (2006) *Bodies at Work.* London, Sage.

Woodhead, L. (2005) 'Kendal, Cumbria – A Spiritual Laboratory', *CeNtre WoRdS: Centre for North-West Regional Studies*, New Series No. 4: 17–26.

—(2007) 'Atheism: are we really turning away from a belief in God?', p. 55 in *Britain in 2008.* Economic and Social Research Council, London.

Woodhead, L. (ed.) (2001) *Peter Berger and the Study of Religion.* London, Routledge.

Woodhead, L. and Catto, R. (eds) (2012) *Religion and Change in Modern Britain.* London, Routledge.

Woodhead, L. and Heelas, P. (2005) *The Spiritual Revolution: Why Religion is Giving Way to Spirituality.* Oxford, Blackwell.

Woodhead, L. and Heelas, P. (eds) (2000) *Religion in Modern Times: An Interpretive Anthology.* Oxford, Blackwell.

Woodward, J. and Pattison, S. (eds) (2000) *The Blackwell Reader in Pastoral and Practical Theology.* Oxford, Blackwell.

INDEX